WRITING NEWS FOR BROADCAST

Writing News for Broadcast

Edward Bliss Jr.
and
John M. Patterson

COLUMBIA UNIVERSITY PRESS
NEW YORK and LONDON   1971

Dedicated to the memory of

EDWARD R. MURROW

FOREWORD

by Fred W. Friendly

When I interview candidates for the Columbia Graduate School of Journalism, I often ask them why they want to attend. Too often, their reply is, "I like to write." I then begin a kind of pre-admission lecture, which goes something like this.

While writing is crucial to broadcast journalism, it is only the final step of an involved process composed of many elements. More than anything, a journalist is an explainer of complicated issues. Before he can explain he must understand. Before he can understand, he must search. And before he can do that, he must be predisposed to examine with equal parity facts and personalities he dislikes, as well as those he may support.

He must also know the tools of his trade. The grammar of broadcast journalism not only involves words and sentences, but also includes the vocabulary of sounds, and the dialect of pictures. The broadcast reporter is at once audio engineer, visual editor—and the producer. When he walks into Watts or the village of Cam Ne or Sproul Plaza at Berkeley, he is not only the news explorer, looking for the story, but he is also the artist looking for the key that will unlock the viewer's curiosity.

Writing for broadcast is not only achieved with sounds, but also with silence. Often pictures alone can tell a story. Sometimes, Confucius notwithstanding, a single sound is worth a thousand pictures. When a reporter sits down to write the copy that will lace together the pictures and sounds or, in the case of radio, the actuality tapes, he is assembling a mosaic of several disciplines. If he lets his words get in the way of his pictures, he is an ineffective writer. If he permits his visual or audio images to step on his narration, he is a clumsy writer.

It is spurious to ask who wrote a television documentary or a four-minute take-out on the evening news. Such a question is as inaccurate as the credits which often read "Written by Joe Doe." Writing begins when a subject is selected. It continues throughout the planning, the selection (those to be interviewed), the questions to be asked, and the pictorial ingredients to be included. When Jack Laurence of CBS News did his penetrating reporting of the San Francisco State disturbances of 1969, he actually began his writing when he walked onto campus, arriving the way most of the student body did. He was in effect writing when he told his cameraman what demonstrations to shoot, selected his interviewees, and told his sound men where to place their microphones. In his mind's eye, he could envision the final story he would eventually report. But, before he could write, he had to capture the raw realities that could be distilled into content. As it turned out, his copy, though spare, was dramatic and effective. Some of Laurence's most incisive reporting was in the questions he asked and in the scenes he, his producer, and cameraman chose. Though it was a seemingly spontaneous selection, in reality it was the result of swift but sober understanding of a complex situation.

Understanding the complicated issue and conceiving how to explain it with style and imagination are two of three critical steps of broadcast reporting. The final essential is the narration to tie it all together. Whether that narrative represents 2 percent of the air time, as in a Walter Lippmann conversation, or 15 percent, as in a documentary such as "Harvest of Shame" or "The Tunnel," or 80 to 100 percent, as in a ten-minute radio news show, the linking copy can make or destroy the report.

The copy should be more than caption writing, less than the historian's sweep of generations. It is a medium where the impact of the individual parts—an interesting piece of film, an intriguing burst of sound, both stitched together by the right copy—can make tthe sequence soar above the sum total of the individual elements.

Ed Bliss and John Patterson understand this the way Vince Lombardi understood the fundamentals of ball control football. Their volume is a textbook about the orthodox disciplines that have been refined and improved from the World News Roundup of 1938 to the World News Roundup of 1971 (still the demonstration broadcast in its field). Their book is about the flair and imagination pioneered by Ed Murrow in London during the Battle of Britain, Jay McMullen for "Campaign American Style," Andy Rooney for "An Essay on Bridges," and Morley Safer during the agonies of Vietnam.

Bliss and Patterson have learned excellence from working practitioners and they have in turn taught these same correspondents how to improve.

They know that leanness and economy of language is the message of this verbal medium. They know that every sentence which can be deleted and every phrase which can be sharpened not only serves comprehension but also saves crucial time for the actualities of the story.

In the newsroom Patterson and Bliss strove for clarity, content under pressure, and swiftness. They fought against adjectives, the recitation of the obvious, and showing one's tripod. Working with professionals—from Raymond Swing to Murrow to Smith to Sevareid to Cronkite—they have served a generation of pioneer newsmen. As teachers at the Columbia Graduate School of Journalism and at American University, they have inspired a generation of journalists who may yet bring maturity to a profession which had to learn to shout before it could whisper, had to set records before it could set standards.

This is a text for the bold investigator and the careful reporter, and the lesson of the book is that you can't be one without the other. In between the lines is the respect which Bliss and Patterson have for fairness and for the fair men and women with whom they practiced their craft. They know the benchmarks which indicate where reporting ends and preaching begins because they understand that most reporting worthy of the name is interpretive, that most hortative lectures are not really journalism at all. Each of them carries in his wallet a description of what news analysis is, written thirty-five years ago by Ed Klauber, the "founding father" of CBS News:

What news analysts are entitled to do and should do is to elucidate and illuminate the news out of common knowledge, or special knowledge possessed by them or made available to them by this organization through its sources. They should point out the facts on both sides, show contradictions with the known record, and so on. They should bear in mind that in a democracy it is important that people not only should know but should understand, and it is the analyst's function to help the listener to understand, to weigh, and to judge, but not to do the judging for him.

From their "special knowledge" Bliss and Patterson have performed in the Klauber tradition and created a tool that ought to be in every broadcast journalism classroom, next to Webster's, *The Careful Writer* by Theodore Bernstein and *Public Opinion* by Walter Lippman. Come to think of it, all working newsrooms could use the set as standard equipment.

ACKNOWLEDGMENTS

We are in debt to the American Broadcasting Company, the Columbia Broadcasting System, the National Broadcasting Company, and to the Writers Guild of America for their cooperation in making scripts available. We also are grateful to many individuals, including Eric Sevareid, Howard K. Smith, Charles Kuralt, Robert Trout, David Brinkley, Dallas Townsend, Av Westin, Les Midgely, Wallace Westfeldt, William L. Shirer, Hinda Glasser, May Dowell, Harry Reasoner, Richard Hanser, Emerson Stone, Allan Jackson, Frank Reynolds, and Thomas Houghton for their helpfulness, though certainly any mistakes are our own. Our special appreciation goes to Mrs. Edward R. Murrow, Fred W. Friendly, Walter Cronkite, Robert J. Tilley of the Columbia University Press, and Dr. Robert O. Blanchard of American University for their valued suggestions and encouragement.

Excerpts from *In Search of Light*, by Edward R. Murrow, on pages 5, 19, 20, 21, 57–58, and 169 (Copyright © 1967 by the Estate of Edward R. Murrow) are reprinted by permission of Alfred A. Knopf, Inc.

EDWARD BLISS, JR.
JOHN M. PATTERSON

June 1, 1971

CONTENTS

WRITING NEWS FOR BROADCAST

INTRODUCTION

This book is for broadcast journalists, present and future. It is about writing. No skill in broadcast journalism is more basic. The correspondent broadcasting from London or New Delhi, from Washington or Fort Worth, is reading a story he wrote. Often he has less than two minutes on television—one minute on radio—to tell his story. The newsroom writer, for the same story, may have only 20 seconds. A special economy in language, a most sophisticated kind of editorial judgment, is required if in that limited time he can report what is essential—the undistorted essence—of what took place. And this must be done gracefully. Writing for broadcast, whether radio or television, demands a style which is "comely and clean."

So what we have written is really an expanded stylebook. There is very little theory in it. The goal was a set of practical guidelines. Indeed, one network—CBS—already has adopted much of the material in this book as a guide for its all-news stations. Inevitably, among the guidelines are some rules. But the book makes no pretense of being the last word. Each network, each station, has its broadcasters, each of whom has his or her own individual style.

But there are ways which make for good writing. No rule exists for whether you do this from a crouched position, or by using the touch system, or with two fingers, or by dictation. (You'll need your own private office for this last method!) You will find scant reference in this book to grammatical rules. However, you must be grammatical in what you write. You must be accurate. You must be conversational. And you must be succinct. Think of each wasted word in your broadcast as a wasted second. Through such waste, in longer broadcasts, whole minutes are lost. Whole stories are dropped.

The trick is how to be accurate—how to report the essential facts—and be conversational and brief at the same time. No other medium matches broadcasting's insistence on clarity and compression. In no other newsroom is such high premium placed on the writer's craft. This is because the writer of newscasts is challenged to meet two inimical requirements: 1) the requirement to keep within the time allotted and 2) the requirement to report, with accuracy and clarity, the important elements of each story. The news must be written as lucidly as possible because the listener has to understand at once what he hears—there is no going back to listen again.

It is no accident that the so-called "stars" of television news are, first of all, good writers. If there were no TV, they could support themselves comfortably with their typewriters. Eric Sevareid and Howard K. Smith both have written books, including best-sellers, and many magazine articles. Chet Huntley wrote a tremendously appealing story of his boyhood in Montana. Edward P. Morgan is a syndicated columnist. Alexander Kendrick wrote *Prime Time*, the best-selling biography of Edward R. Murrow. For years, Walter Cronkite was a foreign correspondent for the United Press, now United Press International, and William L. Shirer, one of the early greats in broadcast journalism, has revealed a high degree of writing ability, as well as scholarship, in his histories of Hitler's Germany and the fall, in 1940, of the Third French Republic.

David Brinkley, Harry Reasoner, Allan Jackson, Ed Newman, and Charles Kuralt all began their broadcasting careers as news writers. So did Reuven Frank, president of NBC News, and George Herman, moderator of "Face the Nation." The list could be expanded. The point is: Don't embark on a career in broadcast journalism if you can't write. You may say, "I don't plan to write. I want to produce documentaries. Producers don't have to write." Well, you are wrong. The best producers do write—beautifully—starting with Norman Corwin in the 1940s and coming up through the '50s and '60s, and into the '70s, with Henry Salomon, Richard Hanser, Donald Hyatt, Fred Friendly, Irving Gitlin, John Secondari, Fred Freed, Lou Hazam, Jay McMullen, Andrew Rooney, and Perry Wolff.

In this book you will find examples of the kinds of writing heard in broadcast journalism—hard news, commentary, features, leads, voice over film —several of which are classics. The authors are indebted to the broadcasters who made these scripts available. One of the early practitioners of the art was Robert Trout. In response to a request for examples of his work, he wrote from Paris, where he is in semiretirement, "For a time I occupied a one-room apartment and somehow managed to afford a girl to come in and clean up. Alas, the girl did not understand that papers piled on the floor are not necessarily trash but invaluable records of the recent past. Doesn't everybody file papers on the floor? So gone are many of the old scripts and treasured newspaper clippings." But examples of Trout's craftsmanship with words do appear, notwithstanding.

The graduate in broadcast journalism enters an expanding field. Each year, more hours have been devoted to news programming. Licenses are being granted to more FM stations. UHF stations are multiplying. News writers are needed not only at radio and television stations, and at the networks, but at AP and UPI. Both press associations have increased their broadcast services. They employ writers for their radio wires; other newsmen specializing in audio reports are assigned to overseas bureaus.

Networks and group stations, like those belonging to Westinghouse (Group W), syndicate news, and this service requires editors and writers. Cable television promises opportunities for the broadcast journalist which cannot yet be measured.

When Charles Kuralt heard that this text was in preparation, he wrote: "Good luck. Lord knows, writing is the principal shortcoming with television news. Good writers always get promoted to producers or editors or correspondents and they don't write much any more." This is another reason for the demand for good writers in the broadcast media. Do not misunderstand. The demand is for GOOD writers. The other kind are plentiful enough.

Surely a word about responsibility belongs in the introduction to a book such as this. More people turn to radio and television for news of what is happening than to other media, and this makes it incumbent upon the broadcast journalist to fulfill with integrity his informational role. Truth *is* the only justification of the profession. Ed Murrow said, "There is a great and perhaps decisive battle to be fought against ignorance, intolerance, and indifference." He also said, "The trouble with television is that it is rusting in the scabbard during a battle for survival." Television is a double-edged sword. The cutting edges are picture and sound. For the companion weapon, radio, it is sound alone. And most of the sound is the spoken word.

This book is about the art of using words, man's most important invention, in man's most influential media. Of necessity, the practitioners of broadcast journalism have created a specialized style to suit their media—a new verbal form. To help you learn this form is the authors' purpose after spending an aggregate of more than forty years trying to learn it themselves. The text is written in spoken English. The sign in the window might read:
No Pedagogic Jargon Spoken Here.

1

A NEW KIND OF REPORTING

In the beginning was the word, and in radio it was man's word, not God's, and the air was filled with screwball comedy, crooners' songs — and suds. Not every word was designed to sell or amuse. In 1920, a Pittsburgh station, KDKA, went on the air to report the returns in the presidential election in which Warren G. Harding defeated James M. Cox. Newscasts were heard for the first time. The voice of Lowell Thomas became as well known as the voice of the President of the United States. A king abdicated the throne of England — on radio. And almost continuously for eighteen days, in 1938, H. V. Kaltenborn analyzed Chamberlain's nightmarish talks with Hitler for "peace in our time." And when war did come, radio news came of age, and America listened.

The role of radio in that time — the role of words heard simultaneously by millions — cannot be measured. Eric Sevareid has observed: "Never, surely, in the history of human travail had so many owed so much to so few human voices. . . .Churchill speaking to the world. J. B. Priestley speaking to his own people. Ed Murrow speaking to America each night, the timbre of his powerful, steady voice reflecting the spirit of England and persuading millions of Americans that the cause was not lost even when it seemed beyond saving. Raymond Swing speaking from America to the British via the BBC each week, letting them know in his intimate fatherly tones that America had got their message, that America understood."

What were the words of these men? How did they write? Here is an excerpt from a Murrow script, vintage 1940:

Christmas Day began in London nearly an hour ago. The church bells did not ring at midnight. When they ring again it will be to announce invasion. And if they ring, the British are ready. Tonight, as on every other night, the rooftop watchers are peering out across the fantastic forest of London's chimney pots. The anti-aircraft gunners stand ready. And all along the coast of this island the observers revolve in their reclining chairs, listening for the sound of German planes. The fire fighters and the ambulance drivers are waiting, too. The blackout stretches from Birmingham to Bethlehem, but tonight over Britain the skies are clear.

This is writing news for broadcast. The sentences are readable. They are short. They are to the point. There is no fancy, involved writing. No "inverted pyramid" with the answers to who, what, why, where, and how crammed into the first couple of sentences. The style is simple and straightforward. This is copy written to be read aloud, to be heard once and, with only that one hearing, to be understood.

For years it has been the habit of teachers of journalism to illustrate broadcast style by comparing it with the style of writing found in newspapers. So will the authors of the present text, but only in passing. The writing found in newspapers today so closely resembles the writing in news broadcasts that the comparison has become almost—not quite—irrelevant. Here are the leads to five stories that appeared on June 11, 1970, on the front page of the *New York Times*:

President Nixon made public today the outline of a revised, expanded welfare program that he hopes may prove more acceptable to Congress than the bill that stalled there six weeks ago.

Premier Aleksei N. Kosygin reported today that the seven months of talks with Chinese Communist officials in Peking had failed to make any appreciable progress.

South Vietnamese and American military planners are expected to give the South Vietnamese Army a greatly expanded role in fighting the North Vietnamese main force in the next few months.

The House passed today a clean air act that went considerably beyond earlier legislation in the stringency of its antipollution standards and in the penalties imposed on industry for noncompliance.

A United States military attache was killed by Palestinian guerrillas at his home in Amman today and the United States Embassy came under sniper fire several times in the second day of heavy fighting between the Jordanian Army and the commandos, the State Department announced today.

Of these five leads, only the last is written in the old, gradually disappearing newspaper style. Far too much information is crowded into this sentence for the comfort of listeners to radio and television. The sentence is too long for the broadcast media, and it is unnatural. No one speaks this way. In normal conversation, the clause attributing the information to the State Department would come at the beginning of a sentence, not dangle at the end. Or the attribution might be given in a separate sentence. You might say

The State Department reports that an American military attache has been killed by Palestinian guerrillas in Amman.

Or

According to the State Department, an American military attache has been killed by Palestinian guerrillas in Amman.

Or you might tell what happened and then, after the first few sentences, say

That's the latest word from the State Department.

Or you could tie in the attribution with other facets of the story:

In announcing this, the State Department expressed concern for those other Americans whom the guerrillas are holding hostage.

In short, however you report attribution, do it as you would in normal speech. Think of the broadcaster as someone who SPEAKS. He will be grateful. And if you write for yourself, you will be doing yourself a good turn. (On more and more stations, the writer and broadcaster are one and the same.)

The changes the broadcaster would make in the other four leads are small, but they are important. The first lead, for example, would be better broadcast copy if it were broken up into two sentences.

President Nixon today made public the outline of a revised welfare program. He hopes it will prove more acceptable to Congress than the bill that stalled there six weeks ago.

Generally, shorter sentences are easier to read *and* easier to understand. The fact that Mr. Nixon proposed an expanded program is omitted from the first sentence. The main point is that the President has revised his program with the hope Congress will approve it. The writer's next step is to tell HOW the program was revised, and the expansion proposals are part of that. The listener should not be told too much all at once. Besides, the phrase "a revised, expanded welfare program" is a bit clumsy.

You will notice that today now comes before, instead of after, made public. This places the word in a more conversational, less stilted position in the sentence. It would have been just as good to have said, "Today, President Nixon made public, etc."

In the fourth lead, today again is used awkwardly. The construction "The House passed today. . ." is awkward because passed is a transitive verb and should be followed as closely as possible by what was passed—namely, a clean air bill. "The House today passed a clean air act. . ." is a much more straightforward way of reporting what happened. The House did not pass today. It passed a piece of legislation. Be literally correct. Don't raise hurdles, however slight, to understanding. Help the listener every way you can.

Incidentally, it helps the broadcaster in his pronunciation if you hyphenate words like *antipollution* and *noncompliance*. *Anti-pollution* and *noncompliance* are easier to read.

In the second lead, Premier Kosygin is preferable to *Premier Aleksei N. Kosygin*, when you are writing for broadcast. Here, the first names and initials are excess baggage. It's interesting that the *New York Times* omitted this surplus impedimenta for Nixon and not Kosygin.

The third lead reporting plans to give the South Vietnamese Army an expanded role in the fighting is a little long for broadcast journalism, but it is written in good conversational style. This is, basically, broadcast style. It is a far cry from the style prevalent early in this century when most newspaper stories followed Victorian formulas as rigid as the type in which they were set. That was an ornate, pretentious style for which the chief rule seems to have been to try to make sentences as long and convoluted as possible while, at the same time, cramming them with more facts than they could decently hold and the reader, with one reading, could readily digest.

Came the Revolution

Gradually, this newspaper style changed. A quiet revolution took place in the way news was written. In this, radio played an important, unpublicized role. The authors saw it happen. In 1944, CBS News Director Paul White asked his editors to cooperate in an experiment being conducted by the International News Service. INS, the Hearst news-gathering organization, had no radio wire. It wanted its regular press wire to be written in such a way that it could serve its radio clients as well as newspapers. Network newsmen were asked to check the INS copy and suggest how to make it more readable — more listenable.

This was done. INS issued a brochure saying that, henceforth, its stories would be written in a "modern, simplified style." Research, it said, had "found that, rather than a conflict, there was a close relationship between writing for the eye and for the ear." INS boasted that, as a result, its news wire had been restyled to make it "easier to read, easier to broadcast, easier to understand."

At the same time, the United Press made a study of its news reports. When the study was completed, Earl Johnson, UP's general manager, issued a memorandum which said in part: "Much of the news these days is of such vital importance that it deserves to be presented in terms that can be understood by the widest possible audience. Let's have more periods and fewer complex words. Watch that lead sentence. Keep it short and simple. Then let the lead set the pace for the whole piece."

A similar campaign against obfuscation took place at the Associated Press. Everywhere, what the INS brochure described as "the 1890-style hangover" was being discarded. Even the good, gray *New York Times* began publishing stories that were "easier to read, easier to understand," so that when Astronauts Neil Armstrong and Edwin "Buzz" Aldrin landed on the moon, *Times*man John Noble Wilford wrote this historic lead:

HOUSTON, July 20 — Men landed on the moon today.

It is difficult to imagine a clearer, more concise, more readable lead sentence. Compare it to this tortured lead which appeared in the *Times*, issue of July 30, 1912:

Lieut. Charles A. Becker, the one-time head of Police Commissioner Waldo's strong arm squad, whose name has been mentioned in connection with the case ever since Herman Rosenthal, the gambler who had threatened to "squeal," was murdered in front of the Hotel Metropole last July 16, was arrested last night, immediately indicted for murder in the first degree and locked in the Tombs, there to await a further hearing a week from yesterday.

This kind of lead appeared frequently in the nineteenth and early twentieth centuries. Compare it to Murrow's "Christmas Day began in London nearly an hour ago" and Wilford's "Men landed on the moon today."

The revolution — evolution, really — in news style is continuing. Throwbacks to earlier unnatural journalese still occur, though rarely is the language as tortured as that found in the story of Lieutenant Becker's indictment in 1912. Here, for comparative purposes, are more recent examples taken from two leading American newspapers. First, the *New York Times*:

The discovery in mountains near the South Pole of the fossil remains of a reptilian counterpart of the hippopotamus that lived, as well, in Africa has established "beyond further question" the former joining of all the southern continents, according to a leading authority on the subject.

Now, the lead for the same story as it appeared in the *Washington Post*:

Scientists have found a 200-million-year-old reptile skull in Antarctica that they said "establishes without further question" that the earth once consisted of one or two continents that split into the present seven.

The *Washington Post* lead not only is the more conversational in structure, but it is interesting to note that the writer, Stuart Auerbach—whether he knew it or not—adhered to broadcast style in writing the figure 200,000,000 as 200 million for easy comprehension.

None of this is to suggest that newspapers never would have clarified their language if it had not been for broadcast journalists. However, broadcast journalism did have its direct effect. As Paul White said, "It wasn't until radio really got going that news reached Americans in simple, direct English." It created a new style for writing news.

The Eyewitness Medium

What about television? Television added picture to the word. At its best, television shows history as it is happening. In covering a tragedy such as the assassination of President Kennedy, or a triumph such as man's first walk on the moon, television journalism is unsurpassed. "Seeing," as the *Times* observed during the mission of Apollo 11, "is still believing." Television not only records history; it changes history. It was America becoming eyewitness to war, through television, that helped build up public revulsion against the Vietnam War. And television is revolutionizing politics.

But seeing is not always understanding, and ideas—issues—are not easily shown. Watch the evening news and notice how many words are spoken by the anchorman, by staff reporters, and by persons—public officials, witnesses at Congressional hearings, visiting dignitaries, and so forth—who made the day's news. If you turn off the picture, you will miss only one or two stories reported in the whole half-hour.

Here's another test. Can you think of a single Washington story reported on television in the past week which you could not have understood almost as well if you had listened with your eyes shut? If you have trouble thinking of such a story, don't be surprised. After all, the first definition of the verb *to report* is "to give an account of, to relate, to tell." You can, of course, tell a story with pictures. In television journalism, this should be done whenever physically possible and editorially feasible. But ideas, as we said, are difficult to show. And news, in large part, consists of what newsworthy people say. Again, as in the beginning, the word.

The same is true of some documentaries. In the case of Senator Joseph McCarthy, it was McCarthy's own words, broadcast on nationwide television, and Murrow's devastating summation — "We will not walk in fear, one of another" — which helped destroy McCarthyism. But in most television journalism, word and picture are complementary. Each reinforces the other. It might be said that the best television news program is that in which voice and picture, combined, produce revelation, new insight — truth.

Television owes its life to both microphone AND camera, to sound as well as to sight. You hear natural sound — traffic noises, grenades exploding, a dog barking — and you hear human voices, some wise, some foolish, and these voices speak in words. Respect the word.

As word and picture, together, make television effective, radio and television complement each other as instruments of electronic communication. At this writing, many radio stations are switching to an all-news format, presenting nothing but news — and commercials! — around the clock. Consequently these stations require more newsmen who can write, as well as read, broadcast copy.

Broadcasting is, of course, the swiftest of all media. This very swiftness affects the way stories are written, and we'll go into that later. In general, radio is still faster than television. It is less cumbersome. (Fred Friendly once called television a two-ton pencil.) It also is more accessible to the public. As you read this sentence, millions of motorists are listening to their car radios. The appetite for news is increasing in both radio and television. As radio steps up its news programing, so does television. The news schedules at all the TV networks have been expanded. Public television is increasingly news conscious, as well it might be.

News is broadcasting's most important product. It is to broadcasting that the public turns for information in this time of crisis; it is broadcast news more than any other kind of news they trust. In this other, journalistic sense, broadcasting is a public trust. It follows that the writer in broadcast journalism — and he really is an editor — must be a responsible practitioner of the art.

In the next chapter, we shall take a look at some of the pioneer writers in broadcast news. We'll see how they wrote. (Often, as today, the broadcaster and writer were the same person.) Then we shall get down to the A, B, C's.

2

THE FIRST GENERATION

In the beginning of broadcast journalism there were those first "big names," the stars of the late 1920s and '30s that people listened to night after night for the news. Names like Floyd Gibbons, Boake Carter, Lowell Thomas, Walter Winchell, H. V. Kaltenborn, and Edwin C. Hill. Graham McNamee and Ted Husing might be added to the list. They became best known as sportscasters—Husing was No. 1—but McNamee covered the Republican National Convention in 1924, and Husing broadcast the arrival of the *Graf Zeppelin*, that lighter-than-air dream ship, after its first trans-Atlantic flight in 1927. He also helped cover the presidential election of 1928—Herbert Hoover versus Al Smith.

Some of these names are forgotten today, but they were giants in their time—as big as Brinkley or Cronkite—and it comes as rather a shock, poking around the electronic ashes, to realize that the only one you can still hear as this is written is Lowell Thomas, who has been broadcasting every weekday night on radio for years!

Thomas' writer for more than half of those forty years was Prosper Buranelli, who was dean of radio news writers at the time of his death in 1960 and perhaps the highest paid. Buranelli had been a feature writer for the old *New York World*, where he developed a narrative style which he carried over into radio. His formula in writing for Thomas, he said, was "everything storified." Buranelli would dictate two or three stories at a sitting, chortling over the news as he worked, delighting in its surprises. "Ha!" he would exclaim, whether or not anyone else was in the room. Or he might be heard to mutter under his breath, "Well, I'll be damned!"

Here is a story he wrote from the old United Press wire:

The ancient city of Naples gives us a blood-curdling comedy. A young couple, frustrated in love, seeking to end it all in a melodramatic way. Antonio Mainardi and Nuncia Majonie were in despair because their families objected to their marriage. So they made a suicide pact—more fantastic, I think, than anything you will find in an opera. They meet in a narrow street, each armed with a knife, and cut each other's throats.

Well, they went through with it as well as they could. They slashed. The only result was Nuncia got scratched a bit and started bleeding, whereupon Antonio fainted. Nuncia thought she had killed him, and *she* fainted. People on the street thought they both were killed and the two bodies were taken to a nearby hospital and placed on slabs. There, they came to, saw each other and went into an ardent embrace. Whereupon the nurses fainted. Love and death in Naples!

It is the kind of story Lowell Thomas —and his listeners—go for. Buranelli custom-styled his language, carefully, to conform with Thomas' own way of writing. The broadcaster is a devotee of the participle, and the writer gave him the line: "A young couple, frustrated in love, seeking to end it all in a melodramatic way." Beyond the proper names of the principals, not a single hard-to-pronounce word appears in the script—no tripping combination of sibilants, no word of more than three syllables. And the sentences are short and simple. The 13 sentences average only 12 words each.

And see if you can tell the same story, in the same appealing way, in fewer than the 156 words this expert used.

Of course, this is strictly a feature story. But Buranelli tended to give the same feature treatment to other news. For example, to France's action in giving up its last possession in Hindustan. Normally, this would not interest many Americans, but Lowell Thomas had traveled widely on the Asian subcontinent. HE was interested in Hindustan. Buranelli knew it. So he referred to Thomas' files and wrote a personalized version of this relatively minor story, endeavoring to make it just as interesting as possible for the radio audience—in fact, using a bit of psychology to suggest to Thomas' listeners that if they had any sense of history at all, they WOULD be interested!

People with a fancy for history will meditate over this item in today's news: India gets Pondicherry. France losing her last possession in Hindustan.

Today the municipal councillors of Pondicherry voted to join India. France has agreed—the fate of that city of renown to be decided at a meeting of the councillors. They voted 170 to 8. The decision also including the town of Karikal, another tiny French possession in India.

Well, it all goes back to the historic days of the seventeenth century, when the French and the British fought it out for the domination of India. The French had their stronghold at Pondicherry. In bold military moves, they lined up Indian principalities, making the fabulous nabobs their allies and puppets. The British played the same game, and there were wars between Indian states. The French backing one side, the British backing the other. Great Britain had the sea power—and also Clive of India. That fantastic genius who won the victory for England. When it was all over, the magnificent land of Hindustan was—British India. France retaining only a few scattered points. The chief of these—Pondicherry.

I, myself, have a vivid recollection of the city. Traveling far and wide in India, I suddenly saw a bit of Old France on the Coromandel coast. The boulevards—like those of a French metropolis. But teaming with an exotic population, India. Pondicherry, one of those beautiful paradoxical cities that a traveler always remembers well.

Again the short sentences, again the participle clauses. And the use of dashes to alert Thomas to pause for effect. The Thomas file and the *Encyclopedia Britannica,* and the UP wire, had given Buranelli what he needed to give the story the background necessary to make it come alive. He had striven through research and skillful writing (note the crafty use of adjectives) to sell the story.

There is a rather important point to be made here. On occasion, a news writer should indicate to the radio or TV audience WHY a story deserves attention. In the case of Pondicherry, Buranelli's effort was self-serving. But there are times when a significant story appears routine. Then it is the writer's obligation to point up that significance, if only with a sentence. For example, in January, 1970, the government released figures showing that industrial production was down in December. For the news writer not to report that industrial production in the United States had dropped for the FIFTH consecutive month would have been irresponsible. This is what is meant by saying that the best news writers are good editors. A news writer must think continually of what a story means.

An early broadcaster who stayed on the air almost as long as Lowell Thomas was Gabriel Heatter. Like Walter Winchell ("Hello, Mr. and Mrs. America and all the ships at sea!"), Gabriel Heatter's style was hypoed, full of excitement, and replete with personal reference. It is curious how a commentator who began most of his broadcasts with the line "There's good news tonight!" so often took a pessimistic view.

Here is a sample of Heatter's intimate, first-person style, as broadcast on ABC at 9 P.M., October 1, 1946, the day the captured Nazi leaders were sentenced at Nuremberg:

Well, I said last night there was one place anyway where the Allies did achieve unity, where they were in complete agreement. And that place was Nuremberg courtroom. But I was wrong. For there, too, there was disagreement. With the Russian judge opposed to life imprisonment for Rudolph Hess. He wanted him to hang. . . .During the war, in the grim days of war, there were people who said this man Heatter is a wishful thinker. Foolish enough to believe that Hitler would never get to England when he was only 18 miles away. Foolish enough to believe that Stalingrad would hold out when there were only two thousand yards left. When so many people were sure Hitler would conquer all Russia in eight weeks. Well, I know some real wishful thinkers tonight. They're the people who really believe shooting [sic] Goering and a handful of Nazis will end the chapter and spare the children a war in their time. They're the wishful thinkers. Those men whose names were called today, they were the rabble, the window dressing. The real masters of Germany were never in that courtroom.

We're setting up a new German government. We're turning Germany back into German hands. She'll have goods and probably credit and perhaps in time a fat loan. Better look carefully at the hands into which we turn it back. Better look carefully for marks on those hands lest our children pay for it as our sons paid and their fathers before them. . . .

Let's examine some of the craftsmanship to be found here. Notice the first five sentences. They really are ONE sentence:

Well, I said last night there was one place anyway where the Allies did achieve unity, where they were in complete agreement, and that place was Nuremberg courtroom, but I was wrong, for there, too, there was disagreement with the Russian judge opposed to life imprisonment for Rudolph Hess.

Through the strategic placement of periods, Heatter—or his writer—broke this long sentence up into five sentences for easier reading. And notice the underscoring of thought through repetition:

. . .where the Allies did achieve unity, where they were in complete agreement.

This is good technique in writing commentary. The commentator's meaning is nailed down. As Ed Murrow used to say, "You tell them once, and you tell them again." The same thing happens farther down in Heatter's script:

During the war, in the grim days of war. . . .

and

Better look carefully at the hands in which we turn it back. Better look carefully for marks on those hands. . . .

Heatter continually reinforces his meaning, expands on it, and you get a picture, not just words. The whole script, in fact, is full of rhetorical devices. The phrase <u>foolish enough</u> is a device he uses to dramatize how right he has been all along, and again he heightens the effect through repetition. This is an old oratorical trick, fine for certain types of commentary. But it is NOT for hard news.

The most celebrated of the early commentators was H. (for Hans) V. (for Von) Kaltenborn, who first went on the air in 1921. Kaltenborn's instant, round-the-clock analyses during the Munich crisis made him a living legend. When he was not ad-libbing his pieces, he wrote them. In a later chapter we'll examine Kaltenborn's role.

In August, 1939, CBS hired Elmer Davis. A former Rhodes scholar, Davis had gone from cub reporter on the *New York Times* to editorial writer for that paper. He wrote a history of the *Times*, numerous short stories, and at least five novels. Shortly after Pearl Harbor he resigned from broadcasting to become director of the Office of War Information. When he died in 1958, the *Times* hailed him as a veritable Mount Everest, "towering in serenity and grandeur over the foothill Cassandras of his time." (Language which surely would have made Davis squirm.) Speaking at Columbia University, Eric Sevareid said: "Davis. . .knew that to be a regular reporter or commentator on a nationwide network is so different in degree from writing for a publication with a coterie of readers who read it because they find it generally agreeable—so different in degree as to be almost different in kind. It is the difference between riding inside the stage coach, however hot and bumpy, and riding shotgun, exposed to the endless hailstones and the pointed arrows." Then Sevareid said, "His life was too short for our common need."

Here is vintage Davis as he reported on the Columbia Network, as it was known then, in the early days of World War II. You will notice that he ignores some of the guidelines for good broadcast style. His lead sentence is longer than it should be—28 words. (The next sentence is 43 words!) His lead also violates the rule that the source of information—the attribution—come at the head of the sentence. Davis until this time had been writing for newspapers. A news style peculiar to broadcasting had not been developed. But Davis pulled it off. He was writing for himself. It was HIS script. And that makes a very great difference indeed.

Note the careful qualification and elucidation, and trust in his own man on the scene. It is a no-nonsense, unpresumptive report—pure Elmer Davis.

Serious riots are going on in Milan and elsewhere in Northern Italy, according to information reaching diplomats in Yugoslavia and reported by our correspondent in Belgrade, Winston Burdett. There seems to have been some sort of military rising, either against the Fascist Party or against the German troops, who are reported as numerous in Northern Italy, for three high Italian officers are said to have been killed by Germans who intervened. And blackshirt units are assisting the Germans in repressing the disorders. German soldiers are said to have occupied the Milan railroad station and telephone, telegraph and radio offices, and also to be guarding the principal factories. Turin and various other places in the Po Valley are also the scene of rioting, and the casualties are said to run up into the hundreds. This information is not yet corroborated from other sources, but Mr. Burdett is the correspondent who got the first news of the arrival of German troops and planes in Italy. And our correspondent Harry Flannery reported from Berlin tonight that papers there speak of endless trainloads of Germans going through the Brenner Pass toward Italian soil.

There is a great deal of news here, packed into only a little more than one minute of copy. Notice the absence of highly colored adjectives. Indeed, there are hardly any adjectives at all. The report is straightforward, completely unsensational. It is objective. The Germans are not described as an invading horde, or even as Nazis—relatively few German soldiers were members of the National Socialist Party.

Elmer Davis was factual, but he did not hesitate to interpret. He once said, "All of us in the news business ought to remember that our primary responsibility is to the man who buys his newspaper or turns on his radio, expecting us to give him in so far as is humanly possible not only the truth and nothing but the truth, but the whole truth." He was endeavoring to report the real story "so far as humanly possible" when he said, "There seems to

have been some sort of military rising." This was his professional interpretation—not the same thing as personal advocacy or attack.

The First Roundup

In the shadow of war in Europe, radio journalism produced its first World
News Roundup. The multiple-pickup program, aired on March 13, 1938, was
the culmination of a year's planning by CBS. Nothing like it had ever been
done before. The studio clock in New York showed 8 P.M., but it was 1 A.M.
in Western Europe. Relay points across the Continent were skeleton staffed.
Reporters were standing by in four European capitals. Would it work? Then
William L. Shirer was up on the shortwave circuit from London—a good signal. Robert Trout, the anchorman in New York, began the introduction: "The
program 'St. Louis Blues' will not be heard tonight. . . ." Shirer made his
report, and then the American people heard the direct firsthand reports of
Edgar Ansel Mowrer of the *Chicago Daily News* from Paris, Pierre Huss of
the International News Service from Berlin, Frank Gervasi of the same news
service from Rome, and Edward R. Murrow from Vienna, which had just
been occupied by German troops.

Twenty years later, on March 13, 1958, Murrow participated in an anniversary broadcast and told how it was in those days, working in a fledgling medium.

Before the Anschluss [Hitler's takeover of Austria], arranging broadcasts from
Europe was a leisurely, civilized sort of business. Plenty of time to read and to see
your friends. It involved such things as relaying to this country the Vatican choir at
Easter time, a speech by DeValera, folk music from Scandinavia, the song of a
nightingale in a Surrey wood. After the Anschluss, things became rather more
interesting and considerably more hectic. We began to recruit our own staff of
reporters.

A radio reporter is a special kind of animal. He requires to know what he is writing
about, must be able to write it and, after that's done, he must be able to read it in
such a fashion as to be believable. In putting together our crew in Europe, I tried to
concentrate on finding people who were young and who knew what they were talking
about. Without bothering too much about diction, phrasing and manner of speaking.
There were occasional complaints from the home office on this score, which were
generally answered by saying that we were trying to collect a group of reporters
who would be steady, reliable and restrained—even though they might not win any
elocution contests.

In those days, before and during most of the war, we were not permitted to use recordings. Everything was live and moved directly from the reporter's microphone into your home. There were no editors or rewrite men who might tone down or hot up the copy as a result of their working in a more detached and tranquil atmosphere. We had no budget. Nobody gave orders. New York asked us only to find the news, try to report it and keep our heads. When we made a mistake, we tried to be the first to correct it. I don't recall that anyone ever objected to an assignment. And we never developed a habit of second-guessing each other on stories. Risks were run as a matter of course, and no one tried to examine how the other fellow felt about it or expound about his own reaction. You get more of that kind of stuff on a dull evening on television than I heard in Europe, North Africa and Korea.

I think it would be fair to say that we were pridefully serious about our job but not too serious about ourselves. And we all felt that words were puny things indeed to use in the effort to collapse distance between the men who were fighting and those who were at home. . . .

Another capsule description of what it was like in those days is given by Eric Sevareid, broadcasting from Rome on August 22, 1969:

Anniversaries are subject to the law of diminishing returns. The fact that as of this week I have been reporting almost daily over CBS for 30 years seems remarkably unimportant. If my superiors in New York think otherwise, it is probably out of astonishment that anyone could remain intact and in place so long in such a high pressure, rapidly changing profession. I share the wonder.

I began here in Europe when the Great War began. A reporter then enjoyed the sweet simplicities of radio. A portable typewriter, strong legs and a microphone in an office or a truck were all that he required. It was television that altered his life, his work and his nerve ends. In those early days of fine, careless rapture, a new form of journalism was created—certainly the most personal form ever known. We had to find, by trial and error, techniques and standards. Whether we knew it or not, or did it well or badly, we were creating a tradition, so to speak. Some bold spirits broke the path, including the superb Edward R. Murrow, who telephoned me from London 30 years ago and asked me to try this new kind of work.

Some of us, like me, were youngsters in our twenties. It seemed a fearful responsibility for callow youth, but war requires those leg muscles and youth has them. So we were educated at the public's expense. But we have tried at least, as some particles of wisdom may have gathered in place, to repair that—to repay that debt.

Over the years, other things change in one besides the muscles. You find yourself more and more tuned to the long waves, to the historical view of men and affairs. In the midst of much suffering, as the human race continues to make life rough for itself, you remain conscious of how it used to be, here in Europe and in your own land, and you know that yours has been a generation of healing from far more awful social ills—no guarantee, of course, against relapse.

Now, among some of the earnest young, a different concept of journalism is developing—mission oriented journalism, they call it. Commitment to cause or doctrine, based on the proposition that objective reporting or explanation of the news does not exist, since all reporters are human and conditioned one way or another. We used to call this propaganda. Pure objectivity may not exist. What counts is the aim, the effort in that direction.

After 30 years, only one commitment, one passion, remains to a journalist who loves and respects his profession and his colleagues: to find the truth of things as best he can and to relay it with what skill he can command.

Read these reminiscences for more than "background purposes." They offer contrasting examples of the essay type of broadcast. They concern writing—and rather importantly. Murrow found words "puny" for collapsing distance but used them powerfully. Sevareid speaks of "techniques and standards" and a new concept of journalism's role in society. Both would agree on the journalist's commitment: "To find the truth of things as best he can and to relay it with what skill he can command."

"This is the News"

Murrow once said: "I have a peasant's mind. I can only write about what I see." It is true he was a great eyewitness reporter. Note how, in this report on the German blitz against London, he uses words to help the listener, visually, share his experience:

Up toward London we could see billows of smoke fanning out above the river and, over our heads, the British fighters climbing almost straight up, trying to intercept the bombers before they got away. It went on for two hours, and then the all-clear. We went down to a nearby pub for dinner. Children were already organizing a hunt for bits of shrapnel. Under some bushes beside the road there was a baker's cart. Two boys, still sobbing, were trying to get a quivering bay mare back between the shafts. The lady who ran the pub told us that these raids were bad for the chickens, the dogs and the horses. A toothless old man of nearly seventy came in and asked for a pint of mild and bitters, confided that he had always, all his life, gone to bed at eight o'clock and found now that three pints of beer made him drowsy-like so he could sleep through any air raid.

Before eight the sirens sounded again. We went back to a haystack near the airdrome. The fires up the river had turned the moon blood-red. The smoke had drifted down until it formed a canopy over the Thames. The guns were working all around us, the bursts looking like fireflies in a Southern summer night. The Germans were sending in two or three planes at a time — sometimes only one — in relays. They would pass overhead. The guns and lights would follow them, and in about five minutes we could hear the hollow grunt of the bombs. Huge pear-shaped bursts of flame would rise up on the smoke and disappear. . . .It was like a shuttle service, the way the German planes came up the Thames, the fires acting as a flare path. Often they were above the smoke. The searchlights bored into that black roof but couldn't penetrate it. They looked like long pillars supporting a black canopy. Suddenly all the lights dashed off and a blackness fell right to the ground. It grew cold. We covered ourselves with hay. . . .

As World War II began, *Variety* said, "Murrow in London always gets close to the dramatic and human element, and furnishes an account which is clear and to the point." There could be no better dictum for the correspondent for radio or television: Be clear and to the point.

Clarity was the hallmark of Murrow's writing. His leads were simple, short, declarative sentences. The sentences in the body of his broadcasts often were written in the same simple, direct style. Here are the first two paragraphs of Murrow's broadcast of April 22, 1945, reporting the fall of Leipzig to American troops:

"Tell them resistance was slight!" That's what a GI shouted to us as we entered Leipzig. There were two tankers dead at the corner. Somebody had covered them with a blanket. There was a sniper working somewhere in the next block. Four boys went out to deal with him, then there was silence.

The Gestapo headquarters had been evacuated in a great hurry, but they had taken all their files with them. Down in the air raid shelter the floor was covered with money — Belgian, Polish, Hungarian — wherever the Germans had been. The money was ankle deep, and it was dirty. And it had no meaning.

This is eyewitness reporting of the first order, recalling Murrow's descriptions of the Battle of Britain and his firsthand account of the bombing of Berlin. The writing is dramatic — without dramatics. No fancy words are used, almost no adjectives. When an adjective IS used, it is used with telling effect. For example, with reference to the money, "and it was dirty."

Here is an excerpt of Murrow's report on the liberation of the wretched inmates of Buchenwald:

Men and boys reached out to touch me. They were in rags and the remnants of uniforms. Death had already marked many of them, but they were smiling with their eyes. . . .When I reached the center of the barracks, a man came up and said, "You remember me. I'm Peter Zenkl, onetime mayor of Prague." I remembered him but did not recognize him. . . .I asked how many men had died in that building during the last month. They called the doctor. We inspected his records. There were only names in the little black book, nothing more —nothing of who these men were, what they had done, or hoped. Behind the names of those who had died there was a cross. I counted them. They totaled 242—242 out of 1200 in one month. As I walked down to the end of the barracks, there was applause from the men too weak to get out of bed. It sounded like the handclapping of babies, they were so weak.

Edward Weeks, the great editor of the *Atlantic*, said of Murrow: "His manliness and compassion were never more touching than in his broadcast on Buchenwald, spoken the day that President Roosevelt died, and in his tribute to the British on V-E Day, ending with these poignant words: 'Some people appear not to be part of the celebration. Their minds must be filled with memories of friends who died in the streets where they now walk, and of others who have died from Burma to the Elbe. There are a few men on crutches, as though to remind all that there is much human wreckage left at the end. Six years is a long time. I have observed today that people have very little to say. There are no words.' "

Of Murrow's style of writing, Weeks said it was a vivid one. And, he said, "the timing was such that he had to be economical, and he favored the understatement." Then the magazine editor—no broadcaster—made one of the best judgments of what good writing for broadcast journanlism is by saying, "Broadcasting is writing for the mind through the ear, and it is quite different from writing for the eye, a distinction not always appreciated by professors [!]. Sentences must be short; words with a high vowel content make a much sharper impact. Consonants are likely to fluff and be missed. And the sentence structure must accentuate one image or one idea, not an assortment."

During World War II, no one wrote for Murrow. He wrote distinctively, for himself. However, with the start of the nightly radio program "Edward R. Murrow and the News" in 1947, he was assisted in his writing chores by Jesse Zousmer, a CBS News editor. For the next eight years, Zousmer wrote the hard news that made up the first six or seven minutes of the program, while Murrow wrote an analysis, or commentary, filling out the rest of the 15-minute broadcast. The program received more awards than any other news program in the history of radio, and Zousmer was recognized as the best news writer in the business. (He died in a plane crash in 1966.)

Zousmer's news summaries, of classically simple design, can be taken as models today. The sentences are lean, almost completely devoid of adjectives. Verbs are active. The language is conversational, yet never chatty. One searches in vain for exaggeration—no impression is given of knowing everything. Sources, where necessary, are identified.

Here is a sample, written on January 17, 1951, during the first year of the Korean War. It is a complete broadcast, including Murrow's analysis of the major story of the day. Both styles, however, are Murrow's, for Zousmer patterned his writing after Murrow. And Murrow, of course, edited everything. So what we have is a contrast in methods —one style for summarizing the news and another for analyzing it.

This is the news:

Communist China has rejected the United Nations' peace plan. The Communists have offered their own plan. The United States calls it unacceptable. In a few minutes I'd like to review these developments and where they leave us now.

In Korea, according to the reports available to us, things are very quiet. We have word of the enemy massing his troops below Seoul for a possible attack. Military sources are remembering that this type of lull preceded the Chinese attack in late November. But we are told only of small patrol actions all along the 130-mile front. A late United Press dispatch says an Allied reconnaisance patrol entered Wonju late today and found it deserted.

In Indo-China, the French claim a great victory. They say Communist troops have fallen back north of Hanoi with "tremendous" casualties after four days of battle.

In Burma, Dr. Gordon Seagrave, the American doctor who is widely known as "the Burma surgeon," today was convicted of high treason and sentenced to six years in prison. Dr. Seagrave told reporters, "I sincerely hope the American people will not judge the people of Burma by the action of a few." He is appealing the decision.

In this country, a high government source (who doesn't want his name used) says we're going to have a freeze on prices and wages within the next week. Mobilization Chief Wilson is reported to have decided that voluntary controls just won't work. Mr. Wilson may explain his position in a speech he's making tonight to the Poor Richard Club in Philadelphia.

Another report from Washington has it that the soft coal industry has decided to give the miners a voluntary 20-cent-an-hour wage increase, with the consumer eventually paying for it through a price increase.

The auto industry told the government today that it's going to cut production 20 to 30 percent below last year's record of 8-million cars and trucks. That would mean the production of from five-and-a-half to six-and-a-half million vehicles.

The President said today he's going to try voluntary controls to get the most out of our available manpower. He said, "Each individual will be expected to serve in the capacity in which he can contribute the most to the total mobilization program." If this doesn't work out, the President will ask Congress for power to prevent "indiscriminate" shifts of workers from one job to another, power to say how many skilled workers an employer can hire, and power to compel employers to make full use of women and handicapped and minority groups.

Defense Secretary Marshall today formally asked Congress for permission to draft 18-year-olds. He promises that none of these boys will be sent into combat before they are 19, except in dire emergency. But he does *not* want a ban on sending 18-year-olds overseas. He feels that this would "cripple the services in meeting any sudden, ruthless and violent action by our enemy." Today, senators heard the heads of five colleges — M.I.T., Princeton, Tufts, Williams, and Johns Hopkins — support the draft of 18-year-olds.

The Air Force has suspended its recruiting, at least until the end of the month. Its basic training facilities are swamped.

The Air Force says it is building up quickly from the present authorized 84 groups to 95-to-100 groups. And it's doubling the number of officers and men it had before Korea.

General Vandenberg, the Air Force chief, said in Tokyo today that there is no fool-proof defense against air attack. But if an enemy were to strike at us, we would have "certain indications" that would help us retaliate almost immediately.

In today's foreign policy debate in Congress, Republican Senator Mundt of South Dakota demanded that the President assure the country immediately that he will not send troops overseas without the advance approval of Congress. Democratic Representative Flood of Pennsylvania said it would be "monumental folly, akin to courting disaster" to limit the President's power in this fashion. House Speaker Rayburn urged that the foreign policy debate be conducted on a high level. He said, "Any jackass can kick a barn down, but it takes a carpenter to build it."

The House has unanimously approved a 2-billion-dollar naval construction program.

French Premier Pleven is coming to Washington a week from this Monday to discuss "important questions" with the President.

Britain's Prime Minister Attlee has reshuffled his cabinet. Health Minister Aneurin Bevan has been shifted to labor minister, the job Ernest Bevin held in the last war. Aneurin Bevan, leader of the Labor Party's left wing, would be the man assigned to keep unions in line for Britain's stepped-up rearmament program.

Here Murrow's own commentary begins.

Another chapter in the effort to achieve a cease-fire in Korea and a peaceful settlement with Communist China is closed, marked "FAILURE." The United Nations, by a vote of 50 to 7, had offered the Chinese an immediate cease-fire, the withdrawal of all non-Korean forces from the peninsula, the Koreans to choose freely their own government. Then there was to be a conference, including the United States, Britain, Russia and Communist China, to talk about Far Eastern problems, including the future of Formosa and China's representation at the United Nations. Our government supported this proposal because most of our allies pressed us to do so, and we wanted to maintain as much unity as we could. (Just for the record, we never agreed to turn Formosa over to the Chinese Communists, or to give them a seat at the U.N. We merely agreed to discuss these matters after the cease-fire and after the non-Korean troops had left the peninsula.)

Today the Chinese Communists turned down the proposal, saying that it was merely a device to let our troops in Korea rest and regroup. The Chinese said they must be seated at the U.N. *before* any talks began. The Chinese Communists further insisted that all foreign troops leave Korea, that a conference on Far Eastern problems, including Formosa, be held — the representatives to be Communist China, the Soviet Union, Britain, the United States, France, India and Egypt. And they insisted that the conference be held in China. Within two hours of the unofficial receipt of the Chinese answer, Secretary of State Acheson termed the reply "a complete rejection of the U.N. cease-fire proposal." He said the Communist counterproposal is unacceptable, and he had no doubt it would be unacceptable to the United Nations generally.

Warren Austin, our chief delegate to the United Nations, said this refusal "begins a new chapter of action for the United Nations to meet and repel the aggressions of the Chinese Communists." That action will take the form tomorrow, or the next day, of a broadly sponsored resolution at the United Nations, condemning Communist China as an aggressor in Korea. The only voice raised against this proposal, so far, comes from India's Prime Minister Nehru, who says that if the West brands Communist China as an aggressor, it will "bar the door to a peaceful settlement in the Far East." Mr. Nehru thinks that should be avoided at all costs and that most of the trouble in the Far East arises from the failure of the rest of the world to recognize the arrival of a great new power in China.

Lester Pearson of Canada, a member of the cease-fire committee, said, "We've gone farther than most of us would have gone to meet the Chinese, and there certainly won't be another cease-fire proposal." A British spokesman (whose country recognized the Chinese Communists and who pressed us to vote for the proposal) thinks now there is no alternative but to declare China the aggressor. The terms, he said, were very liberal, and they "strained the patience of the Americans to accept them."

So another formula for ending the war in Korea has failed. There has been no appeasement. We have gone as far as we could — indeed, many people thought we went too far — to demonstrate our willingness to talk. This latest failure brings an increase in the tension between China and this country and makes subsequent efforts at compromises more difficult, if not impossible. The fact that we made the effort will undoubtedly increase our support at the United Nations when the time comes, as it soon will, for the nations, including those that have recognized Communist China, to stand up and be counted. They must belatedly decide whether sending a million or more troops across a frontier and engaging in full-scale war is an act of aggression. It seems to me that our support of the cease-fire resolution, even though it was turned down by the Chinese Communists, has strengthened and reinforced the moral ground upon which we will stand in the future.

The Chinese refusal will, of course, give added ammunition to those who urge that we blockade and bomb China. I have seen enough of bombing, both from the ground and from the air, to doubt that bombs on China would substantially relieve the pressure in Korea, or prevent the eruption of the Chinese Communists into Indo-China or elsewhere. I think it was Clausewitz who laid it down that the first duty of a nation at war is to recognize its enemies. Our prinicpal enemy is the Soviet Union, and bombs on China will not damage that enemy.

Study these scripts. Note the simplicity of Zousmer's lead:

Communist China has rejected the United Nations' peace plan.

No adverbs. No adjectives except the one essential adjective <u>peace,</u> modifying the monosyllabic noun <u>plan</u>, which Zousmer chose over <u>proposal</u>, which is multisyllabic and takes three times as long to say. No fancy phrasing. No editorialization. Completely conversational. It's as though you are a newscaster and a friend sees you on the elevator.

"What's new?" he asks.

And you say, "China's rejected the United Nations' peace plan."

Always think, when you write for broadcast, what you would SAY. Ask yourself how you would tell the story in your own words.

Notice the absence of triteness. After the foreign news — the war news from Korea and Indo-China — Zousmer leads off the first domestic story with the phrase <u>in this country</u>, eschewing the thin-worn phrase *here at home*. (Yes, it was thin-worn more than twenty years ago!) The listener is oriented by the use of similar prepositional phrases: in Korea, in Indo, in Burma. Before Murrow reported the story, the listener knew where it happened. Such phrases, which act as datelines, enhance ease of understanding.

The lead story is told in the perfect tense. The next story from Korea is reported in the present tense. So is the story from Indo-China. But the report of Dr. Seagrave's conviction is told in the past tense. The tenses vary throughout the broadcast, avoiding monotony.

Note also the absence of verbal fat. Try excising words from Zousmer's script. Attempt this, and in almost every case the sentence will bleed. An important element will be lost. See if you can tell the story in fewer words by rewriting it completely. You will have a job on your hands.

Go through what Zousmer wrote, and what Murrow wrote, and you will see demonstrated most of the practices for writing news for broadcast which we have discussed. Neither of these scripts is perfectly written. Neither writer, working against a deadline, realized that he would be studied. But both writers were good at their craft.

Murrow edited Zousmer's script; he rarely rewrote it. One story he did rewrite concerned the arrival in San Francisco of a shipload of World War II dead. The date was October 10, 1947. The war had been over for more than two years. Zousmer wrote:

A ship carrying 3-thousand Americans who lost their lives in the war arrived in San Francisco today. It paused briefly in the bay while a memorial service was held on shore. Then it moved to the dock at the Oakland army base and started unloading. There were many men there today. . .reporters, longshoremen, army officers. . .who noticed a sign erected long ago. It was meant for the cheering soldiers who started coming home after the Japanese surrender. It was not without meaning today. The sign read: "Welcome home. Well done."

The story was well-written. Murrow rewrote it because he wanted to use the incident in his commentary on the United Nations, which was then in session. The story appeared in this new form:

About noon today a United States Army transport came in through the Golden Gate. Cargo: three thousand brown, steel caskets containing all that is mortal of men who did not flinch—men who lived a life, not an apology. There will be many more shiploads of those caskets coming home before the dead of the Second World War are returned to the land that was never far from their thoughts while they lived.

The transport came in past the birthplace of the United Nations. And at the Unite Nations today there were more speeches that missed fire, more oral bombs that didn't explode, more confusion and chaos in the ranks as nation strove against nation for petty paper advantage. The chair-borne army of diplomats is no worthy successor to those who made it possible for them to sit there in comfort and security. It is one of the lessons of history that young men suffer and sacrifice and achieve victory, and then the old men come out and try to rebuild in the image that they knew. The men who came home today are beyond words or worry. They bought us another chance. Their job is done. Ours is beginning. And if we fail, history will take its revenge and retribution will not limp.

Perhaps most prominent among other radio correspondents of World War II was William L. Shirer, known today for his two readable histories, *The Rise and Fall of the Third Reich* and *The Collapse of the Third Republic*, which is subtitled *An Inquiry into the Fall of France in 1940.* Shirer was hired by Murrow, and in the early days of the war his soft, untrained yet authoritative voice was heard by millions of Americans in direct reports from Hitler's own capital, Berlin.

For several years after the war, he continued broadcasting. Here is his first report on returning to America after the German surrender. The style of writing is vastly different from Murrow's. The language is casual, such as that which a well-informed, literate person would use in writing to a friend. But always conversational. The report is for the ear. Shirer was speaking. Listen!

What a wonderful — and fantastic — land of ours it is to come back to! No matter where you've been, or for how long. That is always your first impression when you come home. But to leave Europe yesterday, as I did, and arrive in New York this afternoon is to leap awfully rapidly from one world to a very different one indeed.

I've only been back four hours or so, but already one marvels at the contrasts and — may I say it? — our blessings. From the plane coming down New England today you could see the picturesque landscape covered with snow. A week ago, also in a plane, I watched the German and French landscapes. There was snow there, too, but nearly every town you flew over was in ruins. And from the houses no smoke rising, as from the New England houses I watched this afternoon. There's no fuel to heat the houses of Europe this Christmas.

When I stepped off the plane this afternoon my two daughters promptly dragged me off to some Christmas show at their school. The show was excellent — the singing, the pantomimes and all that. But what really impressed me was the look of four or five hundred American school kids. They looked so healthy. They looked so different from the youngsters I'd just seen in England or France or Germany who don't get enough milk or warm clothes or heat in their homes and schools, and are scrawny and pale and many the victim of rickets.

Just before I came up to the CBS studio, I walked down Fifth Avenue. It was jammed, of course, with shoppers, and though I heard some of them remark that there wasn't much to buy this year, I must say most of them staggered under Christmas bundles. And the store windows were, to me, quite fantastic.

I suppose the fundamental contrast is that we've recovered from the war — already forgotten it, in fact — and that in Europe they're just beginning to dig themselves out of the war. I guess what we Americans forget is the tremendous dislocation of the old world — the destroyed cities, the ruined lives, the starvation, and the cold. We forget that, and we forget how really lucky we are.

The report was for the ear — easy to listen to, easy to understand. The language is informal. Shirer was dragged to school by his two daughters. He uses phrases like school kids and and all that. He supposes and he guesses. He was talking, intimately, to his fellow countrymen. He was appealing to America's conscience.

3

BASIC WORK RULES

Bernard Shaw said, "Style is a sort of melody that comes into my sentences by itself. If a writer says what he has to say as accurately and effectively as he can, his style will take care of itself."

Shaw never wrote news for radio or television. Nonetheless, in his summing up of what style is, and how it comes about, he was saying something relevant to news writing. If the news writer says what he has to say accurately and effectively, he need not worry much about style. He has it made.

This book's whole purpose is to help you, in the specialized work of writing news for broadcast, to say what you have to say as effectively as possible.

Two questions are to be answered: What is effective writing in broadcast journalism? How, by what devices, do you make your writing effective?

Before exploring these techniques, let's look at some basic work rules. These rules have mostly to do with format. They concern how you make up your script.

Not every newsroom prepares its copy the same way. In general, however, these rules hold. For they ARE rules. They are as basic as turning on the ignition when you start your car.

Format

Triple space. When writing for radio, use the full page, allowing about an inch for margins. In television, use the right half (or two-thirds) of page for news copy. The left side of the page is for video information — visual effects, film or video tape rolls, on-camera talent, etc. If the broadcaster does voice-over (V/O), that is shown, too. There is also room on the left side of the page for the director to scribble in his cues and timings. (For examples of television scripts, see chapters 9, 13, 14, 15, 17, and 19.)

Type all news copy in upper and lower case UNLESS instructed otherwise. Some broadcasters prefer all caps. There are at least two reasons why copy usually is typed in upper and lower case. One is that video information frequently is typed in capital letters to set it apart from what the broadcaster reads. It LOOKS different, so the chance of mix-up is reduced. (Anything that reduces the likelihood of mix-up in television operations is to be welcomed.) The other argument for upper and lower case in news copy is that it enables the broadcaster to recognize proper names and the beginning and ending of sentences more readily.

Make at least one carbon copy of what you write. (Some television newsrooms require a total of seven copies, with distribution to broadcaster, producer, associate producer, director, associate director, prompter, and news editor. In most TV news operations, four copies are enough.)

DATE the first page of your script. Type your initials (or last name) in the upper left-hand corner of every page.

Use paragraphs. When you start your story INDENT.

In radio, number the pages of your script. Use a separate page for each story or write several stories on the same page, whichever procedure is followed by the station or network where you work. The advantage of using separate pages is that the order can be changed, and stories added or dropped, without marking up your script.

In television, the STORIES are numbered. Pages are arranged according to story numbers. And each story is on a separate page. If a story runs more than one page — and this goes for radio or television — write more in parentheses at the bottom of the page.

If more than one page is required, make the sentence at the bottom of the first page a COMPLETE sentence. If possible, make it a complete paragraph. Pages sometimes get out of order, and it is a nightmarish experience, on the air, to turn the page in the middle of a sentence and find the rest of the sentence missing. (It's bad enough to find the rest of the STORY missing! Almost any night, when you tune in to Walter Cronkite, you'll see him checking to see if his stories are in the right order. He's not play-acting during those few seconds when he is being introduced.)

If it takes ONLY another line to complete a story, and you have come to the bottom of the page, don't start another page for just that one line. Type it in at the bottom of the other page.

Turn in a CLEAN script. Retype the story if you have made revisions and time permits. (You always will be fighting the limitations of time.) The broadcaster may want to do some further editing, and his revisions, plus your own, can make the final script difficult to read. Professional writers pride themselves on clean copy.

Corrections

When you cross out a word, REALLY cross it out. Black it out completely. Leave nothing ambiguous in your script. The last thing the broadcaster wants is confusion in what he is trying to read.

If you make a correction in spelling, REWRITE THE ENTIRE WORD. If you are using a pencil or ballpoint pen to make your correction, print the corrected word PLAINLY. Do NOT use proofreader's marks to make corrections. The corrections in

Four persos are reported dead a in priva te plane cash near ironton, Ohio

are small help to the broadcaster. They may do for the typesetter, who has time to translate, but the man on the air wants a completely readable script. This is how the sentence should have been corrected:

Four ~~persos~~ **persons** are reported dead ~~a in privaate~~ **in a private** plane ~~cash~~ **crash** near Ironton, ~~Oiho.~~ **Ohio.**

Notice that in the properly corrected sentence the period was brought up NEXT to the last word, Ohio. In making such corrections, keep punctuation marks and the words they follow together. Again, this reduces confusion. With the word Ironton, it was easier for the writer, as well as less confusing for the broadcaster, simply to superimpose the capital "I." This kind of minor correcting can be done in those cases in which it IN NO WAY MAKES THE SCRIPT MORE DIFFICULT TO READ.

Do not cross out consecutive words individually. Take the sentence

He will report when they turn in their findings after the first of the year.

Do not edit down the sentence so that, in your copy, it looks like this:

He will report ~~when they turn in their findings~~ after the first of the year.

The edited sentence, if you choose to cross out those six words, should, instead, look like this:

He will report ~~when they turn in their findings~~ after the first of the year.

That is, if a succession of words is to be eliminated, cross them out without leaving space between the crossed-out words. Separately crossed-out words in succession tend to confuse. The eye is conditioned to regard such linear units as words.

And here is an example of horrendous "steeplechase" editing from an actual script:

However, the United States attorney's office ~~said~~ it ~~would~~ not ~~aks~~ for ~~an~~ a jail sentence. [*handwritten above: says will ask*]

Such verbal hurdles are inexcusable in a script. In this case, most of the second line should have been crossed out and corrections made like this:

However, the United States attorney's office ~~said it would not aks for an~~ a jail sentence. [*handwritten above: says it will not ask for*]

Clarity of language — all meaning — is annulled if your corrections of typographical errors, or other mistakes, cause the broadcaster to stumble about in the sentence you tried so hard to write simply and well.

Punctuation

Don't overpunctuate. With rare exception, the only punctuation marks you need in writing for broadcast are the period, comma, question mark and dash. (Note that no comma appears in the preceding sentence between *question mark* and *and*. In journalism, the comma before *and* in such a succession generally is omitted.)

Forget the semicolon.

Place commas after phrases like, "In London," "Here in this country," "At the United Nations," etc. when used at the start of a sentence.

NEVER hyphenate at the end of a line. Give the broadcaster only complete words.

Regardless of what Webster says, hyphenate words like *semi-annual, non-fiction, co-defendant, anti-pollution* and *non-proliferation.* By ignoring the dictionary in such cases, you are helping the broadcaster read what you have written. The only excuse for punctuation in your script is the help it gives the broadcaster in reading, so that the listener, in turn, can better understand what he hears.

The dash is TWO hyphens. It is useful in indicating pauses and for setting off parenthetical phrases.

Three periods (. . .) are used in much the same way as the dash. Adopt whichever style the broadcaster prefers.

Do NOT use the three periods to indicate omitted matter in a quotation. The listener can't hear the three periods, so they serve no purpose. In editing quotes, care must be taken not to distort what was said. Repeat: Be careful in editing what a person says. Do not distort.

It is not necessary to start and end a quotation with the verbal quotation marks *quote* and *unquote*. Usually a quotation can be adequately identified by inflection of the voice or by such attributing phrases as employed in the following:

He attacked the program, <u>calling it</u> "a boondoggle and a sham."

The mayor was, <u>in his words</u>, "full of promises God Almighty cannot redeem."

He said — <u>and we quote him</u> — "The lady is a tramp."

That would be, <u>as he expressed it</u>, "a cold day in hell."

Sometimes — not often — *quote* is used at the start of a quotation and *unquote* not used at the end.

She said <u>quote</u>, "The people yearn for another Dwight Eisenhower to lead them back to peace."

It can be argued that here, too, the <u>quote</u> is unnecessary. And we are inclined to agree. We probably would have rewritten the sentence to read:

She said that the people yearn for another Dwight Eisenhower to lead them back to peace.

As simple as that. If the language of the quotation is not too distinctive, the indirect quote serves.

Be careful where you place quotation marks, which one broadcaster has described as "those pesky little marks which look so pretty in print but which utter not a sound on the air." This sentence, read on the air, is confusing:

The defendant said that, if released on bail, he would go "where I always go."

The listener does not know whether I refers to the defendant or to the broadcaster. The sentence would be much more understandable if it read:

The defendant said that, if released on bail, he would go where he always goes.

Always consider what a direct quote adds to your story. What information, what insight, does it contribute? Avoid direct quotations that ramble on for three or four sentences. When you use long quotations, it's difficult to tell where the words of the person being quoted stop and the broadcaster's own words begin. You can solve the problem to some extent by saying something like "That's the end of X's statement," or, "We've been quoting the senator." But this doesn't remove the uncertainty in the listener's mind during the long quotation. Besides, if the statement is THAT good, shouldn't you use a piece of sound film or audio tape?

Don't try "personalized" punctuation — i.e., far out ungrammatical punctuation designed to make copy easier to read — UNLESS you are writing for yourself or you have had experience with the person you're writing for and KNOW how he wants it. Some broadcasters, for example, frequently pause before verbs. They believe the sentence sounds better — that THEY sound better — if the pause is made. But it would be a mistake to sprinkle commas indiscriminately before verbs because the broadcaster who effects this style of reading does not pause before every verb. You may not be able to sense which pause is right.

Stick to the general, accepted rules for punctuation until you know a broadcaster's peculiar needs.

Abbreviations

Most abbreviations are to be avoided. As a general rule, words used in broadcast copy should look the way they are read.

Names of states are written out in full: *Arizona*, not *Ariz.*; *New York*, not *N.Y.* The rule also applies to countries. Two exceptions are *U-S* and *U-S-S-R*, though *U-S* is less used than *United States* in general conversation and has a stilted sound when used repeatedly in a news broadcast. (Henry Wefing, one of CBS' first news editors, advocated use of *U-S* as the adjective and *United States* as the noun. But, when tempted to overuse *U-S*, don't forget that *American* is a perfectly good adjective, too.) *Russia* or *the Soviet Union* is preferable to *U-S-S-R*. If you want to say *U-S-S-R*, be sure you have first said either *Russia* or *the Soviet Union*.

Names of the months and days of the week are written out in full: *January*, not *Jan.*; *Monday*, not *Mon.*

Military titles are written out. Never abbreviate rank as *Pvt.*, *Capt.*, *Gen.*, and *Adm. Pfc.* may be regarded as an exception. This because *Pfc.* frequently is read *P-F-C* as well as *Private First Class*.

Avoid such abbreviations as *Adj. Gen.*, *Dist. Atty.*, and *Asst. Dir.*

The abbreviations *Dr.*, *Mr.*, and *Mrs.* are fine. *Prof.* for *professor* is frowned upon.

The abbreviations A.M. and P.M. are permissible. Other time abbreviations like *E.S.T.* and *E.D.T.* are not.

Abbreviations like *U-N*, *I-O-U*, and *T-N-T* should be punctuated (not written *UN*, *IOU*, and *TNT*) to facilitate the reading as separate initials. The punctuation may consist of hyphens or periods, whichever the broadcaster prefers. We, and most stylebooks, prescribe hyphens because the final period in the abbreviation can be mistaken for a period marking the end of a sentence.

A good rule of thumb is to punctuate when each initial is read separately. It is NOT necessary to use the hyphen (or period) in abbreviations like *NATO*, *NASA*, and *HUD* which are read as one word.

Generally, the full name of the organization—not the initials—should be reported when it is mentioned in a story for the first time. Exceptions are initials like F-B-I, G-O-P, and Y-M-C-A which practically everyone recognizes.

Other sets of initials like *U-A-W*, *A-I-D*, *F-C-C*, and *F-E-P-C* may be used ONLY after the full names of the organizations—United Auto Workers, Agency for International Development, Federal Communications Commission, and Fair Employment Practices Commission—have been given. The initials may be readily recognizable by you, but many listeners have forgotten, or never knew, which organizations or agencies such initials represent.

Numbers

Write out numbers *one* through *nine*. Use figures for 10 through 999. After 999, write out *thousand, million, billion*, etc. For example, write:

> 6-thousand 23, instead of 6,023
> 3-million, 8-thousand, instead of 3,008,000
> 8-billion, 600-million, instead of 8,600,000,000

The reason for this is that whereas the eye can readily take in, and the mind almost instantaneously translate, a three-digit number such as 213, the mind finds it more difficult to translate a figure like 3,008,000. You, the writer, translate for the broadcaster when you write out the number as *3-million, 8-thousand.*

Round off large numbers. For example, if the allotment for a federal project is $6,510,000, you can say that the allotment is *six and a half million dollars.*

The listener assumes that you are not reporting the allotment down to the last dollar and cent. If you want to be more precise, you can say that the allotment amounts to *a little more than six and a half million dollars.*

NEVER write the figure as $6.5 million. It's not much better to write the figure as *6 point 5 million.* Why not say *six and a half million* as people usually do in conversation?

Don't write, as one newspaper correspondent did:

The French government decided today to reduce the value of the franc to 18.004 United States cents from 20.255 cents in an effort to bolster France's ailing economy.

This detailed information is useful. The newspaper reader can digest it—that's the advantage of the print media over radio and television. In newscasts, such figures carried to the thousandth place are indigestible. The broadcast version of the story should read something like this:

France decided today to bolster its economy by devaluing the franc. It reduced the value of the franc to 18 cents. The franc had been worth a little more than 20 cents.

A place where figures most frequently are simplified on the evening news programs is the stock market report. The Dow Jones industrial index may be down 2.18 points, but the newscaster will say, "The Dow Jones industrial index lost a little more than two points today."

This business of rounding off, and translating, figures in the interest of making news stories less complicated, and hence more understandable, can be carried too far. For example, it would be inexcusable to say a hundred persons died in an airplane crash when 103 persons died. But it would be not only excusable but preferable to report that B-52's bombed an enemy base a hundred miles northwest of Saigon when the target actually lay 103 miles away. Or the broadcaster might say that the target was "*some* hundred miles northwest of Saigon." The point is that in this story the three miles does not really matter.

Incidentally, most stylebooks say that *one thousand, one million,* etc., are preferable to *a thousand, a million,* etc. The reasoning is that, to a listener, *a thousand* may sound like *eight thousand.* This may be, but we have observed that almost every time a figure like *one thousand* appears in a script, the broadcaster reads it as *a thousand* on the air. And *a thousand* is more conversational. We know of no actual case of a listener mistaking *a* for *eight,* and are inclined to go along with the broadcasters on this.

Sometimes distances—inches, feet, and yards—can be roughly translated to make a smaller figure. Thus, 36 inches can be translated into three feet, or a yard, and 5,000 feet into nearly a mile.

Fractions always are written out: *one-half, three-fourths*, etc. Fractions can be used to simplify — again by translating. "One-third of the money will go for housing" is better broadcast copy than "Thirty percent of the money will go for housing." And isn't it easier to say, "Food prices have almost doubled," than it is to say, "Food prices have risen 95 percent?"

One last word about numbers — the fewer of them you throw at the listener, the more understandable you are. Bear in mind that the listener cannot read the numbers, he has to remember them. And he has to remember, at the same time, what you said about them. So when you are thinking of using a figure — any figure — think twice. Ask yourself if it is necessary. If it IS necessary, give it to the broadcaster AND to the listener in its simplest form.

Dates

In writing the day of the month, add the *st, nd, rd*, or *th* which the broadcaster would add to the date if you did not. For example, make it *May 14th*, not *May 14*, but *January first*, not *January 1*.

Symbols

Don't use them. Symbols such as $, %, and # are anathema to the broadcaster and will not be suffered. Instead, use *dollar, percent*, and *number*. Also shun *No.* as in No. 007. Write it *Number 007*. (Some broadcasters would favor Number Double Oh 7, just as they would favor N-double A-C-P.)

Active Voice

Whenever possible, use verbs in the active voice. This is one of the basic principles in writing news. "The car hit him" is a much more forthright statement of what happened than "He was hit by a car." Comparatively, the passive voice is weak.

Grammar

News directors frequently complain over their writers' ignorance of English grammar.

Harry Kevorkian, news director of WNDU, South Bend, reports that in hiring writers "for the most part our basic problem is that we generally are training people from scratch. And in some cases it's a task to remind them of basic English, let alone about refining leads."

Russ Thornton, news director at WBAP, Fort Worth, says, "An amazing number of newsmen come to us with college degrees and leave us wondering how they ever passed freshman English."

Instruction in English grammar is beyond the province of this text. If you have trouble with grammar, better brief yourself. The library or any good bookstore can provide what you always wanted to know about grammar. It IS important.

4

NAMES AND PRONUNCIATION

In any reporting, the most important thing about peoples' names is to get them right. Still, in broadcasting, names are treated differently than in other media — they are simplified wherever possible. That is, where communication does not suffer for it, first names and initials are left out. The broadcaster says *President Nixon, Premier Kosygin, Secretary of State Rogers*, or even just *Secretary Rogers* if the name appears in a context which leaves no doubt that you are talking about the secretary of state. The broadcaster does NOT say *President Richard M. Nixon, Premier Aleksei N. Kosygin*, or *Secretary of State William P. Rogers.*

This is consistent with the guiding principle in writing news for radio and television, which is to tell your story clearly and accurately — as effectively as possible — in the fewest number of words. You are no less accurate when you say *Secretary of State Rogers* than if you use his first name and initial, and you have saved time. In fact, through simplification you have improved communication between the broadcaster and the person who is listening. The listener's mind isn't being cluttered with nonessentials. The "shape" of your message has cleaner lines.

In national stories, first names and middle initials can most often be dropped from the names of governors and members of Congress.

Examples:

>Governor Rockefeller of New York
>Senator Griffin of Michigan
>Representative Albert of Oklahoma

In broadcast terms, this language is better than

>Governor Nelson A. Rockefeller of New York
>Senator Robert P. Griffin of Michigan
>Representative Carl Albert of Oklahoma

Now it gets a little more complicated. When party affiliation is not apparent from the context in which the name appears — and identification of party is important — this style usually is used:

>Republican Governor Rockefeller of New York
>Republican Senator Griffin of Michigan
>Democratic Representative Albert of Oklahoma

This is better broadcast style than

>Governor Rockefeller, Republican of New York
>Senator Griffin, Republican of Michigan
>Representative Albert, Democrat of Oklahoma

and MUCH better than

>New York Republican Governor Nelson A. Rockefeller
>Michigan Republican Senator Robert P. Griffin
>Oklahoma Democratic Representative Carl Albert

"Freight train" phrases like those are abhorred by all broadcasters, and writers who perpetrate them deserve to read their own words.

When a member of Congress is chairman of a committee, his chairmanship often becomes more significant than the fact that he is a senator or a representative. Thus *Senator Fulbright of Arkansas* gives way to *Chairman Fulbright of the Senate Foreign Relations Committee*, and *Representative Hébert of Louisiana* gives way to *Chairman Hébert of the House Armed Services Committee*. Likewise, Senator Mansfield of Montana often is referred to as *Senate Majority Leader Mansfield.* His position in the Senate lends special importance to what he says. The same is true of all majority and minority offices, including Speaker of the House. In such instances, the office usually precedes the name.

Remember, these are guidelines. None of this means you should never use the first names of members of Congress. It means you can usually leave them out. By leaving them out, you make a less complicated sentence. But there is nothing wrong, for example, with saying

The chairman of the House Armed Services Committee, F. Edward Hébert, said today that he strongly disagrees.

although

Chairman Hébert of the House Armed Services Committee said today that he strongly disagrees.

says the same thing and saves two words.

There is almost no case for using initials. The initial is something for the broadcaster to read — and the listener to hear — which is totally unnecessary. It makes the reading of the script more difficult. More importantly, it gives the listener a superfluous fact — one which must be comprehended, added to other, essential facts, sorted out in the mind of the listener, and finally discarded in the process of achieving understanding of what is significant. It is a waste of the mental process. And it is a waste of time. In a broadcast, as elsewhere, small wastes add up.

In this boycotting of initials, the big exception is the initial (or middle name) which is popularly — and permanently — associated with the person. Usage must be respected with such names as George M. Cohan, D. W. Griffith, John L. Lewis, Edward R. Murrow, Robert Penn Warren, and William Carlos Williams, to name a few. The initials and middle names are their trademarks.

More About Names

It is permissible to start a news story with a well-known name — "J. Edgar Hoover made one of his rare appearances on Capitol Hill today." But NEVER start with a name that is unfamiliar to most listeners, as in this story by the Associated Press:

CONCORD, N.H. — AP — MIKE DOMBROSKI, 28 YEARS OLD, A UNIVERSITY OF NEW HAMPSHIRE GRADUATE STUDENT, ANNOUNCED HIS CANDIDACY TODAY FOR THE DEMOCRATIC NOMINATION TO OPPOSE REP. LOUIS C. WYMAN, REPUBLICAN OF NEW HAMPSHIRE.

The story for broadcast might be written:

A graduate student at the University of New Hampshire announced today that he will run for Congress. The student is Mike Dombroski, and he's 28. He is seeking the Democratic nomination to oppose Republican Representative Louis Wyman of New Hampshire.

The reason for not starting with an unfamiliar name is that listeners probably will miss it. The strange name takes them by surprise. They have to be prepared for it. The "preparation" consists of reporting the person's occupation, function, title — whatever makes him newsworthy — FIRST and his name SECOND. Don't write

Dr. William Dix, president of the American Library Association, today denounced encroachments on what he called "the right to read."

Instead, write

The president of the American Library Association, Dr. William Dix, today denounced encroachments on what he called "the right to read."

The name is now "teed up." When the listener hears the words "president of the American Library Association," he expects to hear a name and is listening for it. He is not taken by surprise.

It is especially important in the treatment of names to remember that you are writing for the ear. (That phrase again.) Unlike the newspaper reader, the listener cannot dwell on a name. He hears a surname — sometimes for the fraction of a second — and it is gone. So never give a person's name in the lead of a story and then, in the rest of the story, keep referring to that person as *he* or *she*. Repeat the name. Failure to do this is one of the most aggravating "sins of omission" in broadcast journalism.

Similarly, do not refer in your copy to *the former* or *the latter*. This is a carry-over from print journalism, where the reader can look back. It imposes on listeners, who cannot look back, an unreasonable obligation to remember and translate. You must give listeners, in every instance, what John Chancellor has aptly described as "understandable information."

And don't bother with meaningless names in the news. If the governor of a Philippine island appeals for emergency aid after a typhoon, just say the governor made the appeal. Not only might the broadcaster have difficulty pronouncing the governor's name, but the name contributes nothing to an understanding of what happened. Indeed, it can distract. A pretty good rule is to report those names which listeners recognize or will come to recognize because of subsequent events. In short, names which to the listener mean something.

KIGH-roh Is the One in Egypt

This heading is stolen from the *New York Times*, which did an article on the trouble newscasters have with pronunciation. The article observed, among other things, that if a newscaster confuses *KIGH-roh* in Egypt with *KAY-roh* in Illinois, "a certain amount of precious credibility goes out the window."

Mispronunciation does damage credibility, and broadcasters know it. The well-worn dictionaries in station libraries are used more for pronunciation than for spelling, and the networks have lists of easily mispronounceable names for the guidance of their news staffs. NBC has compiled its own book on pronunciation, and for more than thirty years CBS has enjoyed the services of Dr. Cabell Greet, a professor of speech at Columbia University, as its special consultant. It is due to the instruction of Professor Greet that on CBS you hear *junta* pronounced *JUN-ta*. Until he intervened, most newsmen had given it the Spanish pronunciation, *HOON-ta*. He reasoned that *junta*, pronounced *JUN-ta*, had been in English usage since 1623 and should be spoken that way. In his research, he found that the Spanish pronunciation, *HOON-ta*, was not introduced in the United States until after 1898, when it was brought back by soldiers who had served in Cuba during the Spanish-American War.

Until 1939, the BBC employed an advisory committee on spoken English. Its first chairman was the poet laureate of England, Robert Bridges, who said, "We are daily establishing in the minds of the public what correct speech should be." But a later chairman, Bernard Shaw, called the committee a ghastly failure. "It should be reconstituted," he said, "with an age limit of thirty and a few taxi drivers on it." This from the creator of Professor Higgins, the most celebrated phonetician of them all!

Today the BBC has a Pronunciation Unit with a staff which maintains, and constantly is expanding, a card file of more than 60,000 pronunciations.

Experts on the pronunciation of certain words are not hard to find—IF you look in the right place. When the identification of Robert Kennedy's assassin was bulletined, you could hear Sirhan Sirhan's name pronounced a dozen different ways. No authority seemed to know the correct pronunciation. Then someone thought to ask the defendant's mother. Why, yes, she said, the name is pronounced *sir-han* rhyming with *pan*. CBS had been pronouncing it *seer-hahn*. NBC's pronunciation had been *SEER-hahn*. ABC hadn't committed itself. Other ways you may have heard the name that day include *sir-HAN, sir-HAHN, SEER-han, seer-HAHN* and *SIR-AHN*!

Of course, the best source is your dictionary, with its pronunciations of the names of people and places. Unabridged dictionaries are especially good in this respect. *Who's Who* comes in handy. But many names are not to be found readily in print. What do you do then?

There are various things you can do. If you don't know the pronunciation of the name of an official of a foreign country, or how to pronounce one of its towns or provinces, call the consulate of that country. If you're in Washington, call the embassy. New York stations often are helped in their pronunciation problems by the United Nations. If it's the name of a politician, call his office or the local political organization. If it's the name of a labor leader, call union headquarters. If it's a member of a black organization, try the organization.

Be resourceful. On occasion, when we were desperate for the pronunciation for a seldom-heard-of-town, we turned to "Mother Bell." We simply called the telephone operator in that community. We'd ask, "How do you pronounce the name of your town?" Sounds crazy, but it cost nothing. And it worked. One of us boasts that from his desk in New York he got the correct pronunciation for Elizabethton, Tennessee, in fifteen seconds. (It's *Eliza-BETH-ton.*)

The best advice that can be given on the pronunciation of names is not to assume you know. The NBC News editor, Bill Monroe, tells an amusing story about an announcer's mispronunciation of the name of Fred Preaus, a Louisiana politician. The announcer snatched a piece of copy from the AP radio wire and, reading it word for word on the air—with total disregard for what he was saying—declared pontifically:

Fred Preaus, whose name rhymes with moose, today announced his candidacy for governor.

Besides reading the AP advisory on pronunciation, which he was not supposed to read, the announcer compounded his mistake by giving *Preaus* the French pronunciation *pro*. He assumed this because the name is French. A lot of listeners, hearing the reference to *moose*, must have done a double-take.

There is a real lesson here. If you are reading, don't pontificate. If you stumble in your arrogance, you fall farther, and harder, because you are revealed as a fake. And don't assume.

Know What You Are Reading

In pronouncing place names, never trust the way a word looks. For example, *Pago Pago* is pronounced *PANG-o PANG-o*. (A student intern at a station in Washington D.C. won a five-dollar bet on that one!) Within a matter of minutes, a network correspondent who should know better was heard pronouncing *Edinburgh* as though it rhymed with *Pittsburgh* and *Gloucester*, the Massachusetts fishing port, *GLOW-ster* instead of *GLOSS-ter*. Such mispronunciations do make you wonder if the newscaster is well-informed. They do damage credibility.

There is an inconsistency in the pronunciation of place names. *Miami*, for example, frequently is pronounced *my-AM-a*, not *my-AM-ee*, by people living in Miami, and citizens of Cincinnati often say *sin-sa-NAT-a*, instead of *sin-sa-NAT-ee*. Likewise, *St. Louis* sometimes is pronounced *saint-LOO-ee*, as in the song, "St. Louis Blues." Of course, the generally accepted pronunciations for all three cities are *my-AM-ee*, *sin-sa-NAT-ee*, and *saint-LOO-iss*. Visitors to New York City often pronounce *Houston* Street like the city in Texas. But it's pronounced *HOWS-ton*.

We began this section by noting the difference in *KIGH-roh*, Egypt, and *KAY-roh*, Illinois. Other look-alikes pronounced differently are:

> *BO-fort*, N.C. and *BU-fert*, S.C. (Beaufort)
> *BURR-lin*, N.H. and *Burr-LIN*, Germany (Berlin)
> *Cal-las*, Maine and *Cal-aye*, France (Calais)
> *CAN-ton*, Ohio and *Can-TAWN*, China (Canton)
> *KWIN-see*, Ill. and *KWIN-zee*, Mass. (Quincy)
> *LYE-ma*, Ohio and *LEE-ma*, Peru (Lima)
> *MYlan*, Ohio and *Me-LAHN*, Italy (Milan)
> *Moss-cow*, N.Y. and *MOSS-co*, Russia (Moscow)
> *NEW-erk*, N.J. and *NEW-ark*, Del. (Newark)

Listeners like to write to broadcasters, correcting them on their pronunciation. The "corrections" are not always right. A listener in Malvern, Arkansas, wrote to Murrow: "I listen to your broadcasts but have one fault to find with them. You pronounce words like *essential* and *effective* as though they were spelled *ee-sential* and *ee-fective*. However, you don't put a cow in *Mosco(w)*, for which I am pleased. I hope this reminder will prove *ef-fective*."

In this case, the listener was wrong. So was Murrow, if he indeed did pronounce the first syllable of *essential* and *effective* like the *e* in *eve*. According to Webster, the first syllable of both words is pronounced like the *e* in *end*, and that's not the *ee* sound the listener referred to. It's more like the sound of a very old man who can't quite hear what you say and asks, "Eh?"

There are instances when uncommon though correct pronunciation impresses the listener as affectation. Few American newscasters, for example, have—or in most cases should have—the temerity to pronounce *either* as *EYE-ther*. As Fowler says in the preface to his *Modern English Usage*, "Display of superior knowledge is as great a vulgarity as display of superior wealth."

Don't ignore listeners' critiques on pronunciation. They're often right!

A name that took broadcasters unawares early in 1970 was *Pnompenh*, the capital of Cambodia. For weeks it was called *Nom-pen*, then gradually became *P-nom-pen*. At the conclusion of a broadcast, Harry Reasoner shared this pronunciation problem with his nationwide audience, to wit:

Those of you who hang on my words may have noticed that earlier [in this broadcast] I pronounced the capital of Cambodia P-nom-pen for the first time, instead of Nom-pen. I've given in on this because I believe in the theory that it is better for all broadcasters to pronounce something the same way, even if it's wrong. I yield my contention that Nom-pen is closer to what the Cambodians say. Also, my record on pronunciation is not so good that I can enter an argument as the favorite. And it's a small matter for a man of my reasonable p-sy-chol-o-gy.

We have gone into considerable detail on this subject of pronunciation because 1) it is fascinating, and 2) it is a problem with which, as writer or broadcaster, you are going to live. In many newsrooms it is the writer's responsibility to check pronunciation for the broadcaster. In any case, the broadcaster is going to want to know. If the writer does not provide him with the correct pronunciation, or if he writes his own script, the person going on the air will research the word himself.

This information—the correct pronunciation of a word—should be written into the script. The pronunciation should be typed IN CAPITAL LETTERS, IN PARENTHESES, either above or immediately after the word in question. Examples:

Ecology (EE-KOL-OGY) was the major subject discussed.

　　　(EK-O-LOGICAL)
They discussed the ecological aspects of the problem.

The pronunciations are given in capital letters to set them apart.

The radio wires operated by the Associated Press and United Press International have adopted a system of phonetic spelling for hard-to-pronounce names—teletypes cannot transmit the pronunciation symbols used by biographical dictionaries and gazeteers. These phonetic spellings provided by the wire services are given in parentheses after the names, not above them, for obvious reasons. They are provided ONLY on the radio wires.

Once, when she presented daily commentary on the *New York Times* station, WQXR, that newspaper's celebrated women's news editor, Charlotte Curtis, did a three-minute broadcast on the problems of pronunciation. As a newspaper woman turned broadcaster, she had become increasingly conscious of the way words—especially proper names—are pronounced. She told her radio audience:

Europeans can complain all they want about the pronunciation difficulties of the English language. They've had their revenge with all the foreign words that are bedeviling us poor Americans.

For instance, in spite of Commander Whitehead's curiously refreshing commercials, many Americans still order "Shweepeeze" or "Shweppus" instead of Schweppes [Shweps]. Beer drinkers ask for "Michael Loeb," who's a very charming fellow, or "Michele Lobb," who's not. When they're really thirsty for Michelob [MICKelobe]. When it's time for cigars and cognac, Remy Martin [Reh-mee Martan] sounds more like the name of a European movie star—"Remmy Martin" if she's English or "Reemie Marteen" if she's French.

Drinkers aren't the only Americans with a foreign language bugaboo. Pity fashion-conscious ladies. The makers of Jean Naté Friction pour le Bain finally gave up trying to get Americans to say "Zhan Natay." They compromised and called it "Jean Natay" and let the Friction pour le Bain go down the drain. Sun-worshipers desperately stumble over the first two words of Bain de Soleil [Ban deh Solay] and then ask for the sun cream with the French name.

Speaking of la belle France, the country of the boutique, [boo-teek] which many still pronounce "boh-teek," she has sent us the ultimate in unpronounceable boutiques—the St. Laurent Rive Gauche. St. Laurent has been giving Americans trouble for years—mostly in the pocket books. But Rive Gauche is a new phrase to master. For the record, Rive is not like *sieve* or *hive* and Gauche is not "gowshie" or "goshay" but "Reeve Goh-sh." Simple, n'est-ce pas?

Now that you're an expert on these foreign words, you may start working on such all-American places as Illinois, Washington and Nevada. In the Middle West, but rarely in Chicago, Illinois is pronounced "Illinoise"—as if there really were a big noise in Winnetka. And lots of people put an "r" in Washington, making it a very warlike Worshington.

Then there's Nevada—Nevada to Easterners and "Nevaaduh" to the Nevaaduhans. One of Nevada's most charming little towns would seem to be Verdi, named for the Italian composer. Yet the natives call it "Verdye," and "Verdye" it is.

And I'll end this nonsense by telling you what the Kentuckians have done to the pronunciation of what the French so lovingly call Versailles, even though it may well ruin your evening. It's "Versayles," if you can stand it — Versayles, Kentucky.

This is Charlotte Curtis. I'll be back tomorrow.

Miss Curtis had devised her own system of phonetic spelling which, she says, "works for me." Her favorite pronunciation story involves the word *halcyon*. "WOSU, the Ohio State University station, was forever having bright young people who wanted to use enchanting off-beat words on the air. Hence, *halcyon*, which they pronounced as if it rhymed with pelican. No amount of complaining helped. And for all I know," she says, "they're still mispronouncing it."

Pronunciation is serious business. It is bad enough not to know how to pronounce a foreign name, but to be ignorant — and there is no kinder word for it — of how to pronounce a good American word is embarrassing for all concerned. As Allan Jackson said in one of his broadcast journalism lectures, "Nothing is quite so distracting to a listener as a news broadcaster who can't pronounce the words of his own language."

The actor, David Garrick, said of the preacher, George Whitefield (*WHIT*-field), "He could make men laugh or cry by pronouncing the word *Mesopotamia*." Many a writer could weep over the pronunciation a newscaster gave a word selected oh so carefully. And many a listener, hearing that word, has laughed.

Do not assume because the person for whom you write is intelligent and well-traveled that he knows. Make sure. Then there will be no need to laugh OR weep.

The preceding two chapters on handling corrections, punctuation, abbreviations, numbers, dates, symbols, names, and pronunciation really constitute a primer. These rules are elementary. They are NOT arbitrary. They evolved from the experience of thousands of radio and television newsmen in the first half-century of broadcast journalism's existence. They have been proven in practice. They do make the script more readable and the news easier for the listener to understand.

So much for the work rules. On now to broader fields!

5

TELL YOUR STORY

The time: Seconds before 5:47 P.M., April 12, 1945.
The place: New York City

Editors on the second floor of the Times Building discuss their lead story: Three United States armies—the 1st, 3rd, and 9th—are pressing toward Berlin. Armored elements of the 9th Army have crossed the Elbe River in force. Also on Page One will appear the report of new air strikes against American warships off Okinawa. We have lost a destroyer, and the Japanese have lost 118 planes.

Across town, on the seventeenth floor of the CBS Building, John Daly is writing his evening newscast. He is due to go on the air at 6:15. The news he intends to report has, basically, the same portent as that which is being set in type at the *New York Times*. Victory in Europe is imminent. More hard fighting appears inevitable in the Pacific.

In those few seconds, an era ends. At 5:47 P.M., bells begin jangling on the International News Service teletype at both the *Times* and CBS, and in all the newsrooms that subscribe to INS. CBS World News Editor Lee Otis walks quickly to the teletype and reads the flash: FDR DEAD. Two minutes later—at 5:49 P.M.—CBS engineers have interrupted the radio serial "Wilderness Road," and Daly, at the microphone in Studio 9, is saying:

We interrupt this program to bring you a special news bulletin from CBS World News. A press association has just announced that President Roosevelt is dead. All that has been received is that bare announcement. There are no further details as yet, but CBS World News will return to the air in just a few moments with more information as it is received in our New York headquarters. We return you now to our regularly scheduled program.

And now let's make an interruption of our own for some critical comment regarding his historic bulletin. The news that Roosevelt had died should have been repeated. Of the five sentences in the bulletin, only one sentence makes direct reference to the fact that the President of the United States was dead. The source of this unexpected news should have been clearly identified as the International News Service. And press associations don't ANNOUNCE the death of presidents; they REPORT it. Also, it is surprising that after receiving this news the network rejoined its regularly scheduled program, even for a few moments. That would not happen today. As when President Kennedy was shot, all networks would start giving continuous coverage. As it was, within two minutes after giving his bulletin, Daly was back on the air, reporting the cause of death—cerebral hemorrhage—and plans for the funeral.

Funeral services will be held Saturday afternoon in the East Room of the White House. Interment will be at Hyde Park.

Through the night, coverage of the death of the President continued on CBS and the other radio networks. It was the first death of an incumbent President to be covered by journalists of the new medium. Eighteen years would pass before a comparable tragedy again challenged their technical and reportorial skills.

At the *New York Times*, reporters, editors, printers grappled with their biggest story since D-day. The original front-page dummy was scrapped. The American advance on Berlin—Hitler's own Gotterdammerung—became the No. 2 story. The headline across the top of the page now reads:

PRESIDENT ROOSEVELT IS DEAD;
TRUMAN TO CONTINUE POLICIES;
9TH CROSSES ELBE, NEARS BERLIN

Arthur Krock, chief Washington correspondent, wrote the lead story:

WASHINGTON, April 12 — Franklin Delano Roosevelt, President of the United States and the only Chief Executive in history who was chosen for more than two terms, died suddenly and unexpectedly at 4:35 o'clock P.M. today at Warm Springs, Ga., and the White House announced his death at 5:14 o'clock. He was 63.

This initial coverage by CBS and the *Times* can be compared in many ways: speed of communication — immediacy — depth of coverage, audience. But let's look at one aspect — the language used by the two media, the difference in reportorial style.

John Daly was telling what happened.

"A press association has just announced that President Roosevelt is dead. . . .Funeral services will be held Saturday afternoon in the East Room of the White House."

This is how people speak. "I just heard Mrs. Smith died. The funeral will be Friday afternoon at the home." The style is conversational. It is natural. It is right.

In broadcasting the first bulletin, all Daly had before him was a slip of yellow paper from the INS machine bearing the two words: FDR DEAD. Later he ad-libbed from wire copy from all three wire services — AP and UP, as well as INS — before switching to Washington for firsthand reports:

He had gone again to Warm Springs to try to get new strength to face the San Francisco Conference, to shape there with his own hands, as much as he could, the course of the peace to come, to lead there men of all nations and all faiths, to sit down together around the council table and to give the gift that he had always wanted — the gift of peace that would last beyond our time, perhaps beyond our children's time, and to the time of our grandchildren.

That is an extraordinarily long sentence — 87 words — much too long according to every style book that has been written for broadcast news. But if flows. It is conversational, albeit in Daly's individual, rather ornate style. And because it is beautifully structured — full of pauses — it is completely understandable. It is also very eloquent.

Now compare the broadcast language of John Daly with the print language of Arthur Krock. For the ear alone — without sight — Krock's language in insufferable. He starts with the name of the President, then spends the next 19 words identifying him. You are deep in the sentence before you are told what happened, that the President died. The sentence would confuse listeners with its conglomeration of facts and figures: Franklin Delano Roosevelt. . .only Chief Executive. . .history. . .two terms. . .died. . .4:35 o'clock

P.M. . . .Warm Springs. . .White House. . .5:14 o'clock—all in one sentence. Also, phrases are used which practically no one employs in conversations: 4:35 P.M. o'clock and 5:14 o'clock. You just don't talk that way. Imagine a friend saying, "I'll meet you in the lobby at 8 P.M. o'clock!" Of course, Krock's next sentence—"He was 63"—is ideal broadcast copy, although the figure is piled onto 4:35 and 5:14, which is not the kind of thing you want to do in writing for radio or television.

Recall how the distinguished editor, Edward Weeks, in analyzing Murrow's style, said that "sentence structure must accentuate one image or one idea, not an assortment." One reason Daly could deliver an 87-word sentence and not confuse the listener is that he was accentuating one idea—Roosevelt's desire to do what he could to make a lasting peace. One idea to a sentence is an excellent guide. Arthur Krock's lead held a devastating assortment.

So here are four differences between writing news for the ear and writing for the eye:

> Broadcast news is telling—not chronicling—what happened. The style should be conversational, informal, but not cozy.
>
> No array of facts—especially figures—can be thrown at the listener all at once. The fewer figures the better.
>
> Each sentence, ideally, should contain only one idea or image.
>
> And sentences generally should be brief.

Ernest Hemingway has been quoted as saying, "Good writing is good conversation, only more so." Nowhere is this so true as in broadcast journalism. The "more so" means the writer of news for radio and television will be more selective in what he talks about and in the way he says it than he might be while chatting with friends. But his writing, to earn the adjective *good*, will have to be conversational.

If you want a recipe for telling a story, an approach, here's one from CBS News correspondent John Hart, who says, "I think it's the same thing as when you come home from the office. You say to your wife, 'Honey, guess what happened today.' You don't tell her, "I sat at my desk for eight hours. I wrote a report on 350 different conclusions on how many whatever.' You don't report to her the humdrum. You report to her something that is extraordinary, and you say, 'What I saw was this guy come up to this gal at the water cooler, and do you know. . . .' Then you go on to tell her something juicy.

"Well, in a way we are gossips. Gossip doesn't mean untruth. It means telling fascinating tidbits about fascinating things. We're more than gossips, of course, at our best. We tell them things people need to know. We tell them about cyclamates, we tell them about crooked politicians, we tell them about other things when we're doing our best work. But it's a form of gossip. We come on the air and we're saying, 'Hey, folks, guess what I saw today. Nelson Benton, what did you see today?' And Nelson Benton comes on and says, 'Guess what I saw today,' and then he begins his story. He doesn't say it, but it's implied. That's the preamble to everything. We're just telling, reasonably accurately, what we saw. And what we choose to report on is what we think will be interesting when we come home at night at 6:30 in people's homes and say what the husband said to his wife.

"That's the way I feel about it. We're engaged in the gossip of history when we're at our very best."

The Enemy Is Complexity

Just as the person who writes science articles for a popular magazine must be able to translate complicated scientific data into layman's language, the writer of broadcast news must be able, without demeaning them, to make complicated stories sound simple. Few listeners, for example, have the background necessary to understand the workings of the Common Market. A story concerning the market must be written in such a way as to be universally meaningful — that is, meaningful to the mechanic in Youngstown as well as to the economist at Yale. More than two centuries ago, Daniel Defoe said, "If any man were to ask me what I would suppose to be a perfect style of language, I would answer that in which a man speaking to 500 people all of common and various capacities should be understood by them all." Instead of writing to be understood by 500 people "all of common and various capacities," the broadcast journalist may be writing for 5 million. He must sort out the facts — the essential from the nonessential. Then he must make the essential understandable. He must translate.

Take, for example, the quotation from Defoe. The idea expressed is excellent. But for radio or television, Defoe's style is horrendous. Even in print, you may need to read the sentence twice to capture its meaning.

In broadcasting, understanding must be immediate. It avails you nothing if your facts are straight and your copy is clean and your grammar faultless IF the listener makes no sense out of what he hears or, worse still, misunderstands. In writing news for the ear, the "perfect style of language" is that language which makes your meaning — what you are reporting — clear to the harassed motorist in rush-hour traffic and to the housewife trying to prepare dinner with a brood of children round about, pleading to be fed.

There are many requirements for good style, but in writing news for broadcast the first requirement is clarity. Not just clarity for listeners with college degrees but clarity for people of "various capacities." Remembering the rule, "Never underestimate the listener's intelligence or overestimate his knowledge," you write down to no one. But the language must be catholic. You are writing for all manner of men who depend on you to be informed.

It makes no difference how good you are, or how important what you want to say, if you are not understood.

The Challenge

A great deal of news is, of itself, confusing. Therein lies the challenge.

Take as an example the following story which appeared on the "A" wire of the Associated Press:

A233WX

SCHOOL FUNDS NL 500

WASHINGTON — AP — THE SENATE SOUNDLY DEFEATED WEDNESDAY A SOUTHERN-LED DRIVE TO STRIP THE GOVERNMENT OF SOME OF ITS MOST POTENT SCHOOL DESEGREGATION WEAPONS.

A LEADER OF THE SOUTHERN FORCES CALLED THE SETBACK "TRAGIC" AND SAID IT WOULD HURT NOT ONLY THE SOUTH BUT THE NATION AS A WHOLE.

"THE WORST THING ABOUT IT IS THAT IT IS THE SCHOOL CHILDREN WHO MUST SUFFER FROM THESE UNREALISTIC POLICIES OF FORCED INTEGRATION." SAID SEN. JAMES O. EASTLAND, D-MISS., CHAIRMAN OF THE SENATE JUDICIARY COMMITTEE.

FOR THE SECOND STRAIGHT YEAR THE SOUTHERNERS HAD SOUGHT TO AMEND THE BIG HEALTH, EDUCATION AND WELFARE APPROPRIATIONS BILL TO FORBID USE OF FEDERAL FUNDS TO FORCE BUSING, SCHOOL SHUTDOWNS OR PUPIL REASSIGNMENT AGAINST PARENTAL WISHES.

THE AMENDMENT APPROVED BY THE HOUSE AND BY THE SENATE APPROPRIATIONS COMMITTEE WOULD IN EFFECT HAVE AUTHORIZED THE FREEDOM OF CHOICE APPROACH TO SCHOOL DESEGRATION ALREADY RULED INADEQUATE BY THE SUPREME COURT. BUT, AGAIN FOR THE SECOND STRAIGHT YEAR, THE SENATE ACCEPTED A SUBSTITUTE WITH QUALIFYING LANGUAGE THAT SOUTHERNERS SAID NULLIFIED IT.

THE SUBSTITUTE, SPONSORED BY REPUBLICAN LEADER HUGH SCOTT OF PENNSYLVANIA, WAS ADOPTED 52 TO 37 ON THE SECOND DAY OF OFTEN HEATED DEBATE.

THE SENATE IN AN ANTICLIMACTIC SECOND VOTE THEN TABLED 60 TO 28 ANOTHER AMENDMENT THAT WOULD HAVE DIRECTLY AUTHORIZED FREEDOM OF CHOICE. IT WAS OFFERED BY SEN. JAMES B. ALLEN, D-ALA.

WITH ITS FIRST MAJOR CIVIL RIGHTS CLASH OF THE SESSION OUT OF THE WAY, THE SENATE TURNED TO THE VOLATILE ISSUE OF CAMPUS DISORDERS.

AN AMENDMENT BY SEN. JACOB JAVITS, R-NY., SOUGHT TO STRIKE OUT OF THE BILL A COMMITTEE-APPROVED PROVISION THAT WOULD HAVE REQUIRED COLLEGES AND UNIVERSITIES TO TAKE ACTION TO CURB CAMPUS DISORDERS OR LOSE FEDERAL AID.

THE SENATE APPROACH DIFFERED FROM THE HOUSE WHICH LAST SUMMER APPROVED AN AMENDMENT BARRING FEDERAL AID TO STUDENTS ENGAGING IN DISORDERS.

AS APPROVED BY COMMITTEE, THE APPROPRIATIONS BILL WOULD HAVE PROVIDED $20.8 BILLION FOR THE FISCAL 1970 OPERATIONS OF THE DEPARTMENT OF HEALTH, EDUCATION AND WELFARE, PLUS THE LABOR DEPARTMENT AND SOME RELATED AGENCIES.

IN FLOOR ACTION, HOWEVER, THE SENATE ADDED MORE THAN HALF A BILLION DOLLARS, MOST OF IT RESTORING TO THE OFFICE OF ECONOMIC OPPORTUNITY ITS AUTHORIZED $2.08 BILLION. THE COMMITTEE HAD APPROVED APPROPRIATIONS OF $1.6 BILLION.

THE COMMITTEE-APPROVED AMENDMENT RESTRICTING USE OF FEDERAL FUNDS TO FORCE SCHOOL DESEGREGATION WAS KNOWN AS THE WHITTEN AMENDMENT FOR ITS SPONSOR-REP. JAMIE L. WHITTEN, D-MISS.

IT SAID: "NO PART OF THE FUNDS CONTAINED IN THIS ACT MAY BE USED TO FORCE ANY SCHOOL DISTRICT TO TAKE ANY ACTIONS INVOLVING THE BUSING OF STUDENTS, THE ABOLISHMENT OF ANY SCHOOL OR THE ASSIGNMENT OF ANY STUDENT ATTENDING ANY ELEMENTARY OR SECONDARY SCHOOL TO A PARTICULAR SCHOOL AGAINST THE CHOICE OF HIS OR HER PARENTS."

THE SCOTT AMENDMENT LEAVES THAT WORDAGE INTACT BUT ADDS AT THE BEGINNING THE PHRASE "EXCEPT AS REQUIRED BY THE CONSTITUTION. . . ."

OPPONENTS SAID THIS PHRASE NULLIFIES THE INTENT OF THE WHITTEN AMENDMENT AND ADMINISTRATION OFFICIALS CONCEDED PRIVATELY THAT IT WOULD HAVE NO EFFECT ON THE PLANS THEY SUGGEST FOR DESEGREGATION OF SOUTHERN SCHOOLS, MANY OF WHICH INCLUDE BUSING AND CLOSING OF INFERIOR SCHOOLS.

ONE OF THE CHIEF QUESTIONS ARISING DURING DEBATE WAS THE POSITION OF PRESIDENT NIXON AND THE ADMINISTRATION.

SCOTT SAID HIS AMENDMENT HAD THE BACKING OF THE PRESIDENT. BUT SEN. JOHN C. STENNIS, D-MISS., FLOOR MANAGER OF THE SOUTHERN CAMPAIGN, DISAGREED.

STENNIS TOLD THE SENATE THAT NIXON HAD COME OUT STRONGLY AGAINST BUSING DURING THE 1968 CAMPAIGN. HE INTRODUCED INTO THE RECORD WEDNESDAY A SERIES OF NIXON COMMENTS AND THE DATES THEY WERE MADE WHICH HE SAID PROVED THE PRESIDENT WAS AGAINST IT.

WHAT WILL HAPPEN TO THE SCOTT LANGUAGE WHEN THE APPROPRIATIONS BILL GOES TO CONFERENCE WITH THE HOUSE IS IN DOUBT, DESPITE THE RESOUNDING ENDORSEMENT OF THE SENATE VOTE.

THE HOUSE LAST YEAR APPROVED AN AMENDMENT RESTRICTING USE OF FEDERAL FUNDS TO FORCE DESEGREGATION AND THE SENATE APPROPRIATIONS COMMITTEE APPROVED IT THEN, TOO.

ON THE SENATE FLOOR IT WAS TONED DOWN TO SAY FEDERAL FUNDS COULD NOT BE USED TO "OVERCOME RACIAL IMBALANCE," BUT A JOINT HOUSE SENATE CONFERENCE COMMITTEE KNOCKED OUT THE PHRASE. THE SENATE THEN BALKED AT FINAL PASSAGE AND THE WORDS WERE PUT BACK.

JC335PES DEC 17

That's the story as it moved on the AP wire. Your editor hands it to you and asks you to rewrite it for the 4 o'clock news.

"How much do you want?" you ask.

He says, "Thirty seconds."

So you must boil down a 500-word story into 30 seconds. You realize after a careful reading of the wire story that in your 30-second version you can't possibly include the campus disorder angle. You also realize that the story is extremely complicated. You have to understand it yourself and then write it so the viewer will understand. So that, in DeFoe's phrase, it will be understood by all. But, we repeat, first YOU must understand it. Then you tell the story. Do not write in the fashion of reporters whose medium is print. Your style is conversational. TELL what happened. The man on camera will then be telling it to the viewing audience.

If you want to test yourself, write your own version of this AP story, remembering that instead of telling it in 20 words or less you are allowed no more than 30 seconds.

Ready?

All right, here is how Frank Reynolds told it on "The ABC Evening News":

With backing by the Administration, the Senate today rebuffed an attempt to slow down school desegration. The House had added amendments to an appropriations bill that would have curbed the power of the Health, Education and Welfare Department to push desegregation. The House amendments would prevent HEW from denying federal funds to school districts that did not take desegregation moves. Today the Senate added its own amendment. . .a phrase reading: "Except as required by the Constitution."

A great deal of detail has necessarily been omitted. But the essence of the story has been reported. The House attempt was rebuffed, and the viewers know how it was done. Moreover, the story has been written in such a way that it can be TOLD. Still, do you see ways in which it (bearing in mind the 30-second limitation) could be improved?

But what if you have a minute — twice as much time — to tell the story? How would you tell it then?

This is how a congressional correspondent, Roger Mudd, reported the Senate action for "The CBS Evening News with Walter Cronkite," after Cronkite's introduction saying that the Senate had cleared the appropriations bill after a two-day fight:

The South tried again to slow down the pace of school desegregation. They failed again, even though this time they were supported by 15 Western and New England Republicans. The issue was the power of the Department of Health, Education and

Welfare to cut off federal funds from stubborn school districts. An amendment, attached in the House to the big HEW appropriations bill, would have prevented the use of HEW money to force pupil busing, school shutdowns or pupil reassignment against the parents' wishes.

But today the Senate, at the Administration's request, added the crucial words, "except as required by the Constitution." The vote was 52 to 37, and the Southerners must now take their fight into conference with the House, which last summer voted heavily against forced busing. John Stennis of Mississippi declared the Federal Government has made a wilful decision to concentrate on the South but was avoiding the North because, he claimed, it would be political poison to attempt, by busing or student reassignment, to break up the big Northern city ghettos.

Here again is the simple, straightforward lead — a short sentence you might use in conversation with a friend. The style is conversational, though factual, throughout. Notice that in broadcast journalism the word *parental* used by the wire service has become <u>parents</u>. *Sen. John C. Stennis, D-Miss.*, has become <u>John Stennis of Mississippi</u>. Nor will you find any dangling attributive phrase such as *said Sen. James O. Eastland*, which occurs in the third paragraph of the AP story. Because Mudd covered the story firsthand, he has information not carried by the wire service, such as the fact that quite a few Republicans from New England and the West supported the House amendment. But, of course, the AP story is more complete, even though the TV correspondent did take a few seconds more than the allotted one minute.

A Broadcaster's Nightmare

Compare the style of these two stories. The first was broadcast from London by Edward R. Murrow on June 11, 1944, five days after D-Day. The second was carried on the radio wire of United Press International on March 3, 1969. We shall call them Exhibit A and Exhibit B.

Exhibit A:

In Normandy, the battle is raging furiously. It is a swaying struggle, but so far as we know the day has brought no important change in position. Troops are in continuous contact from east of the River Orne to a point northeast of Sainte Mère Église. This is a distance of something like 50 miles, but at no point is the penetration deeper than 11 miles. About 500 square miles of the Continent has been occupied by the Allies, but two million more are still controlled by the enemy. We have made a beginning, and a brilliant one, but it is still only a beginning. The battle has started, but it has not been fully joined.

Exhibit B:

(PERU)

LIMA — THE MILITARY GOVERNMENT SOLVED A WEEKEND CABINET CRISIS TODAY BY APPOINTING NEW MINISTERS FOR FINANCE AND DEVELOPMENT.

GEN. FRANCISCO MORALEZ BERMUDEZ TOOK OVER THE FINANCE POST FROM GEN. ANGEL VALDIVIA, WHO RESIGNED FRIDAY, WHILE GEN. JORGE FERNANDEZ MALDONADO SUCCEEDED GEN. ALBERTO MALDONADO, NO RELATION, WHO RESIGNED THE DEVELOPMENT BERTH SATURDAY IN SOLIDARITY WITH VALDIVIA. SEARING-IN [SIC] OF THE NEW CABINET MEMBERS WAS CARRIED OUT AT GOVERNMENT PALACE IN THE PRESENCE OF OTHER GOVERNMENT MEMBERS.

THE WEEKEND CRISIS FALRED [SIC] WHEN VALDIVIA RESIGNED TO PROTEST THE GOVERNMENT'S ACTION IN NAMING A SPECIAL COMMISSION TO INVESTIGATE ALLEGED FLIGHT OF INTERNATIONAL PETROLEUM CO. [PIC] FUNDS FROM PERU WHILE THE COMPANY AT THE TIME WAS IN THE HANDS OF GOVERNMENT ADMINISTRATORS.

IN BUENOS AIRES, MEANWHILE, PERU'S AMBASSADOR TO ARGENTINA, GONALO FERNANDEZ PUYO, SAID PERU "ACCEPTS TOTALLY" ARGENTINA'S OFFER OF ITS GOOD OFFICES IN MEDIATION OF THE POLITICAL CONFLICT BETWEEN THE U.S. AND PERU OVER THE LATTER'S EXPROPRIATION WITHOUT COMPENSATION OF THE IPC.

3/3 — SW307PES

UPI Radio provides a first-rate professional service. The story presented as Exhibit B, however, is a broadcaster's nightmare. So much is wrong with it that one hardly knows where to begin.

In the first place, the story presents a veritable jungle of proper names. Even Spanish audiences would get lost in their profusion. And the sentences are much too long. The longest contains 41 words. Altogether, the sentences average 28 and a fraction words as compared to 16 and a fraction words in Murrow's wartime report. The sentences not only are long. They are wordy—a felony in radio news writing. Take, for example, the clause *while the company at the time was in the hands of government administrators*. In that sentence, the phrase *at the time* is completely superfluous. The clause should have read simply *while the company was in the hands of government administrators*.

The story is full of booby traps, besides the outpouring of proper names. At one point the initials of the oil company are given as PIC, at another point as IPC. Which is it? The typographical errors—*searing-in* for *swearing-in* and *falred* for *flared*—could "throw" a broadcaster. They are a reminder that wire copy should never, repeat never, be read on the air on sight unless, due to an emergency, it becomes absolutely necessary. (The same goes for any broadcast copy. If a writer must give the broadcaster a story — or bulletin — to read on sight, it is the responsibility of the writer, or editor in charge, to make sure that the story is accurate, free of typos — and "reads." While he is on the air, the broadcaster accepts whatever you hand him on faith. Let him down, and you will be letting yourself down, too.)

The UPI story violates a basic rule in broadcast writing by using the phrase *the latter*. Such phrases as *the former* and *the latter* are outlawed in broadcast journalism because they impose an unnecessary burden on the listener who must try to recall who *the former* or *the latter* is. The story also uses the abbreviation *gen.* for *general*, when the military title should be spelled out. The word <u>company</u> also should have been spelled out. In fact, so much is wrong with the way the story is written that, in order to salvage it, it must be completely done over. The rewritten story might go something like this:

The cabinet crisis in Peru has ended. The crisis was an outgrowth of the expropriation, without compensation, of the International Petroleum Company, in which a lot of United States money is invested. The military government of Peru named a commission to investigate the alleged flight of company funds out of the country. On Friday, the minister of finance quit in protest against the investigation, and the minister of development resigned the next day. Now they have both been replaced. And Peru is said to have accepted Argentina's offer to mediate the dispute with the United States over expropriation of the company.

All the proper names, which would mean nothing to 999,999 out of 1,000,000 North Americans, have been eliminated. Instead of using five sentences averaging more than 28 words a sentence, the story is now told in six sentences averaging 16 and a fraction words a sentence. (It also may make some sense. The original belongs in the journalistic chamber of horrors. And woe be to the unsuspecting broadcaster who, running short of copy, would tear off a story such as this and attempt to read it on sight!)

In comparison with this untypical UPI story, the Murrow copy, which he wrote himself (see Exhibit A), reads like a dream. Besides readability, observe how carefully Murrow maintains perspective:

<u>So far as we know</u>, the day has brought no important changes in position. This is a distance of something like 50 miles, <u>but at no point is the penetration deeper than 11 miles.</u> About 500 square miles of the Continent has been occupied by the Allies, <u>but two million more are still controlled by the enemy.</u> The battle has started, <u>but it has not been fully joined.</u>

In writing news, the responsible reporter in every medium "levels" with his audience. He tells it, to the best of his ability, the way it is. In this instance, Murrow, reporting one of the most crucial battles in history, did not want to mislead the listener regarding the degree to which the Allied landings had been successful. <u>The battle,</u> he said, <u>had not been fully joined.</u>

This is not an example of Murrow's best writing. But it illustrates responsibility, readability, and understandability. This was not an easy story to make understandable in one minute's time. Again, the length of sentences. The longest—only 23 words. There are figures like *50 miles, 11 miles, 500 square miles*, but he makes them as painless as possible by saying <u>something like 50 miles</u> instead of saying *51 or 52 miles*. With <u>11 miles</u> he had to be specific, but then he says <u>about 500 square miles</u>. It's the way you give distances in conversation. He was TELLING. The place names were essential to the story. They were important to listeners, many of whom were following progress of the battle on detailed maps. They became, literally, household words.

Contractions

Contractions are common in conversation, but the person starting out to write news for broadcast seems instinctively to avoid them. Professionals, on the other hand, often contract pronouns with verbs. Example:

I suppose the fundamental contrast is that we've recovered from the war—already forgotten it, in fact—and that in Europe they're just beginning to dig themselves out of the war.

You recognize that as an excerpt from the broadcast William L. Shirer made a few weeks after the end of World War II. But experienced news writers still use contractions today. It is part of the business of writing conversationally. You will notice that each evening when Walter Cronkite concludes his program, he doesn't say, *"That is* the way it is." He says "<u>That's</u> the way it is."

Similarly, forms of *to be* often are contracted with the adverbs *not* and *there*. Examples:

Employees of the company *aren't* eligible.

There's no question he's grateful for the opportunity to speak.

And the older generation remembers Gabriel Heatter's frequent opening, which became his trademark: "<u>There's</u> good news tonight!"

There are times to contract and times not to contract, and usually the choice is determined by a gut feeling as to which is preferable. The contraction is definitely less formal—more casual as well as more conversational. Contractions generally aren't quite as strong—that is, *don't* is not as forceful as *do not*. And sometimes taste is involved. While Cronkite does not hesitate to say, "That's the way it is," the odds are that in referring to the death toll in a major tragedy, he would say, "That is the latest figure we have on the number of persons who died." To cite an actual case, on December 26, 1967, he led his broadcast with this sentence:

There are new danger signals tonight that the war in Vietnam might spread to neighboring Laos and Cambodia.

Besides being of historical interest,* the lead is notable for the fact that Cronkite regarded the possibility of further involvement of too much moment for use of the contraction *there're*. He deemed *there are* more appropriate. There is no rule for this. You have to feel it. It can be generalized, however, that contractions are used more freely in broadcast journalism than in the print media and that, as in the print media, they appear more frequently in feature stories than in hard news.

You Got Rhythm?

Here is another tip. Just as a film-maker knows the value of rhythm in pictorial story-telling, produced by the inter-cutting of long and close shots, or of totally different images, so the professional writer appreciates rhythm in the way sentences are arranged: alternating long and short sentences and alternating simple declarative sentences with sentences starting with those small conjunctions, *and* and *but*. This is true in any writing but especially true in writing for radio and television because, once again, you are writing for the ear.

The Scriptless Story

When news is written for broadcast, it should SOUND told. But because of the nature of fast-breaking news, and because of the nature of broadcasting,

*The "danger signals" consisted of a North Vietnamese drive against positions in Southern Laos and the question whether Allied troops should pursue Communist forces into their Cambodian sanctuaries, the so-called "hot pursuit" issue.

many of the biggest stories ARE told. These are the stories like the death of President Franklin D. Roosevelt which do not wait for a script. The first reports on the assassinations of Dr. Martin Luther King and President Kennedy and his brother Robert were ad-libbed.When man first went to the moon, all the running commentary accompanying the actual landing was unscripted. And, of course, Election Night reporting is mostly ad-libbed. So the biggest story is often a scriptless story, and this places a high premium on the broadcaster with the experience, intelligence, and stamina to perform for long hours under pressure. These are the top-echelon pros.

We mention these scriptless stories because they are fine examples of conversational style. They are not blueprints for the writer to follow—they are not that exact. They are, instead, eminent demonstrations—reminders—that the way to report a story on the air is to tell it. Write it, yes. But write it for the tongue, so that it may be told. And—yes, again!—for the ear, so that it may be heard well and understood.

The greatest ad-lib artist (and we say artist advisedly) in the history of broadcast journalism thus far is Robert Trout, the same Robert Trout who anchored that first World News Roundup program in 1938.

"What I was trying to do," says Trout, "was make the listeners see what I saw as I saw it. The colors and the smells had to be there, as well as the sounds. When the event was finished—let's say a presidential visit to a CCC camp (those letters stood for Civilian Conservation Corps and, although ancient history, sound ecologically modern)—I was finished. Often exhausted, but finished. My colleagues of the press at that point began their labors, uncovering their typewriters, searching for a lead. Some of them said they envied the way I 'wrote' my radio story just by opening my mouth and talking. They wished they could write theirs with the same apparent lack of toil. Aside from the fact that I toiled a great deal, before as well as during the broadcast, what they didn't quite see was that their kind of story was different from mine."

Trout, who first used the phrase "fireside chat" in introducing Franklin Roosevelt to the radio audience, tells the story of a joke once played on him by the New Deal President. Roosevelt, traveling in his special Pullman car, was scheduled to make a major campaign speech. As the hour approached for him to appear on the rear platform, Trout went on the air, ad-libbing a description of the crowd, the train, the railroad station, the weather, filling the time until the President would make his appearance. Trout kept talking. Five minutes. Ten minutes. Still no sign of F.D.R. The broadcaster expanded on his earlier descriptions, reviewed the whole course of the political campaign, recited the role that trains have played in American politics, and, throughout his ordeal, never a hint of dead air.

"And do you know what Roosevelt was doing all this time? He was sitting there in that damned car, listening to me on the radio. He said he just wanted to see how long I could keep it up!"

Trout carried on for thirty-five years after that experience, ad-libbing his way through everything from national political conventions to Thanksgiving Day parades.

6

WATCH THAT WORD!

Eric Sevareid said, "One good word is worth a thousand pictures." In the realm of ideas, words rightly used communicate in a way that is unsurpassed. Think of John Donne's "Ask not for whom the bell tolls," or William Faulkner's creed for writers delivered when he received the Nobel Prize, or Ed Murrow's declaration on freedom to dissent. Think of the power of words. Ptahhotep said it best in 3400 B.C. "Be a craftsman in speech," he said, "that thou mayest be strong. For the strength of one is the tongue, and speech is mightier than all fighting." This is not to disparage film, which shows what is happening. A picture can work miracles in provoking thought. But the word remains man's best tool for the expression of thought. It is the supreme implement.

This chapter will provide some tips on how that implement can be used more effectively—and how some pitfalls can be avoided—by the writer for radio and television news.

More Than a Matter of Four-Letter Words

We come to the matter of taste. This is not a matter of four-letter words. They're out—at least at this writing! Other judgments are more difficult to come by. The boundary between good reporting and bad taste often is poorly defined. For example, in reporting the mutilation of a murder victim, what language do you use? The murderer obviously was a sexual pervert. How far should you go in reporting the grisly details? Or do you intimate the nature of the crime by saying simply that the body was mutilated?

Taste changes in radio and television reporting as in everything else. In the 1940s, a woman was not raped. She was assaulted or attacked. In each case, the verb usually was preceded by the adverb *criminally*. (Was such an act ever committed legally?) Networks rarely reported any crime unless it involved well-known figures, famous or infamous, or was committed under bizarre circumstances. Even local stations carried a small fraction of the crime news they do today.

The subject of venereal disease was taboo. NBC did not permit use of the word *diaper* on the air until 1947, and then only in comedy "for purposes of dry humor." Coincidentally, the network for the first time approved the singing of the lyrics to the torch ballad "Body and Soul." In his *News on the Air*, Paul White told of a murdered woman in whose brassiere police found $3,200. The broadcast version said police found the money "in the woman's clothes," and White lamented that the most interesting part of the story had been left out. But the propriety of using the word *brassiere* might still be argued. (Notice how *brassiere* has been replaced in common usage today by *bra*.) And it was not long ago that a well-known commentator, discussing British economic problems, was not permitted to observe that the miniskirt, which originated in Britain, "besides being economical, exposes hitherto unrevealed assets."

Sometimes it helps, in this matter of taste, to have a dirty mind. At least appreciate how what you write may sound to a person with a dirty mind. Thousands, perhaps millions, of these people will be listening. They may enjoy the joke, but your editor won't. Neither will management. Some angelic words suddenly become devilish when combined with certain other words. There is no place in a news script for double entendre. That's the province of Johnny Carson and shows like "Laugh In."

On the other hand, don't be milquetoast. On the day the Dionne quintuplets were born, the writer of the Lowell Thomas program left the story out of his script—purposely. "It just didn't seem decent," he explained, "having five babies all at once." Thomas, consequently, was twenty-four hours late in reporting the greatest human interest story of the decade. Perhaps the best quote to come out of World War II was General McAuliffe's one-word reply, "Nuts!," when the Germans demanded his surrender at besieged Bastogne. A CBS News writer balked at using the direct quote! When the Lindberghs' first child was kidnapped on March 1, 1932, NBC News did not carry the story at first because it seemed "too sensational." And when President Truman called that music critic an "S.O.B.," all the networks had a fit deciding whether to use the direct quote. It's our recollection that they didn't.

A pretty good rule when deciding whether to quote anyone's profanity is to ask yourself: How important is it? If the statement is important enough to attract attention, and perhaps find its way into the history books, then go with it. "Damn the torpedoes, full speed ahead."

The time has long since passed when adjectives denoting race or nationality may be used to describe persons accused of violating the law. The only exception is when the story loses much, if not all, of its significance when the race or nationality of the person is left out. For example, if police describe someone wanted for a bank robbery and the newsman reports the wanted man's height, weight, and color of eyes, and fails to report that he is Mexican and speaks with a strong Spanish accent, the description is practically worthless. In 1967, when the daughter of the then secretary of state, Dean Rusk, married a young data processor, it was also news that the bridegroom was black. In the same way, mention of race is appropriate, and necessary, whenever a black is named to the President's cabinet or to any other high government post. In the nature of our society, this is news. The test is pertinence. Is the identification an integral part of the story? Is it news? If you can't decide, better leave it out.

And never use terms for race or nationality which have connotations of contempt. Remember the deep trouble Spiro Agnew got into during the 1968 presidential campaign when he referred to *polacks*. A large part of good taste is simply sensitivity for other peoples' feelings. This is not to say that listeners to radio and television should be spared facts which may be unpleasant or even painful. It does mean they should not be subjected to crudities, to careless, purposeless affronts.

Slang can pose other problems. It is good to write naturally, as you speak, but you want at the same time to maintain a certain dignity. Sometimes it is immaterial whether you would say it. Every day we hear *buck* used as a synonym for *dollar*. But you would not write for broadcast, "The mayor's salary was raised by a thousand bucks." Some slang is really a cliché. For example, "His advisers gave him a bad steer." Ridiculous, isn't it?

On occasion, slang can be used to good effect. Much depends on the nature of the story and the personality of the broadcaster. Years ago, when Arthur Godfrey was reading news, he read a story which began:

I wonder how many bachelors are listening this morning because I've got a whale of a tip here on what the modern educated miss thinks about running a house.

You can hear Godfrey saying this. It fits. It's extremely readable if you pause

(Godfrey did) after the phrase <u>this morning</u>. It's also easy for the listener to digest. And it employs slang: <u>whale of a tip</u> and <u>miss</u>. Slang is best suited for the feature story, but that doesn't mean you should use it every time. It should NEVER appear in a story dealing with tragedy, where it adds a note of flippancy.

Some flagrant violations of taste occur because the writer of a sponsored show has not taken the trouble to learn who the sponsor is and where the commercials come in the program. It is appallingly bad taste to go, as one radio station did, from the report of a fire which claimed five lives to a commercial which started, "For that hot, burning sensation. . . ." Know who is sponsoring your newscast. Know what the commercial says. If the story and commercial are incompatible, usually the commercial, or the story, can be switched around. If a story "belongs" where it is because of its news value or context, then the commercial should give way.

Occasionally the position of a story—the order in which it is read—is immaterial. In that case, the story can be shifted. Sometimes the advertising agency, notified of a conflicting story, will want to cancel out of the program altogether. For example, if an airplane has crashed with heavy loss of life and an airline is sponsoring the broadcast, the airline probably will want to reschedule its commercials for another day. That's its privilege.

The juxtaposition of ANY tragedy with a "jolly" commercial is to be avoided. If necessary, insert another story between the report of the tragedy and the commercial. The listener and the sponsor both will appreciate it.

Care also should be exercised in interrupting the program in progress for a news bulletin. How important is the program? What kind of program is it? The career of an editor at one network was blighted because he interrupted an address by the President of the United States. Paul White confessed how he once broke into a program of dance music with a bulletin on the death of a great industrialist and how, immediately after the bulletin, he heard the full orchestra, to his horror, playing, "I'll Be Glad When You're Dead, You Rascal You."

The opportunity for such embarrassment is much less at a local station, where there is likely to be closer coordination between the news and programing departments. Not so many people are involved.

"The Other Network"

Today, what you can say on the air includes mention of "the other network." For years, networks could not bring themselves to identify a competitor's program on the air. Now, in the attribution of a story, it is routine for the networks to name each other. In 1969, for example, when Walter Cronkite interviewed former President Johnson for CBS News, and Johnson said he had never wanted to be President, NBC's David Brinkley reported it as a matter of course, giving CBS as his source.

This "cross-fertilization" of news between networks most frequently occurs as a result of the Sunday panel shows—ABC's "Issues and Answers," CBS' "Face the Nation," and NBC's "Meet the Press." The guests on these programs usually are newsmakers, and the news they make is reported by all networks. Even the videotape of the newsmaker is shared.

So do not hesitate, WITH PROPER ATTRIBUTION, to quote from a story which is exclusive with another station or network. Some old-fashioned managers may object. If they do, try to convince them that news is news and ought to be reported. The industry has come a long way in this regard. There was a day when CBS Radio would not broadcast the time for a special newscast on CBS Television, lest potential listeners abandon radio at that hour and turn on their television sets! To promote a competing program, though it be within the same company, was a sin from the radio advertiser's point of view, and the practice of wearing such blinders continued for a ridiculously long time.

Beware the Cliché

Once upon a time, in a network newsroom, the writers drew a map—not of the moon—but of a cliché-ridden continent washed on the east by the Restless Ocean, in which, clearly marked beside Desperate Straits, lay the Depths of Despair. The eastern shore was labeled Rock-bound Coast. The largest country was Major Power, whose political capital, Mounting Tension, lay west of the Undulating Plains. The crime capital, Dull Thud, was situated at the headwaters of a river called Meandering Stream, just before you come to Sorry Pass. Meandering Stream flowed south a thousand miles and emptied into the Widening Gulf. The principal metropolis on the West Coast was Crystal Clear, washed by the Great Expanse of Water. In the midst of this western ocean large X-marks indicated a score of Watery Graves. At the bottom of the map stretched the Sea of Upturned Faces.

Newsmen have always had fun with clichés. Winston Burdett of CBS tells how, in Tel Aviv, he joined correspondents from ABC and NBC in a contest to see who could make up the longest list of clichés found in dispatches from the Middle East. These included "the strategic 103-mile waterway" for the Suez Canal and "the uneasy head of the desert kingdom" for King Hussein of Jordan.

Too often it has been the "oil-rich" Middle East. It is also the Middle East "powder keg." Charles Coffey of WHAS, Louisville, claims to have had a bad dream in which "roving bands of militant camels began kicking over powder kegs in the oil-rich Middle East." It was a real mess.

Use of such clichés may have been abetted by the old United Press rule that no person's name should be used in the lead sentence, so that the crucifixion of Christ would have been bulletined:

JERUSALEM (SATURDAY) — UP — THE STRONG-WILLED BEARDED LEADER OF THE JEWISH REVOLUTIONARY SECT WAS EXECUTED YESTERDAY IN THE COMPANY OF TWO THIEVES.

Then, of course, there is the story of the UP editor who cabled his correspondents: PLEASE, PLEASE AVOID CLICHÉS LIKE THE PLAGUE!

Russell Baker of the *New York Times* once did a wonderful column on indifference that was not callous, aggression that was not naked—"I had nearly decided that aggression never occurred with its clothes on"—and gall which was mitigated. As for "innocent victim," he found a victim who, far from innocent, had just murdered his cousin.

An old journalistic cliché, smacking of British mystery stories, is *rumpled tweeds*. A writer for the *Saturday Review*, Dereck Williamson, said, "Not long ago I read in the *New York Times* that a man who liked to wear rumpled tweeds had died. The *Times*," Williamson said, "gave no details—not a word about the kind of tweeds or who rumpled them. As the man was quite old, I assume he was a traditionalist who rumpled his own tweeds."

In a lead editorial in the *Times*, chickens came to roost in the White House and the President, after painting himself in a corner, sent his budget back to the drawing board. We are not trying to embarrass the *Times*. We wish only to demonstrate that clichés are sneaky—they creep in. (You may even find a cliché or two in this text.)

Editors abhor clichés. Cronkite, who is managing editor of his news program, once asked a writer to wrap up several stormy weather developments, saying, "You know, a Mother Nature-on-the-rampage sort of thing." The writer knew enough not to give Cronkite literally what he asked for. He would have got hung (repeat *hung*) if he had. Mother Nature is the *grand dame* among clichés. Instead, he wrote, "Nature caused trouble today across much of the country." And Cronkite bought it.

Phrases that once were fresh become clichés through overuse. Thus, in the early 1960s, we had "break-away Katanga" to describe a province that seceded from the Congo. The second half of the decade brought civil war to Nigeria and another cliché, "break-away Biafra." Sensitive writers caught themselves humming these clichés as if they were chants set to the rhythm of primitive drums.

Widespread usage converts brightness into triteness. Barbara Ward demonstrated insight in 1966 when she drew an analogy between the problems of our planet and those of people in a spaceship. By the end of the decade the title of her book, *Spaceship Earth*, had been so overworked it was hackneyed.

A writer once looked up from his typewriter and asked, "Is there such a thing as election fever?"

"I don't think so," a colleague deadpanned. "But call the hospitals and find out."

It's a fever which has infected many scripts.

And take the phrase, "It remains to be seen. . . ." This is frequently used in interpretative reporting. Such was the case at the time of Ho Chi Minh's death, when there was speculation about its effect on the Vietnam War. We once saw a film report on television as Ho's body lay in state, under glass. Now that picture flashes to mind each time we hear a broadcaster say "remains to be seen." And we are not alone.

Test your phrases for aptness and freshness. Both are required in good writing. You should be able to hear, in your head, how sentences will sound when spoken out loud. Then you can judge how listeners will react to the words in combination.

The newsman who commits a cliché must expect a degree of ridicule, if not censure. One radio writer, who shall be nameless, managed this awesome mixture of metaphors and clichés in a single sentence:

The revolt in France during May and June has come home to roost, and it's right in the lap of the French taxpayer.

This writer was ridiculed AND censured.

Watch out for anatomical clichés:

> Finger in the pie
> Foot in his mouth
> Foot in the door
> Ear to the ground
> Nose to the grindstone

Synonyms for the proper names of cities are apt to be clichés:

> The City of Light (Paris)
> The Eternal City (Rome)
> The Film Capital (Hollywood)

Bean Town (Boston)
The City of Brotherly Love (Philadelphia)
The nation's capital (Washington)
The Windy City (Chicago)

Herewith a rogues gallery of other clichés. It does not pretend to be complete, but they're the bromides heard most often in news broadcasts.

Augurs well	Massive attack
Bids fair	Mounting tension
Blast (as in bombing)	Mute evidence
Crystal clear	No uncertain terms
Curb (for *restrict,*	Pack (as in
restrain, reduce)	hurricane-*packing* winds)
Doing as well as can	Predawn attack
be expected	Probe (for *investigate*)
Easy prey	Pulverize (as in bombing)
Few and far between	Remains to be seen
Gone but not forgotten	Roving bands
Hail of bullets	Slate a speech
Hale and hearty	Thick and fast
Here at home	Top advisers
Hold a parley	Vital stake
In my judgment	White stuff (for *snow*)
It all began	Widespread fear
Last but not least	
Loud and clear	

And NEVER let anyone leave in a huff. That was a hackneyed expression more than thirty years ago when Paul White observed that the Huff must be, without question, America's most popular car.

Other Words To Watch For

Be careful of the word *casualty*. In his book, *To Kill a Messenger*, Bill Small mentions Pentagon distress over the fact that the public, hearing a broadcaster report casualties, does not seem to realize casualties include dead AND wounded. Indeed, casualties may refer ONLY to wounded. Many listeners think the word refers to people who are killed. Take care in your copy to avoid this misunderstanding. And KNOW the difference between *wounded* and *in-*

jured. You are *injured* in a fall from a ladder; you are *wounded* by a machine-gun bullet.

It is best to use words you believe the listener understands, but occasionally you may use one about which there is doubt. If you do, remove the doubt with an additional clarifying word or phrase.

Example: While the murder trial of hippie cult leader Charles Manson was still in the jury selection stage in Los Angeles, "The CBS Evening News with Walter Cronkite" took a report from Bill Stout which contained this sentence: "Once the jurors are seated, they will be sequestered—locked up each night in a hotel room for perhaps six months—all at public expense."

Stout was leaving no doubt about the meaning of *sequestered* and providing additional information at the same time.

Be sure YOU know the meaning of the words you use. Be careful of the verb *point out.* The moment you say so-and-so *pointed out* that such-and-such was the case, you are accepting the statement as gospel. The same goes for *disclose.* Only facts can be disclosed.

Be aware of the nuances in words. In World War II, for example, it always was "Washington *says*" and "Berlin *claims.*" Today, script writers have Moscow and Peking claiming much more than London or Washington. It's the other side which claims. Deep down you doubt the veracity of what it says.

Theodore Bernstein of the *New York Times* is a purist when it comes to *claim.* In his book, *The Careful Writer,* he agrees with H. L. Mencken that *claim* in the sense of assert is newspaper jargon. He says, "The verb *claim* should not be used as a synonym for *say, assert* or *declare* except when there is at issue an assertion of a right, title, or the like." Webster also agrees. Still you hear it as a synonym for *assert* or *maintain* almost every day. The authors don't object, but be aware that it is a color word. This is important. Jim Mays, director of news at WTAR, Norfolk, says, "The first guideline for our staff is to tell it straight and watch for the shades of meaning words can convey, even unintentionally."

Remember that *state* is NOT a synonym for *say.* According to Webster, *to state* is "to set forth in detail." The first two definitions given for *to state* in the *Random House Dictionary of the English Language* are "to declare definitely or specifically" and "to set forth formally in speech or writing." *State* is one of the most frequently misused words heard on the air.

Four other frequently misused words are *robbery* and *theft, prison* and *jail.* A *robbery* is attended by violence or threat of violence. The victim is held up, for example, at the point of a gun. *Theft,* the act of stealing, is accompanied by stealth. A *jail* is for minor offenders. A *prison* usually is a place of confinement for persons convicted of more serious crimes. Murderers are sentenced to prison, NOT to jail.

A word overworked as a bridge between stories is *meanwhile*. The adverb should be used ONLY when a close relationship exists in subject matter and intervening time actually is meant. You'll be amazed how well you can write without this crutch.

Avoid Latin prefix words like *semi-starved, pre-armistice, transmit,* and *conclude.* Instead, say *half-starved, before the armistice, send* (so much better than *transmit* OR *dispatch*) and *finish* or *end.* Think of the play *Journey's End.* How much better that title is than *Journey's Conclusion!*

Those Latin Words

In writing the plural of nouns taken directly from the Latin, employ the letter "s" in the following:

> *Ultimatums*, not *ultimata*
> *Dictums*, not *dicta*
> *Referendums*, not *referenda*
> *Honorariums*, not *honoraria*

Ad hoc, sine qua non, per diem, and *quid pro quo* are out. Not all your listeners know Latin. But *data* and *memoranda* are still in.

Medium, as in *television medium*, is a Latin word. That is the singular, although you'd be surprised how may people confuse it with *media*, which is plural. As Theodore Bernstein says, "Unless you suffer from the present-day AD-DICTION, the singular is still *medium* and the plural *media.*"

The man in charge of writing at ABC Radio News is Nick George, managing editor. These are excerpts of a talk he gave at a meeting of the New York State Associated Press Broadcasters Association:

Now in all this writing of broadcast news we use words, and the funny thing about this is that many of the words we use in broadcast news are words you read only in print or hear on broadcast news! You seldom hear these words used in normal, everyday intelligent conversation.

About the only explanation we can give for this is that we are indeed victims of the print tradition. We have not been writing broadcast news the way people talk to each other.

I am suggesting there is a paradox here.

If the purpose of a newscast is to give information—a newscaster talking to a listener—then does it not make sense to talk to that listener in the language and phraseology that he is used to hearing?

We don't do this. . . .Too often we use stiff, stilted passive sentences and phrases.

We *hurl* things instead of *throwing* them.

We *engage* the Vietcong, we never *fight* them.

We say *blaze* when we mean *fire*.

It always seems to be *pact* and never *agreement* or *settlement*.

We always *plunge* when we really mean *fall*.

And we almost never remember that many of these words were first used in everyday print and especially newspaper headlines to accommodate a line count.

And you hardly ever see a *ship* in our copy. A ship always seems to turn into a *vessel* or a *craft*. . . .

The argument is made that it takes longer, takes more words, to write as people talk. Yes, it does sometimes. But isn't it worth four more words to insure understanding? That's better than losing 40 words — wasting them!

The words we write, the phrases we use, the sentences, the facts we write about, the names and places — all these — should get as much care and as much attention as we give to any other phase of news-gathering or news delivery.

It doesn't help much to be first on the scene if your listeners aren't sure what you're talking about.

Here are some other do's and don't's compiled by Russ Thornton, news manager at WBAP, Fort Worth:

Don't use police terms (DOA for dead on arrival, DWI for driving while intoxicated) in straight news copy.

Don't use DA for district attorney in straight news copy.

Autopsy means in part, and in the sense we ordinarily use it, the inspection, and usually partial dissection, of a body. To say an autopsy was performed on the body is therefore redundant and incorrect.

Conflagration — A fire must be particularly destructive to be termed a conflagration. An ordinary fire is never a conflagration.

Chief Justice — Warren Burger is chief justice of the United States, NOT of the Supreme Court.

Demolish — To demolish is to completely destroy. Never say "completely demolished."

Everyone, everybody — Both are singular and take singular verbs and pronouns.

Kind of a — Never to be used. "It was a certain kind of book" is correct.

Only — This word is misplaced in sentences constantly. It should go as near as possible to the word it modifies. "I only went to town once" is awkward sentence structure and incorrect. "I went only once" is correct.

Persons, people — Four *persons* were hurt in an auto accident, NOT four *people*. A crowd of *people*, the people of Europe, etc.

Smithsonian — It is Smithsonian Institution, NOT Institute."

Don't be afraid to use the same word twice, or three or four times, if it is the RIGHT word. Don't strive for synonyms. Your broadcast style should be natural, not contrived.

We are so afraid of repeating ourselves that we have devised six ways of saying President Nixon: *President Nixon, chief executive, commander-in-chief, the American President, the U.S. President* and, simply, *the President. President Nixon, the President* and *Mr. Nixon* should be all we need. Variety is not necessary or even desirable. Notice how Harry Reasoner, reporting the results of sports events, repeatedly uses the verbs *defeated* and *beat*. He feels no need to say *trounced, whipped, walloped, clobbered, toppled,* or *shellacked*.

During World War II, Paul White posted this memo in the CBS newsroom:

This morning within the space of 30 seconds I heard German submarines called *submarines, U-boats, submersibles* and *underseas craft*. The word *submarines* was used once. It should have been used more often. But, my God, *submersibles!* That word should never be used at all.

Jesse Zousmer, who after leaving CBS became vice-president in charge of television news at ABC, believed that when someone said something, the writer should say he *said* it—not *stated, added, asserted,* or *averred*. Anyway, better synonyms for *said* than *stated, added, asserted,* or *averred* are *announced, promised, warned,* and *insisted*. But be SURE these synonyms apply. That is, to use these synonyms there must have been an announcement, a promise, a warning, and an insistence in what was said.

No Moon-tailed Peacocks

In "telling" the news, go easy on adjectives. Adjectives you do use should be selected not only for accuracy but for their quality. Is the adjective unfamiliar to many listeners? Is it pedantic? Logan Pearsall Smith lamented, "Why wasn't I born, alas, in an age of Adjectives; why can one no longer write of silver-shedding Tears and moon-tailed Peacocks? Of eloquent Death?" The answer for broadcast journalists is easy. No one talks that way, and there's no time for all that fancy stuff.

Don't try in the use of adjectives to be erudite. Never write, as a novelist once did, that the eggs were fried longer *to coagulate their mucosity*. Such writing is pretentious—it can't possibly be conversational. (We admit we chose an extreme example, but you get the idea.)

The bigger the story, the fewer adjectives you need—the force is in the facts. No broadcaster ever used fewer adjectives than Ed Murrow. The strength of his language lay in the choice of nouns and verbs.

ABC News once directed its writers to use no more than one adjective per noun. This may have been too arbitrary, but it is worth thinking about. Such a guideline would have prevented a writer for WCBS, New York, from confusing his listeners in reporting the afteraffects of a break in a water main. He said, "It may be weeks before the 48-inch water main break is repaired."

He didn't tell his listeners whether he was talking about a *48-inch main* or a *48-inch break*.

A word of caution about *very*, which can be both adjective and adverb. As an adverb it is overworked. Don Mozley of KCBS, San Francisco, bemoans the fact that "colorful writing to some writers means adding the word *very*." Every time you are tempted to write *very*, try the sentence without it. You'll be (very) surprised.

And take care in the use of superlatives. Think twice, or three times, before you say something is the *smallest* or the *biggest*, or the *first* or the *last*.

In June, 1970, when Alexander Dubcek was expelled from the Communist Party in Czechoslavakia, after being removed as ambassador to Turkey, a prominent newscaster called it "the final humiliation." But only a week later Dubeck was expelled from parliament—another humiliation—and he was yet to face charges that, while in power, he took "massive bribes." Which of these is the "final" humiliation?

The point is that in June, 1970, no one, including the news writer, could possibly know what the final humiliation would be. The authors have found in their experience that at least half the times they have challenged a writer's claim that something is happening for the first time, or for the last time, or that something is the biggest, or the smallest, or the best, or the worst, the writer either found he was wrong or could not substantiate what he said.

Every superlative should carry a winking red light.

Perhaps the best advice on the use of adjectives was given by Mark Twain, who said, "As to the adjective, when in doubt, strike it out."

Prepositions Can Help

Prepositions can help in a special way. They can be used to break up unnatural "freight train" phrases so that they are more readable. Robert Trout has spoken of this. He always revises a phrase like *the public's long-term natural resources interest* to read *the public's long-term interest in natural resources*. In this practice, Trout is not alone. Every good writer does it.

Often the phrase does not have to be so unnatural to benefit from insertion of a preposition. Thus, it is "easier on the ear" to say *the process of registering cars* than to say *the car-registering process*, and it is better to say *a plant for manufactruing tool dies* than to say *a tool die manufacturing plant*. And, again, better to say *Republican Governor Rockefeller of New York* than *New York Republican Governor Rockefeller*.

Used in this way, prepositions break phrases into more manageable pieces which the ear—the mind, really—more readily accepts. They increase readability AND understanding.

THAT Is More Conversational

As your broadcast style develops, you will find yourself making more use of the relative pronoun *that*. This is a good sign. In speech, *that* is used more often than *which*. It's more conversational. And broadcast style is the style of conversation.

On the other hand, *which* is sometimes preferable, though the rules are confusing. Fowler himself calls the relations between *that* and *which* "an odd jumble." According to the grammarians, *which* is correct when the relative clause is non-defining, *that* is correct when the clause defines. This sentence illustrates the correct use of each: "One of the nations *that* emerged was Vietnam, *which* later was partitioned."

The point is that clauses properly begun with *which* appear more often in print than they do in speech. Longer sentences lend themselves to these clauses. So if you are using *which* less often, you should, as a writer for the broadcast media, be enjoying it more.

So much for *that* as a relative pronoun. *That* is also used as a conjunction. For example, "It means *that* no law can be passed" and "He said *that* he would vote." In the interest of tight writing, this conjunction often—not always—can be eliminated. "It means no law can be passed" and "He said he would vote" read perfectly well, and make perfectly good sense, without the *that*.

If the sentence sounds better with *that*, don't kill it. Pay close attention, always, to sound. To readability. To how the sentence flows.

The Sound of Words

The public never sees your words. You are writing for the ear, so think always of the SOUND of what you write. This applies not only to the sound of each word but to the sound of combinations of words.

During the wedding of Princess Margaret, the late British broadcaster, Richard Dimbleby, described Queen Elizabeth's tenseness and "the comforting, tall, friendly and alert figure of the Duke of Edinburgh, on whose right arm she could rely." These words are fastened together, not only by meaning, but by a thread of sound, notably the *l*'s in tall, friendly, alert, and rely. No less effective are the *f*'s in comforting, friendly, and figure and the r's that recur from comforting all the way through to rely. The sounds are woven together to make a whole fabric, subtly, so that the listener, liking the sentence, is not aware how alliteration has been used. If you CONTRIVE such sentences, they fail. They must come to you out of a sensitivity of how words sound. They spring from your subconscious in harmonious array.

Good sentences are written by writers who LISTEN to the words. Watch them at their typewriters and you will see them reading what they have just written, most of them reading aloud, usually in a whisper, testing each phrase, each sentence, each sequence of sentences, for sound. Tom Houghton, news director at WRC, Washington, believes this testing aloud is essential. He asks, "How can it SOUND good if you don't hear it? Better yet," he says, "back up a step. Before you write, read the wire story. Then ad-lib what it means out loud, just like you talk. Now write it, not exactly like you talk—you're probably editorializing when you talk—but somewhere between the way you 'read' and the way you 'talk.' Then, if it still sounds funny, write it again."

Incidentally, an odd-sounding, much over-used formula to be avoided is that which, by modifying a man's last name by his age (x-year-old) makes him appear as a thing. Thus, we have reference to Derek Curtis Bok, president of Harvard University, as "the 40-year-old Bok" and reference to Claude Fly, an American agronomist kidnapped by Tupamaros guerrillas in Uruguay, as "the 66-year-old Fly." These expressions are unnatural enough in print (whoever talks that way?) but, aurally, they are absurd.

Do not hesitate to rewrite—if you have time. Professionals are constantly rewriting copy, especially their leads. A visiting journalism student once expressed surprise that Murrow's writer was preparing parts of the 7:45 P.M. script at one o'clock in the afternoon. The writer was "putting stories in the bank" so that he would have time to deal adequately with stories that might break in the hour or two before Murrow went on the air. By starting early, he MADE time in which to rewrite. And one of the reasons you rewrite is to make the copy sound right—to make it flow.

Just as some people are tone deaf regarding music, some writers are deaf to the "tones" —and "overtones" —of words. The result of such deafness is ineffective writing. Listen carefully to the reports of major broadcasters if you are sensitive to how words sound. Notice how often their sentences end with strong nouns or verbs and how rarely they end with pronouns, adjectives, and adverbs, which tend to make sentences seem to peter out. A strong, meaningful last word gives a sentence definition. It punctuates. You seem to hear the period. And listen to the rhythm in their sentences. One short declarative sentence after another is monotonous. After a couple of these sentences, try to start the next sentence with an *and* or a *but*. Then, after that sentence, go back to the simple declarative. Maintain rhythm.

Shy from sibilants, especially in succession. (Read that last sentence aloud, real fast, and you will see why!) Don't give the broadcaster—or yourself—a line like, "She asserted she was seeking new assistance." Avoid words that slip and slide.

Many sibilants can be avoided simply by dropping unnecessary *s*'s at the end of words. It is better, for example, to write:

"The effect of the *House* action" instead of "the effect of the *House's* action."

"The cosmonauts will make a *two-week* visit to the United States" instead of "The cosmonauts will make a *two-weeks* visit to the United States."

"No *sign* of cooperation" instead of "no *signs* of cooperation."

"He expressed his *hope* for the future" instead of "He expressed his *hopes* for the future."

"She said nothing in *regard* to policy" instead of "She said nothing in *regards* to policy."

"He swam *toward* shore" instead of "He swam *towards* shore."

And, incidentally, don't say, "*Damages* were estimated at two million dollars." Say, "*Damage* was estimated at two million dollars."

Sound-alikes

Be careful in the use of words that sound alike. How misleading such sound-alikes can be was demonstrated when a secretary, transcribing a correspondent's report, quoted him as saying, "That's partly why they excepted Congressman Thomas O'Neill's amendment." What the correspondent had said was, "That's partly why they *accepted* Congressman Thomas O'Neill's amendment."

And think how this SOUNDS: "The Cleveland Indians scored two runs, the Washington Senators one." The writer of a line like that might be saved if the score were flashed on the TV screen. But what if the listener was tuned in to his car radio?

Through and *threw* are two other words which can confuse. "He *threw* out the ball *throughout* the ball game."

Flout and *flaunt*.

And *sex* and *sect*.

Roger Mudd of CBS tells the story of how a politician had fun with words that sound alike — at the expense of his opponent. It happened in 1950, when Senator Claude Pepper was opposed by his protége, George Smathers. Mudd says, "The most famous speech of that campaign was Smathers' play to the wool-hats of North Florida. 'Are you aware,' Smathers asked his rural audience, 'that Claude Pepper is known all over Washington as a shameless extrovert? Not only that, but this man is reliably reported to practice nepotism with his sister-in-law and that his own sister was once a thespian in New York? Worst of all, it's established that Mr. Pepper, before his marriage, practiced celibacy.' " Mudd concluded by saying, "Someone said that Claude Pepper became, on that day, history's first victim of 'guild by assonance.' "

We had to look up *assonance*. It means "resemblance of sound."

7

HOW TO USE THE WIRE SERVICES

A large part of the news you hear on the air comes from the three major press associations—Associated Press, United Press International, and Reuters. Some stations, regrettably, depend entirely on the news gathered by these services. Each service has a tradition of excellence in reporting. The regret is that these stations default on their responsibility to cover local developments. The scope of this deficiency is dramatized by the statement of an owner of several radio stations who said, "Every licensee should be required to maintain a full-time local newsman on its staff." That would appear to be the MINIMUM requirement if a station is to report the news of its community in a responsible, meaningful way.

Since this chapter—indeed, this entire text—is written for news writers, it has no application for those stations where announcers routinely tear copy from the press association radio wire and sit down before a microphone and read. It has no relevancy for these "rip and read" stations except perhaps to show them to what degree, in this respect, their reporting is incomplete.

What the Wire Services Provide

The major press associations provide these services, purchasable by the broadcasting companies:

1. Radio wire. This wire carries news written in broadcast style, packaged for news programing, and transmitted to the client station by teletype. These reports, consisting mostly of five-minute news summaries, are widely used in both radio and television. Still, it is called the radio wire.

2. "A" wire. This is the press association's main wire, providing worldwide coverage for both broadcast and print media. It is the workhorse wire, carrying the heaviest load of news stories, all of which are written in newspaper style. Transmission is by teletype. Although many major stations and all networks subscribe to this wire, most clients are newspapers.

3. "B" wire. Stories on this wire are usually of secondary importance. Occasionally, extremely newsworthy stories appear on the "B" wire when there are too many high priority stories for the "A" wire to handle. The "B" wire also is the wire which carries complete texts, such as the texts of presidential speeches and proclamations.

4. City and regional wires. A large city like New York, Chicago, or Washington is covered by a special city wire. As its name suggests, it carries the news breaking in, or of special interest to, that municipality. The regional wire provides the same service for regions. These often are synonymous with state wires, carrying the news of a particular state.

5. Financial and sports wires. Just what their names imply. Briefer items on business and sports appear on the radio wire.

6. Picture service. This service provides TV stations with news photographs, maps, charts, and other graphics. This visual material may be received by special wire, by mail, or by messenger if the station and picture distribution center are located in the same city.

7. Audio service. This consists of audio tape reports, frequently in the form of taped actualities, which are purchased by radio stations to supplement their own audio reports. This audio service is expanding. AP, for example, sends out twenty different five-minute tapes each week. These include commentaries by Morgan Beatty, who began his news career with AP and worked as an NBC newscaster for twenty-five years.

All these services are available to stations and networks—at a price. Only the networks and the largest stations can afford to pay for so much service. Relatively few stations, for example, subscribe to both the "A" and "B" wires. Few stations can afford to subscribe to the "A" wire service of all three press associations—AP, UPI, and Reuters. This, despite the real editorial advantages in having at hand the product of these three newsgathering organizations. Later in this chapter we will show what some of these advantages are. Right now, let's have a look at one disadvantage.

Handling the Wire Copy

Perhaps we should say "coping with the wire copy" or "not letting the wire copy get the best of you." Because, for the news writer, subscription to four, five, or six wires presents a physical problem. The writer with only one "A" wire may not be as well-informed, but he has an easier time than the writer who must sort out, read, and digest the stories provided by the "A" wires of all three press services. Add to this the "B" wires, taking into account the hundreds of thousands of words moved in each twenty-four-hour period, and you begin to see the dimensions of the problem.

If the writer is not to be overwhelmed by sheer mass of copy, he must have a system. He must have a system whether he is using one wire or six.

Every writer has a slightly different way of handling copy. These, however, are the basics:

Use a ruler to tear your stories. If you use scissors, you are wasting time.

Discard all stories you KNOW you won't use. Exercise editorial judgment. If you don't winnow out the less newsworthy stories at this stage, you will have an unmanageable accumulation of wire copy by the time you start to write. And remember that stories keep coming in as you write. You must keep up with them. As Paul White said in *News on the Air*, "Listeners have the right to expect that every story is up-to-the-minute."

File in a drawer (there isn't room on your desk) all stories—backgrounders—you may need for future reference. These are stories outlining campaign issues, condensing Supreme Court decisions, listing new members of the President's cabinet, capsuling the history of the North Atlantic Treaty Organization, etc. Throw away one such story today and, inevitably, you will wish you had it tomorrow.

Plan how you will arrange copy on your desk. This really is a filing system. Use any arrangement which works best for you, but, we repeat, you must have an arrangement—a system for laying out your stories before you in orderly fashion. One system, for example, would be to place all Washington dateline stories you may use in the broadcast in one pile to your right, all other stateside stories in another pile next to that, all European dateline stories in still another pile, and so forth. A writer, when he has finished sorting copy, may have five or six of these categories in front of him. It's a pretty good idea, if there are important running stories like Vietnam and a presidential election, to arrange those stories separately. The whole purpose is to give you easy access to a news story when you want it. Easy access means time saved. TIME IS PRECIOUS.

Label your stories. Make your labels as brief as possible, again to save time. A Vietnam story slugged VIET is just as good as a Vietnam story slugged VIETNAM. Print your slugs—labels—in capital letters so they stand out. Some news writers do this with black crayon pencils or felt-tipped pens for easy identification, and some use their ballpoint pen or No. 2 pencil. There is no rule except to handle your copy efficiently. If we seem to belabor this point, it is because we have seen colleagues in broadcast journalism who lost out, not because of poor editorial judgment or because they did not write well, but because they simply could not cope with the mass of material with which they had to work. In a word, they never devised a system. They were swamped.

Now make a list of your stories. You have read them superficially, enough to know you did not want to throw them away. You still must decide which of these stories will go into your broadcast. Which stories does your editorial judgment tell you to report? Which are the most important, most interesting news developments as of that hour? The list will help you decide.

The next step is to make a new list, a run-down of the stories to be included in the broadcast. You'll probably jot them down next to the original list. In making up this list, arrange the stories in the order they will be reported.

Aside from editorial judgment, which we'll go into later, you usually will group together those stories that are related. That is, it is logical to go from a story on the fighting in Vietnam to a story on efforts to end the war, or from a story on a government crisis in Italy to the reported death of a former premier of France. Unusual developments in the weather, plane accidents, economic announcements lead naturally to wrap-ups in your script on what is happening with regards to weather, airplane accidents, and economics. There is the same proper tendency to wrap together the reports coming from a specific geographic area, such as Western Europe or the Far East. For example, news items from Hong Kong, Peking, and Tokyo may often be reported together in a sort of Far East package.

With this list, which amounts to an outline, you still are not ready to start writing. You must find out from the news director, producer, or news editor which of these stories will be reported firsthand by a reporter on sound film or audio tape. If a reporter is covering a story, you will need to write a lead-in, introducing him. You will need to know what is in his report. Was there a late development or an important point in the story that he missed? If he missed a significant part of the story, it will be up to you to cover that angle in your script. So it is important for YOU to screen film reports and listen to audio tapes before you write.

And, of course, you must give the wire copy—the raw material from which you must write—a close reading.

Reading Wire Copy

Learn to read wire copy critically. If it says something that appears illogical, or doesn't sound right to you in any way, QUESTION IT. Don't accept it. A poor explanation for an illogical statement in your script is, "Well, that's what the wire says." Editors have little patience with that excuse. If it sounds illogical to you, it will sound illogical to your listeners. It makes the broadcaster look bad. In your news organization, YOU will look bad.

Here's an example. During the 1970 economic recession a wire service reported a "leveling" in the cost of living. It based this generalization on the fact that for two consecutive months the cost of living had risen by four-tenths of one percent. The reasoning was wrong. What the statistics really meant was that, instead of "leveling" or "leveling off," the cost of living WAS INCREASING AT A CONSTANT RATE. The wire service writer had come to an erroneous conclusion, and a network news editor telephoned the service and, tactfully, pointed out the mistake. In this case, the news writer, in his own copy, had used the wire service language. He had accepted at face value, without critical examination, what the wire service said. The news editor had read the copy critically. Be skeptical of what you read on the wire. Ask yourself, "Does this make sense?"

Remember that the story you are reading is the product of someone who, like yourself, is capable of human error. That person's judgment must be subject to review by you, no matter how high the batting average of the wire service may be in this regard. Do not assume because a story comes to you in black or purple print, coughed out from inside an imposing machine, that it is somehow endowed with infallibility. News agencies do commit errors of fact. They do make mistakes in editorial judgment. And that is why, as soon as errors are discovered, they file corrections.

And here is another warning. You must catch these corrections when they move on the wire. Reading through the mass of teletype copy, tearing the stories, you can easily miss a correction. If you do, your story perpetuates the mistake, compounding it as a large audience listens. And before you call a wire service about a mistake, check the wire carefully to see if it has moved a correction. It's embarrassing to call and be told that a correction already has been made. It means you haven't been alert. It also means you are wasting your time and the time of a busy wire service editor.

But do not hesitate to call if a significant mistake appears to have been made. (Don't bother the wire service about typos!) If you are working in New York, query the headquarters of the AP, UPI, or Reuters. If you are working outside New York (which is most likely), query the local bureau. It, in turn, will query New York. If the bureau does not have an answer for you by air-time, skip the story IF it is "skippable." Or it may be that you can omit just that part of the story which is questionable. Here is one of the advantages of subscribing to more than a single service. What does the other wire service say? How does *it* handle the story? By comparing reports on different wires you usually can find out what you need to know. One wire complements the other.

Of course, if your station has its own reporter on the scene, that is whom you should call. And "go" with what your reporter tells you. It's his story. He won't be wrong often and still be around!

All right, you say, but what if you have no reporter who covered the story? And what if none of the wire services makes clear exactly what happened? And what if you have struck out in your telephone call to the local bureau?

What then?

There is, under these circumstances, no sure formula for getting the information—except to be resourceful. Turn reporter yourself. Both of us have called the offices of governors and U.S. senators to supplement, or clarify, the information in wire stories. That's fairly common practice. We also recall Walter Cronkite phoning General Eisenhower, after his retirement, to check on a wire story involving the general's future plans and—within a min-ute—chatting with him on the phone. Not everyone has the status which en-ables him so readily to get in touch with former Presidents. But the incident illustrates a good way to check out stories. Phone the source.

Generally, the availability of more than one news service enables a writer to turn out a more accurate, more intelligible script. But sometimes the disagreement in agency reports can be confusing. UPI, for example, may report 20 persons dead in a bus accident in Virginia. According to AP, 18 persons died. Reuters sets the death toll at 15. What do YOU say? Or UPI refers to Richard Nixon as the thirty-sixth President of the United States when he is inaugurated, and the AP calls him the thirty-seventh President. Which is he? Or UPI says torrential rains are "pounding" Rome, sending rivers over their banks, while AP, in the same hour, reports clearing skies over Rome, "easing the threat of widespread floods." Which story do you choose?

The answers to the first two questions are easy. You say at least 15 persons died in the bus accident, taking the lowest figure. You may say that one report places the death toll as high as 20. You don't have to choose ONE figure. Level with your listeners. Let them know the figures vary. Any reference work, such as the *World Almanac*, will settle the question whether Richard Nixon is the thrity-sixth or the thirty-seventh President. The answer is that he is the thirty-seventh, though he is the thirty-sixth person to hold that office. (Grover Cleveland was both the twenty-second and the twenty-fourth. Benjamin Harrison was the twenty-third President.)

About the only way to check out the flood story is to call Rome!

The truth is that, as a writer, you will find yourself trusting some press association correspondents more than others. You will feel safer with one version of what happened simply because of the by-line. Thus, during World War II, the dispatches filed by Frank Bartholomew of the United Press and Wes Gallagher of the Associated Press were given special credence in broadcast newsrooms. Both correspondents were known for the accuracy of their reporting. Both became high executives in their respective news agencies.

Advisories

In reading wire copy, pay close attention to advisories as well as corrections.

The advisories can be crucial in writing a story. They may inform you, for example, that an important speech that was marked for 6:30 P.M. release is now for immediate release because someone, somewhere, broke the embargo. This information enables you, if you are preparing the 6 P.M. news, to go ahead and write the story. You may want to make it your lead.

Advisories can also tell you about congressional hearings which have been canceled and news conferences which will—or will not—be held. Or the advisory may simply say, "So-and-so will meet with newsmen immediately after today's swearing-in ceremony." Usually the advisory will tell you the time and place where the meeting will occur. Besides helping you plan the content of upcoming broadcasts, by letting you know a certain story will be breaking, it enables your station or network to arrange coverage.

An advisory may tell you that eight Eskimo children have a 3 P.M. appointment with the President. Surely here are picture possibilities. Another advisory may say that a White House statement on such-and-such a subject is expected momentarily. In other words, stand by for a new story. If you already have written a story on that subject, it will have to be revised. (Remember that news never stops. Stories often have to be updated, even as you write.)

Kill any story which the wire service commands you to kill. Such stories usually are loaded with libel, and you want none of it.

Bulletins

The wire services precede major late-breaking stories with the words FLASH, BULLETIN, and URGENT. The flash is rarely seen. It is reserved for news of transcendent importance, such as the death of the President. Bulletin matter is more common. First reports of a mine disaster will be bulletined; so will the final score in the World Series. The label URGENT is still more common. It signifies that the wire service regards the story as more than routine.

In broadcast journalism, bulletin treatment is accorded a story much less often than on the wires. The wire bulletin interrupts the flow of other news. The station or network bulletin frequently interrupts other programing. Unless a news program is in progress, most bulletin material is saved until the next newscast, usually within the hour. On all-news radio, of course, the wire service bulletin goes on the air at once.

The Skeds

Early each morning the press associations file their schedules, or "skeds," listing the major stories the wires will carry for the P.M.'s — the afternoon papers. Again, early each afternoon, they file similar schedules of stories to be carried for the ayems — the morning papers. The schedules consist of one-line summaries of the stories to be filed. They also tell you approximately how many words there will be in each story. They are, in effect, the menus of the news to be served by the agencies to you, their client, and they are of obvious benefit in helping you plan your news broadcast. They tell you not only what stories will be moved but which stories the press associations believe to be most important. The first story listed is deemed, in their judgment, to be the lead story. On this, quite naturally, agencies do not always agree. Nor need you agree with any of them. But these schedules — or budgets, as they sometimes are called — do show you the thinking of some of the nation's top editors, and their thoughts are valuable to you in making your own editorial judgments.

So when the "skeds" come in, save them to refer to.

Study the Copy Thoroughly

This takes time. You feel the pressure to finish your script, and every minute counts. But unless you are working right up against a deadline, and the show is about to go on the air, read EVERY WORD of the wire service story. Resist the temptation to start writing after the first four or five paragraphs, when you THINK you know what it's all about. READ THE COPY ALL THE WAY THROUGH. It takes only a little longer. The writer for the wire service may have buried an important fact — a fascinating angle — in the last few lines.

Even a bulletin that comes in on the teletype cannot always be accepted "as is." Press associations compete with each other to get their bulletin matter out first. Because of this competition, this rush, they do not take time to place the new development in perspective. You must do this in rewriting the bulletin for broadcast.

For example, when an American plane was shot down off the coast of North Korea in 1969, the first wire service bulletin made no reference to the U.S.S. *Pueblo*, captured by the North Koreans the preceding year. The experienced news writer knew at once — without waiting for adds on the press association wire — that the two stories were related. He recognized the new incident as an escalation of the earlier story, and he knew Congress would be upset. So he might have written this bulletin, tying in the Pueblo angle:

Here is a bulletin from the_____newsroom. North Korea says it has shot down an American spy plane over the Sea of Japan. If true, this is the second incident of its kind in a little more than a year. North Korea captured the intelligence ship *Pueblo* in January, 1968, and only recently released its 83-man crew. A plane of the type North Korea claims to have shot down normally carries a crew of three men. No word yet on how many, if any, of them survived.

Such treatment of a bulletin is not editorializing — it's good news judgment. There is a world of difference between expressing editorial opinion and placing news in context. Thus, the writer is an editor not only because of what he omits in the broadcast version of a story but also because of what, on occasion, he adds.

Not every story, of course, needs backgrounding. The test is whether significance is lost when background information is left out.

Another reason for careful scrutiny of wire copy is libel. One service used this lead:

LOS ANGELES—A MOTORIST-SNIPER WHO TERRORIZED THE SOUTHWEST AREA OF THE CITY WHEN HE WOUNDED THREE PERSONS IN A PRE-DAWN ATTACK WEDNESDAY SURRENDERED MEEKLY TO OFFICERS AT HIS ATTIC HIDEAWAY TODAY.

This is libelous. The wire service has convicted the man without benefit of trial. What if he was NOT the motorist-sniper who wounded three persons? And even if he was, the wire service had no business convicting him. That was up to the courts.

So STUDY the copy you take from the teletypes. Examine it for accuracy, for possible libel, for "holes"—for essential facts which somehow may have been missed.

And study it so you will have in your mind all the basic elements of the story you are about to rewrite. When you have read the wire copy carefully, set it aside and tell the story in your own words. TALK it into your typewriter. Refer to the wire copy only to check details, such as numerical figures and the spelling of proper names. (It's not a bad idea to circle names, figures, and dates when you are going through the copy. Some news writers also do a considerable amount of underlining. But don't underline so much that it loses its effect.)

Tell the story as you would tell it to a person who has just asked you what happened in Congress, or in Indo-China, or at the U.N.

Plan Your Story

Decide what you are going to say. What detail are you going to leave out? What are you going to put in? And in what order? This planning, which takes only a few seconds, will save you time. Few broadcasters can turn out a script faster than Allan Jackson, but he has the story in his head before he starts to write. He knows what he is going to say. He rarely refers to the wire copy. He tells the story in his own words.

The veteran CBS newsman says, "There are some excellent reporters on the agencies. They know how to dig for all the facts, how to ask questions, and when to look for background. But not all agency reporters are good writers, and even those who are still are writing 'see' copy because, after all, that is their job. And they are writing only one story at a time. The writer for broadcast is — or should be — writing all stories in relation to each other."

"The ABC Evening News" advertises that its news is presented in segments. The ad says, "Each segment consists of news events that are in some way related. For example, one segment might report on new draft quotas, then go to selective service reforms, and conclude with a report on student demonstrations." The ad itself concludes, "It's a nice clear way to get the news. And it makes sense."

It does indeed. And the practice is not exclusive with ABC.

Copying Wire Copy

Students often ask how much of a wire story they can copy. They ask, "What if the UPI says it better than I can? Why not use their language? Aren't you paying for it?"

Yes, you are paying for it. And if the wire service reports a fact simply, and succinctly, certainly it is no crime to use the same wording. But in most cases to copy what the agency man has written is completely wrong. Not only is "A" wire copy written mainly in newspaperese, but usually the story is written at much greater length than your story is to be written. Your job is to tell the story all over again in a shorter, more lucid form.

And beware of copying the "cute" phrase. During a strike of London garbage collectors, the AP had this sentence: "A Buckingham Palace spokesman *sniffed* that court officials had no idea how the royal garbage problem was going to be solved." This cutie wasn't worth copying, but if it were, it still should not be copied. Any piece of especially clever writing in news agency copy is apt to be aired by stations across the country. Worse still, it often is repeated in later broadcasts. The phrase, so original when the agency man wrote it, becomes hackneyed within hours. And it could be minutes if the phrase appears on the agency's radio wire.

As a general rule, don't copy. It's rare language you cannot improve upon, and news directors like their newscasts to be different from every other newscast down the line. They want their newscasts to be the best.

For you, too, it should be a matter of pride.

8

THE TIME ELEMENT

Broadcasting is the "now" medium. Radio and television can report what is happening right now, or what has just happened. Or, for that matter, what is just about to happen. For this reason, the present, perfect, and future tenses are used more than in print journalism. The past tense is used much less. Allan Jackson says: "Just because newspapers and wire associations write everything in the past tense doesn't mean that we on the electronic side of the business must, or even should, follow suit. Nothing sounds sillier than to hear some broadcaster say something to the effect that 'John Doe said he *thought* Christmas was a good idea.' Doesn't he still think so?"

The UPI stylebook says, "Use the present tense when appropriate, but don't belabor the point." Nothing in your writing should appear labored. There ARE times when it is best to use the past tense. If you use the past tense in a lead, you should include the time element.

The Senate voted *today* to reform the draft.

You could, of course, say *this afternoon* or *tonight*, if these apply. In fact, in an evening broadcast use *tonight* whenever you truthfully can. It makes the news sound fresher. In any case, if you use the past tense in a lead, tell when.

An exception would be if you are wrapping together several related stories.

If you report the Senate action on draft reform and go on to report House passage of an anti-crime measure, and conference committee agreement on a public housing bill, there's no need to add the time element to the last two stories. It is taken for granted by the listener, after hearing the first story, that these other congressional actions also took place today. Thus, the leads to the three stories, reported in succession, might read:

The Senate voted today to reform the draft.

The House approved the controversial anti-crime bill.

And a Senate-House committee agreed on a measure to provide public housing for 200-thousand low-income families.

No need in these last two stories to say *today*. It's assumed.

You would not have had to use the past tense in reporting any of these stories. "The Senate has voted to reform the draft" is every bit as good a lead as "The Senate voted today to reform the draft." But, as we said, if you do choose to use the past tense, then you need the adverb *today* or its equivalent.

Avoid a succession of leads containing the word *today*, especially in news summaries when repetition of the word becomes painful. Vary the tenses of your leads. Use the present and perfect tenses when they are appropriate. Your newscast "listens" better if you do this, and you are exploiting the fact that broadcast news is what is happening now. It is not only a natural, correct way to report the news but the most interesting way from the point of view of the listener, who is impressed by the immediacy of what you are reporting. He enjoys it.

You will enjoy it, too. Within minutes after a bulletin moves on the wire — sometimes within seconds — you have shared the news with a vast audience. There is excitement in writing a present-tense lead like

Egypt announces that it accepts the American proposal for a cease-fire in the Middle East.

Reflect the swiftness of the medium in what you write. For example:

It's official now. The French government formally announced a few minutes ago that it will devalue the franc.

So here is another tip on tenses. You are reporting news that is NEW. Let it sound that way. Don't hide it!

The present tense is by no means restricted to such bulletin-like material. It can—and should—be used in such relatively routine stories as

President Nixon is flying to Chicago, where tonight he will make a major foreign policy speech.

Here you can say *is flying* because the President has taken off from Andrews Air Force Base and actually is in the air, flying to Chicago. A newspaper or wire service can't say that. By the time the press reporter's story is published and reaches the reader, the President will already have arrived in Chicago. Chances are, he will also have given his speech.

Here's an example of effective use of the perfect tense in a lead:

Congress has just recessed.

The listener is being told what just happened, and he knows it.

Another reason for using the perfect tense is that we use it so often in every-day speech. Note how "natural" these leads sound:

Rescue workers in Mississippi have found the bodies of 100 more victims of Hurricane Camille.

The Chinese have test-fired another hydrogen bomb.

Those peace talks in Paris have again recessed.

Avoid a succession of perfect tenses in the same sentence. It has an awkward sound. For example, do not write

The White House has announced that President Nixon has decided against going to Europe at this time.

Instead, write

The White House announces that President Nixon has decided against going to Europe at this time.

For the same reason, avoid a succession of pluperfect tenses. THAT sounds even worse.

Do not "gild the lily" by adding *today* when you have used the perfect tense. Do not say

The Senate today has passed a new civil rights bill.

Say either

The Senate passed a new civil rights bill today.

or

The Senate has passed a new civil rights bill.

Choose one or the other, not both!

In some leads, no verb—hence, no tense—is used at all. More about leads later.

Don't Cheat

Don't say *today* when the story broke yesterday. Such practice can prove embarrassing (viewers may have heard the story the preceding day), and it is inaccurate. Be resourceful. Update the story. Move it into the present by highlighting a new fact which you may find through a telephone call or discover buried in the last paragraph of the story which moved on the wire. Don't start your story by saying, "A truce was agreed upon yesterday for the Middle East," even if there is little new to report. If there has been no reaction to the agreement, say so. If there has been no report of the truce being broken, say so. But don't start with yesterday's lead. If you do, you are proclaiming to your listeners that all you have is stale news.

It is perfectly proper to conceal the time someone said something, or something occurred, if the time element is not of consequence. Example: If in mid-afternoon you are using a statement that Pope Paul made the preceding night, it is not necessary to say:

Last night, Pope Paul issued a strong statement condemning the action of Iraq in hanging those 15 persons accused of spying for the United States and Israel.

It is no violation of journalistic principle, in this instance, to leave out the time element so that the story reads:

Pope Paul has issued a strong statement condemning the action of Iraq in hanging those 15 persons accused of spying for the United States and Israel.

What is newsworthy here is the Pope's condemnation of the Iraqi action. But we should emphasize that in some stories the time element is significant and must be reported. If the Pope's statement had been issued one day and an Iraqi statement defending its action was issued the next day, then obviously the timing of the statements is an integral part of the story. The listener must be told. The listener should be told that something happened "yesterday" or "last night" whenever the omission of that fact distorts the story or robs it of meaning. If a winter storm is moving eastward across the country, residents of New York and Pennsylvania have a real interest in knowing that "late yesterday" the storm reached Ohio. So tell them.

Unnatural Usage

In many wire service stories the time element is brought in unnaturally by the scruff of the neck. Example:

QUICK ACTION BY PRISON GUARDS AVERTED WEDNESDAY A THREATENED RACE RIOT IN THE WALLED YARD OF SAN QUENTIN PRISON.

The guards didn't avert Wednesday. They averted a threatened race riot. In normal conversation, you would never place the noun *Wednesday* immediately after the transitive verb *averted*. And you wouldn't say *Wednesday*. You would say *today*. In a newscast, the story might start out simply:

A race riot was averted today at San Quentin Prison.

It should be observed, because so much broadcast copy is rewritten from the wires, that both the Associated Press and United Press International regularly use the name of the day of the week instead of *today* in their night leads. This is in keeping with the special requirements of the print media. The writer of broadcast news should stay with *today*. And, contrary to the wire services, he should use the words *yesterday* and *tomorrow*. It is confusing to a person listening to the news on Friday to be told that something happened on Thursday or will happen on Saturday. He has to say to himself, "Oh, yes.

Today is Friday. When the broadcaster says Thursday, he means yesterday."
Or the listener says to himself, "Today is Friday, so Saturday is tomorrow."
The good professional writer avoids words the listener must translate.

What Time Is It?

The time element can cause trouble in other ways. A major newscaster was
embarrassed on the air when, in introducing a film report by a correspondent
in Prague, he said that it was on the night of August 20, 1968, that Russian
troops invaded Czechoslovakia. The correspondent, in his film report, said
that the Russian invasion occurred on August 21, 1968. They were both right.
It was on the night of August 20, New York time, and on August 21, Prague
time. But such contradictions in script, obviously, are to be avoided. The writer, having previewed the film, should have known the date used by the correspondent and not mentioned it in his introduction. He could, in short, have
written around it.

Pay particular attention to the time element in stories from the Far East. A
wire service story is written in local time. That is, in the time of the place
where the story originates. When something happened in Vietnam on
Wednesday, Saigon time, it may have happened on Tuesday, New York time.
If the story reports that a Communist infiltration raid took place on Wednesday night, the writer of a script for broadcast in New York cannot on Wednesday night, New York time, say that the raid took place tonight. Not only is the
word *tonight* inaccurate, it makes the broadcaster look foolish because, due to
the time difference, listeners to other news programs have been hearing about
the raid all during the day. "How," the listener asks, "can the raid have taken
place tonight when I heard it reported on that other station this morning?"

So we repeat: Don't fudge on the time element to "freshen" your story
because 1) it's wrong and 2) you will be found out.

The Midnight Writer

For the writer of "The Midnight News," the time element offers a special
problem. If, for example, it is midnight Saturday, the news actually will be
heard during the first few minutes of Sunday. How does the midnight writer
refer to an event which occurred earlier in the evening? Does he say it occurred last night? And how does he refer to what happened Saturday and what
will happen Sunday or Monday?

In the first instance, the writer would technically be right in saying *last night*. It already is Sunday. But in the minds of many listeners it still is Saturday night. The phrase *last night* will confuse them. For the same reason, they will be confused by references to *yesterday, today,* and *tomorrow*.

What's the answer?

Probably the best way out is to try, whenever possible, to use the present and perfect tenses without reference to the day. If mention of the specific day is required, say *Saturday, Sunday,* or *Monday*. Also, *Saturday night* is preferable to *last night*. It is awkward, but still the best solution. (In writing the troublesome midnight news, some writers simply say *tonight*, and that seems to work.)

The Advance Text

Be scrupulous in observing the release time on stories. But frequently a dinner speech to be delivered at 8 or 9 o'clock in the evening, local time, will be marked for release at 6:30. This is because the speaker, or the organization he is addressing, wants to "make" the networks' early evening news. The result is that you will be reporting the speech before it is ever made.

How do you write this? Can you report that the speaker said something which he has not yet said?

The answer is, "No, you can't." You CAN say "in a speech John Brown *is going to give* later tonight," or "John Brown says, in the advance text of a speech he *will give* later tonight," or, "according to the advance we have of a speech John Brown *is making* tonight," or, "in a speech he *is scheduled to give* tonight." Speakers often change their speeches at the last minute. You are leveling with the listener if you let him know you are quoting from an advance text. Also, it takes you off the hook if the speaker does not say what you say he's going to say!

We have taken a dinner speech as an example. Of course, the same kind of treatment should be given to any speech, the text of which is released in advance.

9

KEEPING IT SHORT

A long time ago, Mark Twain, giving advice to writers, said: "Use the right word, not its second cousin. Eschew surplusage—but do not omit necessary detail. Avoid slovenliness of form. Use good grammar. Employ a simple and straightforward style."

This is good instruction for journalism in all its forms. But the dicta which apply especially to broadcast journalism are 1) eschew surplusage—don't waste words—and 2) employ a simple and straightforward style. In an interview on "Today," William Saroyan said, "Good writing is irresistibly simple." Each sentence you write for broadcast should be sweet simplicity—deceptively simple and easy to understand. Because you are writing for the ear, the most transitory of all senses, you must use language in a special way. It makes no difference how good a reporter you are if the story you are reporting is not understood. And surplusage—wordiness—is particularly offensive in broadcast journalism where, literally, every second counts.

"Write Tight!"

"Write tight!" is the most common injunction heard in a broadcast newsroom. You must tell your stories in the fewest number of words. It means, as one news director has said, "boiling down a flood of information into a concise meaningful trickle." To do this expertly requires judgment. You must choose—select out—from your notes, or from the wire story, or both, what is essential. You must recognize what is basic—what gives the story meaning. And you must know what words to use in order to be succinct. For example, the sentence, "He wanted to know the reason for her departure," should sound wrong to you. Besides being pretentious, it takes almost twice as much time to read as "He wanted to know why she left." Your choice of words is all-important.

It has become trite to say that all the words used in a half-hour television program would not fill the front page of the *New York Times*. Nevertheless, this bears remembering. It means, as Ralph Renick of WTVJ, Miami, has said, "There is no room for the insignificant." There is no room for stories signifying nothing, or for words signifying nothing, because there is so little time. John Aspinwall, former radio-television news editor of the Associated Press, says: "Broadcast news writing requires special skills because it demands greater compression. It must be terse, but at the same time it must be clear and precise."

The famous editor Herbert Bayard Swope once pointed out that history's best example of compressing a story appears in the Gospel of St. John, in the shortest verse in the Bible which reads, "Jesus wept." Swope said that in those two words John told a great deal more than if he had used hundreds of words "because he allied himself to the imagination of the reader."

Ed Murrow was raised on the Bible and influenced by its language. On a bombing mission over Berlin his plane was buffeted by exploding antiaircraft shells. Murrow was scared. He wrote, "And I was very frightened," a para-phrase of the Bible's "And they were sore afraid." In five words, and in his reading of them, he conveyed—vividly—his fright. He allied himself with the imagination of the listener. And you recall the applause he heard at Buchenwald—"It sounded like the handclapping of babies, they were so weak."

Here is an example from a more recent war—Morley Safer standing ankle-deep in mud, reporting on the mass transfer of American equip-ment—vehicles, ammunition, tanks—to the South Vietnamese. He refers to "all the mechanized might of the world's richest army, the heaviest weapons man can devise," and then he adds, "Somewhere on foot, rifle in hand, is the enemy."

The incisive phrase is not fancy. Sometimes it is plain, like the edge of a knife.

Strive always for clarity. As Frank Bartholomew, head of United Press International, has warned: "There's a crying need for clarity today, and it will intensify tomorrow. Simplicity of language and clarity go hand in hand." And Bill Small says, "Good television journalism presents news in the most attractive and lucid form yet devised by man." In TV, the attractiveness and lucidity depend on the use made of words and pictures. In radio, they depend on the use made of words alone. And neither sentences nor film sequences can be long-drawn-out, discursive, or diffuse. In both media, tight editing applies.

These are generalities. Let's be specific with another example. It's a UPI story on the scattering of the ashes of Carl Sandburg.

GALESBURG, ILL. (UPI) CARL SANDBURG HAS RETURNED TO THE SOIL HE LOVED.

THE ASHES OF THE LATE POET AND AUTHOR OF GRAND MAGNITUDE WERE SCATTERED IN THE SHADOW OF A HUGE GRANITE BOULDER CALLED REMEMBRANCE ROCK IN A 1 1/2-ACRE PARK HERE, BEHIND THE THREE-ROOM COTTAGE THAT WAS HIS BOYHOOD HOME.

ILLINOIS GOV. OTTO KERNER PRESIDED AT A MEMORIAL SERVICE SUNDAY, COMMEMORATING THE PRIVATE CEREMONY AT DUSK SATURDAY. "THEY WILL REMAIN HERE ALWAYS IN THE AREA HE LOVED VERY, VERY MUCH," KERNER TOLD A CROWD OF 2,500.

AS HE SPOKE, TRAINS ROARED DOWN NEARBY TRACKS, REMINDING THOSE PAYING HOMAGE OF HIS DAYS RIDING THE RAILS, GATHERING MATERIAL TO WEAVE HIS PROSE AND POETRY.

In four short paragraphs we are given a torrent of specific detail—the acreage of the park, the kind of stone of which Remembrance Rock is composed, the number of rooms in Sandburg's boyhood home, the time of day the private services were held, the number of people attending the services at which the governor spoke the next day. No mention is made of Sandburg's Lincoln writings, for which he is best known. The phrase "author of great magnitude" is unfortunate. In the last sentence, confusing use is made of the pronouns *he* and *his*.

Let's say a news writer has this piece of wire copy and is told to boil it down to 25 seconds—all the time available for it in a show which goes on the air in 10 minutes. This presents the writer with a real problem. To "tell" the story so that the broadcaster can read it in 25 seconds, he must cut the wire service version of what happened almost in half. He decides at once to skip the reference to Remembrance Rock. He feels that if he mentions it, he must say that Sandburg once wrote a book by the same name. There's not time for that kind of background. He also decides to concentrate on what happened today—Sunday. What happened Saturday is yesterday's news. He leaves out a lot of other detail, and five minutes before air time he's finished. The story, condensed for broadcast, reads:

The ashes of Carl Sandburg have been returned to the soil of his hometown — Galesburg, Illinois. At a memorial service today, Governor Kerner said, "They will remain here always, in the area he loved very, very much." As the governor spoke, trains could be heard passing through, reminding the crowd of the days. . .long ago. . .when the poet and Lincoln biographer was poor and rode the rails.

Some factual information has been sacrificed. But is the listener really cheated? Will he miss not knowing the acreage of the park or any of the other details which have been dropped? Listeners who want these details know they will find them in the print media.

You will notice that mention is made in the broadcast version of Sandburg's role as Lincoln biographer. And, of course, reference is made to Galesburg, Illinois — something the UPI writer didn't have to do because of the dateline on the story, although "dateline" is now a vestigial term so far as wire services are concerned. They no longer give the date in their datelines, only the place.

Sometimes — too often for comfort — you will write a story and discover it runs too long. You must cut. It means killing words, phrases, perhaps whole sentences which you believed, when you wrote them, were absolutely essential.

The same applies to entire scripts. Here is a script Robert Trout wrote for CBS Radio. He says, "Thought you might find some interest in the cuts I had to make when I found this piece was too long. In every case, after I had done the fairly unpleasant job of cutting precious prose, I found that the cuts had improved the piece. That happens so often."

The cuts Trout made are enclosed in brackets. See if you don't agree that the piece is improved.

There I was with a table full of papers, just finishing a long day's work, when the clock jumped. And suddenly everything became clear.

(PAUSE)

You are listening to a man who has just made a sensational discovery. Nothing less than the Secret of Life. Well, anyway, the Secret of How to Live in This Modern World Without Going Mad from the Pressure of Too Many Things To Do and Not Enough Time To Do Them In.

I found the secret in a very pleasant place: aboard a steamship sailing from Europe to New York, where I have now landed. [And I don't know why I missed this discovery before, on previous westbound voyages.] The voyage has to be westbound. That is the secret.

Sailing eastward to Europe in a reasonably fast liner, they set the clocks ahead an hour every midnight. So that when [you think you have gone] you go to bed [at eleven-thirty, it is really twelve-thirty, and you have lost] you lose an hour, which means that you will most likely wake up the next morning feeling grumpy. [And you will get the whole day off to a bad start.] And the next day [it] will be just that much worse.

Sailing westbound on a five-day trip, you gain an hour every night. And everyone who has ever had the experience knows how pleasant that can be. But on this more recent voyage — perhaps because I had a lot of piled-up work to get through while at sea — I discovered that that extra hour is not merely pleasant. It is the secret of survival in this, the Feverish Age.

That book that you never have time to read, those five letters that you put off writing because there is no point in writing just one and letting the other four go again, those physical exercises — running or jumping or just simple deep breathing — they never seemed to fit into a normal day, either. But now there is time for everything. At the end of the 24-hour-day, with all the work done somehow, there is that wonderful extra hour, just standing there, unused, ready for anything. You might even use it to write a play or paint a picture or figure out a system to beat the races. Or just to get an extra hour of sleep [in the hope that that will produce added vim & vigor to tackle the jobs that will be waiting in the morning]. This is daylight saving that really does save time. And presents you with 60 extra minutes of it every day.

As soon as I came face to face with the realization that what the world has been waiting for is the twenty-five-hour day, I began to make plans. These broadcasts, I decided, would come to you each time from a point farther westward on the globe. I couldn't afford to stand still. I saw that. What was needed was a schedule that would take me westward, ever westward, round the world — round and round — always at the steady speed that would add one hour to every 24.

Making use of that 25th hour every day would bring me fame, fortune and satisfaction. And I was busily studying railroad timetables and ship sailing schedules when a disagreeable memory that I was trying to keep buried wiggled its way into the top part of my mind and demanded attention. What I remembered was that the last day aboard ship I did not get all my work done in the twenty-four hours as I had done the first day of the voyage. As we sailed westward, it was taking me a little longer every day to finish the normal tasks, and they were spilling over into that precious twenty-fifth hour.

So the discovery didn't work, after all. The 25-hour-day was defeated by human nature. I was crushed. Then the great idea came to me. Go westward at a faster pace. Gain two hours every day. That is the Secret of Life: the twenty-six-hour day!

Besides being instructive because of Trout's editing, the script illustrates an easy style. It is a small essay written to be spoken. The language is completely readable—and listenable. Note the short sentences: "And suddenly everything became clear," "Nothing less less than the Secret of Life," "But now there is time for everything." Each of these could have been part of a longer sentence. As separate sentences, they increase readability. When Trout wants to emphasize a word, he underlines it. And when he wants special emphasis, he types the word in capital letters, as in the case of TO in the fourth paragraph.

This is a light piece—a radio feature—done with just the right light touch.

Ale for the Ladies?

Let's take another example of how broadcast news is condensed. This time, the elements are a lead-in (read by the anchorman on camera), sound on film (SOF), voice over film (V/O), and closing remarks (again, on camera). We'll give you the script used by the anchorman, Harry Reasoner, and then list some of the details reported by the *New York Times* which he left out. First, Reasoner's script:

REASONER (ON CAMERA):

A court in New York has ruled, in the case of a saloon named McSorley's, that it must reverse an old policy and admit women. This would seem like a natural for one of those light-hearted little pieces of which journalism is so fond, except that the women who are carrying this particular banner get pretty rough when you get light-hearted, and I'm not feeling very strong.

TUMULT OF VOICES, INTERIOR McSORLEY'S
SALOON (SOF) VARIOUS CHARACTERS SPEAK:

" I don't think a decent woman would want to come here anyway, etc."

REASONER (V/O):

We pass over the question of *why* women want to go to McSorley's—it's a pleasant enough place, which with women present would be just another bar. We also concede that the bars where the men go alone at lunch are pleasanter than the places where women go mostly alone, which have a

common tendency to sound a little shrill and
frantic, like a bird sanctuary speaking about
last night's intruder.

REASONER (ON CAMERA):   And we also concede in logic that a head
waiter turning away a woman, because she is
a woman, is the same thing thing as Lester
Maddox with an ax handle turning away a
black. And we do *not* say, as a chauvinist
friend said about today's news event, that
those people are happier with their own kind
at lunch. We just suggest to the ladies that
this might be one struggle which chivalry
would dictate not beginning. And chivalry is
a womanly thing.

Reasoner wrote many fewer words than the reporter in the *Times*. He omitted some interesting facts. He failed to mention that McSorley's is the oldest
saloon in New York. He did not give its location — 15 East Seventh Street. He
did not report that it was a federal court which made the ruling, that the
judge's name was Walter R. Mansfield, and that he made his ruling on consti-
tutional grounds. The broadcaster said nothing about who brought the suit,
nor did he mention that McSorley's owners were expected to appeal.

He left all this out. But from the sound film the viewer got a bar-side seat
and tasted the flavor of the argument at first hand. An added dividend was
Reasoner's essay, which James Thurber, whose favorite bar was farther up-
town, would have loved.

Harry Reasoner was not "rewriting the wires." He had read the wires. He
had been amused by the story in the *New York Times*, where he saw it first.
He had heard — and made — jokes about it in the newsroom where he worked.
He had looked at the cameraman's footage. Then he had sat down and written
his own story, supplemented by film. The mark of his writing was upon the
whole piece.

And do not be deceived. This is remarkably tight writing. It is tight not only
because of the sundries he left out, like the judge's name and McSorley's
address, but because he wrote with extreme economy of language. How can
you start a story more simply than by saying, "A court in New York. . .?" The
whole lead sentence is bare bones.

He saved words through the power of suggestion. You know he was writing
in the context of the militancy of the Woman's Liberation Movement, but he
never mentions the movement. You know it anyway. He doesn't tell you who

Lester Maddox is. The reference to "ax handle" jogs your memory. He doesn't tell you how old McSorley's policy against the admission of women is — it's an "old" policy. You sense that it's quite old. He doesn't specify where women go "mostly alone," as he might have. Why should he? You know. They're those tea rooms and luncheon places in department stores which sound "a little shrill and frantic, like a bird sanctuary speaking about last night's intruder."

The whole thing, of course, is weighted, bald-facedly, on the masculine side. That's part of its charm. And it turned out to be "one of those light-hearted little pieces of which journalism is so fond" after all.

Tight writing is not only for hard news and feature essays. If possible, documentary writing must be tighter still. For no problem in documentary production is more acute than the problem of finding time within the half-hour or hour for adequate examination of the issues. Test these opening lines from the CBS classic, "Harvest of Shame." Do you see a sentence, a phrase, a single word that does not serve a useful purpose?

[MURROW]: This is an American story that begins in Florida and ends in New Jersey and New York State with the harvest. It is a 1960 *Grapes of Wrath* that begins at the Mexican border in California and ends in Oregon and Washington. It is the story of men and women and children who work 136 days of the year and average 900 dollars a year. They travel in buses. They ride trucks. They follow the sun.

The question regarding the expendability of any of this language was rhetorical. The documentary, produced by Fred W. Friendly and David Lowe, was an exposé of the shameful treatment of migrant workers in America. In these six simple declarative sentences, Ed Murrow set the scene.

One of the best writers in television news was the late Alice Weel Bigart. In 1968, when Ford's Theater was reopened in Washington, she wrote the script for a one-hour CBS special, narrated by Roger Mudd. At the top of the show, the producer, Don Hewitt, allowed her one minute to tell (with visuals) the whole story of Lincoln's assassination, including the escape and capture of John Wilkes Booth. Also, in the same minute, she was to provide an introduction to what was happening now, 103 years later.

When you read this, note the wealth of specific detail Mrs. Bigart managed, almost incredibly, to cram into a minute. The detail is executed — written — with such craftsmanship that, instead of being a jumble of incidentals, it reads beautifully and heightens interest. The sentences pack information, but they are lucid.

MUDD (PAN DOWN HANDBILL, MUSIC BEHIND):

Lincoln's attendance at Ford's Theater attracted a new capacity house. It also attracted John Wilkes Booth. It happened near the close of Act 3, Scene 2. Harry Hawk, the actor, had just delivered this rib-tickler: "Well, I guess I know enough to turn you inside out, old gal—you old sockdologizing old mantrap."

DISSOLVE TO ASSASSINATION SKETCH

In Box 8, as laughter rang out, so did a shot. This contemporary sketch shows the President, unguarded, sitting next to his wife. Booth fired once at close range. Lincoln never regained consciousness.

DISSOLVE THROUGH TWO SKETCHES OF BOOTH'S ESCAPE

As the President slumped forward, the agile Booth escaped by jumping onto the stage, 10 feet below. But he broke a shinbone in his fall, and was finally trapped and shot to death in a tobacco shed in Virginia.

DEATH SCENE SKETCH

The dying President was carried across the street, where his long body was placed on a bed in the home of William Peterson, a tailor. Death came at 7:22 in the morning, nine hours after that final act at Ford's Theater on April 14th, 1865. Now, five score and three years later, the world notes and remembers.

The script is a demonstration that brevity—tightness in writing—does not mean wholesale sacrificing of detail. The trick lies in the SELECTION of detail. Notice how skillfully the writer, after telling the story of the assassination in about 50 seconds, brings the viewer back to the theater by saying that death came "nine hours after that final act at Ford's Theater on April 14th, 1865." She is now ready, in just 12 words, to set the viewer up for the next scene—the gala reopening—which is in the present: "Now, five score and three years later, the world notes and remembers."

This is tight, professional writing. In these scripts, Harry Reasoner, Ed Murrow, and Alice Weel Bigart have eschewed surplusage and employed a simple and straightforward style.

"Today, at Mount Sinai. . . ."

Mark Twain also cautioned against the omission of necessary detail. One thinks of the story Bill Small relates of how, if Moses should present the Ten Commandments today, a newscaster's lead might be: "Today, at Mount Sinai, Moses came down with 10 commandments, the most important three of which are. . . ."

In writing a news story, do not simplify—tighten—by leaving out basic elements. Sure you are pressed for time. The cliché is right—time IS a tyrant. Nowhere more than in broadcasting. But abbreviation must never be at the expense of meaning. Sense is not to be sacrificed for the facile phrase. Distortion is not—repeat NOT—excusable "because it's simpler this way" or "because this way it reads better." You must cover what is essential and, with skill, MAKE it read.

In "keeping it tight" you are selecting what to report. That is why, as a news writer, you are an editor, too, with all the responsibility that editorship entails.

The amount of background information which can be included in any news story is limited. In broadcast news there is not the room—or time—for background that exists in print journalism. When a story has been in the news for days, even weeks, it is assumed that the listener knows the background. Only the latest developments in these so-called "running" stories are reported.

The cut-off date for providing such background information is, inevitably, arbitrary. You decide one day, in reporting the story, that by this time the basic facts are generally known. You must, in your judgment, be quite sure of this. There's no use reporting the story if you leave out the element of background which enables the listener to know what the story really is all about.

Here's an example. On May 6, 1970, the Secretary of Defense, Melvin Laird, issued a statement saying that he had supported President Nixon's decision to send American combat troops into Cambodia. This 20-second story was written and turned in to the news editor for a radio station in Washington:

Defense Secretary Laird said today that he "fully supported" President Nixon's decision to send American troops into Cambodia. He said the aim of the Allied action in Cambodia is to destroy the enemy's sanctuary and "get out as quickly as we can." Laird reaffirmed the President's policy not to get bogged down in Cambodia.

The editor killed the last sentence. He didn't like the redundancy in getting out quickly and not getting bogged down. More importantly, he wanted time to include mention of reports, published the previous day, that Laird had counseled AGAINST going into Cambodia. The whole point of Laird's statement was to refute these reports. Not to mention them was to gut the story, to ignore its real meaning. For the last sentence, the editor substituted:

It was reported yesterday that Laird opposed the move into Cambodia.

Thus the Laird statement was reported for what it was—a denial of the published reports. In fact, the story might well have been rewritten so that it led with this angle.

Be careful what you leave out of a story. A Moses of journalism would say: Thou shalt not write stories so tightly that significance is lost.

The Good Word

As suggested earlier, one way to keep your writing tight is to use the good short word that says the same thing as a long word or even a whole phrase.

To illustrate, here is some editing that Murrow did. First, the sentence as originally written, then Murrow's revision:

Mao Tse-tung has *relinquished* one of his top posts.
Mao Tse-tung has *given up* one of his top posts.

The message came *prior to his departure*.
The message came *before he left*.

The Justice Department contends that his naturalization was obtained *fraudulently*.
The Justice Department contends that his naturalization was obtained *by fraud*.

They acted because of an *anticipated* increase.
They acted because of an *expected* increase.

Mr, Eisenhower *reiterated* his proposal for "open skies" inspection.
Mr. Eisenhower *repeated* his proposal for "open skies" inspection.

In the interim, he has waged a *protracted* legal battle.
In the interim, he has waged a *long* legal battle.

Murrow edited his copy to make it tighter, more readable, more direct. Some of the words he shunned are what H.W. Fowler in his *Dictionary of Modern English Usage* calls "stylish" words. It's a mistake, Fowler says, to think you can improve your style by using these words—the effect is apt to be pretentious. Among the stylish words listed by Fowler are: Assist (for *help*), beverage (for *drink*), category (for *class*), commence (for *begin*) and sufficient (for *enough*).

Excess syllables represent waste. A one-syllable word is always better than a two-syllable word, if it says what you want to say. And a two-syllable word is much better than a four- or five-syllable word when it serves the purpose. Often you can save time by using:

ask for *question*	*first* for *initial*
basic for *elementary*	*home* for *residence*
beat for *defeat*	*hurt* for *injure*
big for *prodigious*	*measure* for *legislation*
bill for *measure*	*often* for *frequently*
buy for *purchase*	*on* for *upon*
cost for *expense*	*rebuke* for *reprimand*
cuts and bruises for	*send* for *transmit*
lacerations and abrasions	*speech* for *address*
each for *every*	*start** for *begin*
end for *conclude*	*sure* for *certain*
expense for *expenditure*	*try* for *attempt* or *endeavor*
false for *spurious*	*urge* for *persuade*

Broadcasters prefer the short word. So try—don't endeavor—to make it your preference, too.

---

* A famous TV director used to say, "Let's commence to begin!"

More Than a Matter of Synonyms

Using the short synonym helps, but tight writing is more than that. And more than selecting the important, or significant, detail.

Tight writing is also selecting words and arranging them in such a way that they say as much, or more, then a longer arrangement of words. Again we can explain this best with examples of the actual editing process.

The examples are two pieces of copy—two complete stories—used on "The CBS Evening News with Walter Cronkite." Here is the first story as it was turned in:

[CRONKITE]: Russia, co-chairman with Britain of the 1954 Geneva conference, again has ruled out reconvening the conference in an effort to end the Vietnam war. Soviet Premier Kosygin said such a meeting now would be out of the question. . .not only because of the U.S. bombing of North Vietnam. . .but because neither North Vietnam nor the Viet Cong would be participants in the talks.

Cronkite edited the copy to read:

[CRONKITE]: Russia, co-chairman with Britain of the 1954 Geneva conference, again has ruled out reconvening the conference in an effort to end the Vietnam war. Soviet Premier Kosygin's reasons: The U.S. bombing of North Vietnam and the fact that neither North Vietnam nor the Viet Cong would be participants.

The first sentence is unchanged. Cronkite reduced the second sentence from 36 words to 21 words without sacrificing a single fact.

Here is the second story as it was told by a staff writer. It was difficult to tell on television because of its complexity. There were dates and proper names and a lot of figures.

[CRONKITE]: Until last February, the Federal Aviation Agency required North Atlantic jetlines to fly in corridors 120 miles wide, but then because of the growing need for airspace, the F-A-A reduced the width of the corridors to 90 miles above 29-thousand feet. The Air Line Pilots Association called the narrower corridors a safety hazard. Today, the F-A-A, with Britain and Canada, ordered a return to the 120-mile lanes because, they said, of complexities created by differing regulations for differing heights. The F-A-A says this is only a temporary arrangement during a search for a solution. But the F-A-A asserts it still regards the 90-mile lanes safe.

The complexity of the regulations is reflected in language far too complex for the aural medium. Cronkite rewrote the story so that it is told more lucidly and in two-thirds the length.

[CRONKITE]: Trans-Atlantic airliners fly along prescribed highways in the sky — called corridors. Last February federal authorities reduced the width of the corridors from 120 to 90 miles. Airline pilots screamed, said the narrow corridors were unsafe. Today the government went back to 120 miles but said other technical considerations dictated the change, not safety. And, said the government, after further studies they might change their minds again.

In this case, some facts were sacrificed in the interest of understanding. The listener is not told who the "federal authorities" are. "The Air Line Pilots Association" is translated simply "airline pilots." Neither is the listener told that Great Britain and Canada went along with the United States in ordering a return to the 120-mile lanes. But the listener IS told the "nub" of the story. If more facts — so complex — were poured in upon him, he would lose the story altogether. In his copy, Cronkite eschewed surplusage. He cleared up a piece of murky writing. He did not omit necessary detail. He employed a simple and straightforward style.

You can save words by thinking of every sentence you write as being alive. Every word in that sentence should be an essential part of the organic whole. If a word can be eliminated — cut — without causing the sentence to bleed, then you don't need it. Excise it and good riddance. EXCISE ANY WORD WHICH DOES NOT CONTRIBUTE.

Emerson Stone, CBS' director of news for radio, has picked out some choice examples of wordy writing. Here they are with comments he made in a memorandum to his staff:

General consensus. *Consensus* carries the meaning of a meeting of minds. *General* is superfluous.

The aim of the move was intended to discourage waste. Why not drop *the aim of*?

From whence they came. *Whence* incorporates the meaning of *from*, which therefore can be dropped.

The reason for this, according to Young, is because . . . . Make it, "The reason, according to Young, is that. . . ." *Because* is redundant. You don't need *for this*.

Therein lies an interesting story, not only about a man's sense of duty, but also about West German politics as well. How about losing both the *also* and the *as well*?

He said he allegedly has a witness. Why *allegedly*?

Besides this action, the baseball owners must also decide. . . . *Besides this action* is superfluous.

Thousands have been killed and tens of thousands more are starving. *More* is redundant.

But the true facts came out. Forget *true*. A rose is a rose is a rose. Pigs is pigs, and facts is facts.

We have found these other examples of words wasted in broadcast scripts by using

at this point in time   *prior to* for *before*
  for *now*
do injury to for *injure*   *provide proof* for *prove*
due to the fact that   *sounded their praise*
  for *because*   for *praised*
in an effort to for *to*   *took that walk down the*
                       aisle for *married*!
in order to for *to*   *will be able to* for *can*
is capable of for *can*   *would be able to* for *could*
make changes in
  for *change*

There is a debate over the use of *whether or not*. While print journalists, quite correctly, find the *or not* superfluous, there are occasions in writing news for broadcast when the full phrase serves a useful purpose. That purpose is emphasis. Example:

Negotiations in the next few hours will determine whether or not subway trains in New York City will be running on New Year's Day.

Here, *or not* makes a contribution. The two small words magnify for the listener—dramatize, if you will—the alternatives: Will the subways run, or will they be shut down? Moreover, by employing the whole phrase *whether or not*, the writer has given the broadcaster, like the actor in a play, an opportunity to underscore the alternatives further by his reading of the line. Always remember that as you write for ear, you also are writing for voice.

One means of condensing—keeping it short—is to assume that the listener knows what you are talking about. You assume he knows the background. In the previous chapter, we used the sentence, "Those peace talks in Paris have again recessed," to illustrate use of the perfect tense in writing for broadcast. The same sentence demonstrates the use of the adjective *those* as shorthand, relieving the writer of having to explain who were participating in the talks and in what conflict they were seeking a settlement. The negotiations between the United States and North Vietnam had gone on so long that this was a safe assumption.

The same kind of assumption can be made in a story which has had only a short history. A devastating hurricane may have been in the news only twenty-four hours, but since every newscast and every daily newspaper in the country will have been reporting the storm's progress, it can be assumed that the listener knows of its existence, though obviously there are always a few listeners who have been out of touch. But even the listener who has not heard of the storm understands if you say

That off-season hurricane has struck Havana, killing at least 50 persons. Damage is estimated in the hundreds of millions of dollars.

Two other examples:

All passengers have been rescued from *that* cruise ship sinking off the coast of Portugal.

Doctors report that two of *those* quintuplets born yesterday in Mexico City have died.

Again, the device of using *that* and *those* enables the newscaster to get to the heart of what is new in the story in the fewest possible words.

Where Loss Equals Gain

If the first commandment in broadcast style is to be conversational, the second commandment is to be concise. In his introduction to William Strunk Jr.'s marvelous little book on the elements of style, E.B. White tells how Professor Strunk taught the art of pruning language to make it more effective. White said: "The student learns to cut the deadwood from 'This is a subject which. . .,' reducing it to 'This subject. . .,' a gain of three words. He learns to trim'. . .used for fuel purposes' down to 'used for fuel.' He learns that he is being a chatterbox when he says 'The question as to whether' and that he should say 'Whether,' a gain of four words out of a possible five."

Note that White equates the elimination—loss—of unnecessary words with GAIN. Each word should work for you. A nonworking word reduces clarity, fogs up what you are trying to say, and should be cast off. In broadcast journalism, conciseness carries a double premium. Not only is concise language more effective, making for clarity, but it saves time. And time is the "container" in which news items—film and script—are packaged. The more concisely, cleanly, the stories are written, the more room to report items which otherwise would be left out.

Almost every newscast, regardless of length, is a "tight show" if you are trying conscientiously to report the most important, most interesting developments of the day. If it is a light day and not much has happened, you can use the extra room to explain, perhaps through background, more of the significance of what did happen. When the television networks expanded their evening news programs to a half-hour, they wondered if there would be trouble filling the time. That problem never arose. The problem the producers face is the old one: How best to report the news in the time available to them.

10

MAKING IT CERTAIN

Because of the ephemeral nature of radio and television, they are more susceptible than newspapers or magazines to misunderstanding. The broadcaster's words are fleeting; the picture is evanescent—now you see it and now you don't. This transitory quality affects—SHOULD affect —how you write. An extra effort must be made to avoid confusion in what you say and what you show. Meaning must be clearly established because, as you are told so often, the viewer cannot play back what he has just heard or take a second or third look at what he has just seen.

Some day soon the videotaping of programs at home will be commonplace. When that day comes the viewer will be able to record and replay programs at will. He can review what he has seen and heard. Even then, the basic nature of the electronic media will not have changed. The responsible broadcast journalist still will try to be understood the first time. The premium placed on clarity, simplicity, and precision of language will remain high. Tolerance of careless, ambiguous language will remain low.

In a sense, news writers for radio and television sometimes provide "playback" for their audiences today. On occasion, to remove doubt, they repeat a crucial figure, name, phrase, or even a whole sentence so the listener may be sure what was said. This is good practice whenever a fact needs underscoring because of special importance. For example, a date that determines who will be called up first for the draft, or the description of a deadly poison lost in transit, or a telephone number to call for information in an emergency.

A fact likely to be missed by the listener is where a news event has taken place. He hears that an explosion has occurred killing many persons. He wasn't listening closely until he realized the nature of the story. Now, as the newscaster reads, he listens intently for clues to WHERE IT HAPPENED. He tells his wife to stop talking so he can hear. The newscaster never repeats the location, and the listener "fishes" for another news program or waits for the morning paper. At ABC Radio it is a rule that the location—where an event took place—must be restated somehow, somewhere toward the bottom of the story. This is achieved by using such phrases as "That's at Alton, Illinois" or "That explosion was at Port Arthur, Texas," or simply "The explosion in Port Arthur" at or near the end of the piece which is being read.

Such repetition may not be necessary in every story, though it is interesting that at least one radio network believes so. Certainly no disagreement exists regarding repetition of essential information in a news bulletin.

A most serviceable word is *almost*. The late A. J. Leibling, that astute critic of American journalism, once said, "*Almost* is a very unsatisfactory word, but writers almost never use it sufficiently. It sounds better to say things without qualification, but that is very seldom justified."

"We Interrupt This Program. . . ."

Because of the element of time—generally, commercial time—wordiness, as we said, is a crime. But if it ever becomes a choice between more words and confusion as to meaning, employ more words. Clarity has top priority. This is especially true of bulletins, which often catch listeners off guard. Example: If an airliner crashes, REPEAT the name of the airline (though the public relations people at the airline may not fancy that), flight number, and place of departure and destination. These facts are absolutely essential. If your bulletin is being carried on a network, it's a good bet that thousands of listeners who hear it will, at that very moment, know of some friend or relative who is traveling by air. This procedure should be followed in handling any sudden tragedy involving mass transportation. Such repetition is not only good reporting but humane.

Sometimes the story is so big the broadcaster cannot wait for details, important though they be. If an airliner explodes in midair after take-off, and the airline to which it belongs is not immediately known, certainly the accident should be reported. But the incompleteness of the report must be emphasized. The source of the information must be given. And that first bulletin MUST be followed as soon as possible by another bulletin clearly identifying the plane which crashed. Any inaccuracies in the first report MUST be corrected. The broadcast of erroneous, fragmentary information of tragic proportions is as irresponsible as it is cruel.

Name Your Source

On August 23, 1970, the lead story in the *Washington Post* began:

> The United States has adopted a policy of bombing the enemy in Cambodia where he can be found, according to informed sources here and in Saigon.

It would be a temptation in rewriting this story for broadcast to say, "In Cambodia, the United States is now bombing the enemy wherever he can be found." The writer might then give the background of this country's policy with respect to bombing in Cambodia and let it go at that.

This would be a mistake. The writer must also say that the story appeared in the *Washington Post* and he must attribute the information to sources in Washington and Saigon. The story may be right. But the writer cannot KNOW it is right. There is also the matter of crediting the news organization that comes up with such a story. So the writer MUST name the source.

In 1943, the free world awaited news that American troops under General Patton had closed a pincers on the German forces in Sicily, trapping elements of several enemy divisions. Entrapment would be complete, it appeared, when two American columns linked up at a certain town on the north coast. Reuters moved a bulletin saying that the Americans had indeed reached that town. At CBS, a fifteen-minute news program was in progress. The editor on duty rushed the bulletin to the broadcaster, who scarcely had time to read it before going off the air.

No mention was made of the fact that the bulletin came from Reuters. The editor hadn't taken time to write that in. And, after all, the broadcaster, who was a staff announcer, was also rushed.

The catch was that Sicily has TWO towns of that name. The Americans had entered the other town. There was no closing of the pincers, no link-up at all. Reuters filed further stories, explaining the confusion. Ultimately, the two American columns did meet, but most of the Germans escaped across the Messina Strait to the mainland of Italy.

CBS's news director at the time was the redoubtable Paul White. He demanded to know how the Reuters story got on the air without attribution.

The editor's excuse was that there was little time, and he had trusted what he saw on the wire. White then told the editor a number of things. One thing he said was, "I'd a helluva lot rather be late with a story than wrong."

Weigh all stories on the basis of your news judgment. YOU are responsible. If you decide to go with a story, give the source. It helps the listener to evaluate the story, and you are not going out on such a limb. We are talking here about exclusive stories and stories you want to use which pin their information on a source or sources. Often these sources serve to qualify the report. The *Washington Post* story, for example, is not "hard." There was no official announcement of a change in bombing policy. The newspaper gave its sources. You must give them, too.

This is a question of responsibility. What is the SOURCE of your information? The wire service? A phone call? To report a lobsterman's call that he has just seen a big airliner explode off the coast of Maine—with no further corroboration—is indefensible. If such an accident did occur, confirmation would soon be available from the Coast Guard, from airport officials, from other eyewitnesses, from the police, or from the airline itself. The lobsterman may be right, but often—too often—the "big airliner" turns out to be another type of plane, perhaps a military aircraft, and instead of a tragedy involving the lives of scores of persons, the final death toll stands at three.

Here again, a word of warning. NEVER say "only" three persons were killed. During World War II, Paul White admonished his staff not to use that belittling adverb when he caught a writer, after a massive bombing raid against Germany, reporting, "Only two of our bombers failed to return." His point was that to the men on those planes, and to their families, death was just as real as if it had happened to a hundred other men. It was, he said, like telling a father and mother, "Only your son died." White's policy in such instances was to report the fact: "Two of our bombers failed to return." The fact, unadorned, speaks for itself. The lesson still has not been learned. Today, as these words are written, some newscasters are still saying after a Vietnam battle, "Only five G.I.'s were killed."

Be careful in reporting deaths—any deaths. Allow no room for misunderstanding. It is technically—grammatically—correct to write:

Dr. Ramon Grau San Martin, former president of Cuba and longtime political foe of Batista, died today at the age of 86. He served briefly as president in 1933 and was elected to a full four-year term in 1944.

This may be perfectly acceptable for the wire service, but it is wrong for the medium for which you write. Experience has shown that many people, half listening, will believe it was Batista who died. His name will catch their attention, then immediately after the name comes the word *died*. "Oh," they will say, "Batista died."

There are other objections to the story as it is written. It starts cold with a rather long unfamiliar name. The name needs to be "teed up" in advance—i.e., the listener needs to be prepared for it. Otherwise the broadcaster may have finished reading the name before he has the listener's attention, before the listener really is listening. The experienced writer recognizes that it is not enough for the set to be tuned in. The listener has to be tuned in, too. Another fault is that listeners may be confused by the amount of information thrown at them in the first sentence. They are given, in one gulp, the name of the deceased, the office he held, his political orientation, the fact he died, and his age. Some leads you see—and hear—are worse in this respect, but this is still too much. Don't overcrowd.

A fourth mistake—a bad one—is that Dr. Grau's name appears only once in the story. If the listener doesn't catch it the first time, or is late turning on the set, he doesn't know who died. There are few things more aggravating than to hear a broadcaster keep saying *he* this and *he* that and not know who *he* is. Always repeat the name. Also, in this particular story, it might have been a good idea to identify Batista.

To correct these faults and reduce the possiblity of misunderstanding, the story might have been written:

A former president of Cuba, Dr. Ramon Grau San Martin, died today in Havana. He was 86. Dr. Grau served as Cuba's president in 1933 and again from 1944 to 1948. He was an outspoken foe of Batista, who later seized dictatorial power.

The Elephant's Tail

On January 5, 1970, when Senator Edward Kennedy of Massachusetts flew to Edgartown, on Martha's Vineyard, for the inquest into the death of Mary Jo Kopechne, he was described by a radio newsman as arriving "relaxed and smiling." Several hours later on the Cronkite News, David Culhane at Edgartown described Kennedy as appearing "assured and confident." Homer Bigart, writing in the *New York Times*, said that Kennedy "was solemn as bareheaded he strode into the courthouse with his wife, Joan."

So here we have Kennedy "relaxed and smiling" and "assured and confident" and "solemn" as he came to the inquest into the secretary's death. Probably, at a given moment, each of these descriptions was accurate. You recall the blind men and the elephant, each reaching out and touching a different part of the elephant's body and each giving a description which, for that part of the animal, was accurate. It is altogether possible that, on his arrival, Kennedy saw an acquaintance in the crowd and smiled. At other times, he may have looked "assured and confident." No doubt he was solemn.

It is absolutely essential when you report a story to be accurate in your description and not choose an adjective, or adverb, which distorts what happened or what was said. It is probable that some people, hearing that first radio report, said to themselves, or to the person they were with, "Think of him smiling at a time like that!" Or the listener does not believe the reporter, which means that a credibility gap has been created. The greatest intangible asset a news organization can have is trust.

Say What You Mean

People, unintentionally, say what they DON'T mean all the time. A government office announced that its staff included "people who have strong feelings of *apathy* and understanding." A fire department in Hampshire, England, received a questionnaire which asked, "How many people do you employ broken down by sex?" A student once reported on the campus radio station, "The witness testified with an affirmative 'no.' " And since starting this chapter, we heard a TV weatherman say that a heat wave in the Midwest was "breaking new records."

Think of the literal meaning of what you write.

When Majestic Prince won the Preakness in 1969, after winning the Kentucky Derby, an announcer said, "Majestic Prince now has two legs on the triple crown." Quite a picture! And a newscaster reported that Cassius Clay's wife had given birth to a four-pound, six-*inch* girl."

One of this country's best-known television critics spoke of a broadcast in which "the four-letter word for *excretion* was used." A wiseacre wondered if he meant S-W-E-T, which is the closest to a four-letter word for *excretion* he could come. The critic had not written what he meant to write. A news writer must write what he means.

Avoid words with two meanings. Years ago, the late great sportscaster Ted Husing was heard to say, "I returned from Miami with a dirty linen suit and no trunks." Even if you are right, don't say it if it sounds wrong. Don't say, as the announcer did in a commercial for a Washington bank, that it is "an institution providing the latest in convenience." To the listener, the announcer said *inconvenience*. And it did the bank no good.

Think what you are saying.

11

"FOR YE SHALL SPEAK INTO THE AIR"

H. V. Kaltenborn used to say, "St. Paul said it 1900 years ago,'Except ye utter by the tongue words easy to be understood, how shall it be known what is spoken? For ye shall speak into the air.' "

It is humbling to realize that a preacher more than nineteen centuries ago not only predicted the advent of radio but said just about the most important thing there is to say about writing news for broadcast, which is that the broadcaster, no matter how complex the subject, must report that complexity "uttering by the tongue words easy to be understood."

This means more than avoidance of uncommon words. Such words interrupt the listener's flow of understanding. He stops listening to puzzle over meaning. But the broadcaster does not stop. His voice is a fleeting thing. And it is this fleetingness of electronic news—this speaking into the air—which limits what the writer can do.

He cannot, for example, douse the listener with every detail. Facts vital for an understanding of the story will be lost, just as a juggler trying to keep too many balls in the air drops them all.

The story must be simplified. And it must be complete in itself. You cannot introduce elements of a story and then, because it would get too detailed for the time you have, leave them hanging. For example, if you write

After heated debate over a proposed amendment, the money bill finally was passed.

you MUST tell what the amendment was. You cannot relieve yourself of that responsibility. So before you start to write, decide what is essential. Understand in your own mind what is the essence of the story. Then tell it.

Don't be "clever" in your writing. It rarely succeeds. Again, this is because of the fleetingness of the human voice. The cleverness comes and goes too quickly. There is no opportunity to relish it. It is not absorbed.

One of the loveliest leads ever written appeared in an article in the *Wall Street Journal*. The article was about the magazine *Variety*, and the lead sentence was: "Spice is the life of *Variety*." It was perfect in print. In a broadcast, it would be lost in the onrush of spoken words.

The professional writer in radio and television recognizes this limitation. Andrew Rooney, who won an Emmy for his writing in the "Of Black America" series on CBS-TV, says: "In broadcast journalism there is not much room for clever turns of a phrase. For one thing, people listen slower than they speak, so clever is hard to hear. I remember how, during a New York newspaper strike, CBS used a lot of very good newspapermen on the air, and they were pretty bad. Art Buchwald is usually bad on television because his very clever material does not stand up to being read aloud. I recall Red Smith, who writes sports maybe better than anyone, saying on the air, 'He was a man of many facets — all turned on.' In a column it is clever and adds meaning. On the air it was whadidysay."

Rooney says: "Thoreau gave the best advice. 'As for writing style,' he said, 'if one has anything to say, it drops from him simply and directly, as a stone falls to the ground. There are no two ways about it, but down it comes, and he may stick in the points and stops wherever he can get a chance.' "

"The other thing about writing for broadcast journalism," according to Rooney, "is that it is not essentially creative. Consequently it attracts people who are better organized than most writers. Some of my friends in the newsroom have frequently objected to my characterization of them, but it is true and I don't see why it diminishes their art. It is just different, that's all. Knowing how to say it quickly, completely, and in a style that attracts some attention to the material is difficult, and they know how to do that. They fall into regular writing patterns because there isn't time to do anything else. A lot of people wouldn't hear it if they didn't."

Further insight into this subject is provided, curiously enough, by Daniel P. Moynihan, professor and former White House adviser. In a eulogy delivered on the occasion of the death of Paul Niven, Washington correspondent for National Educational Televsion, Moynihan said: "At CBS, he [Niven] moved from the age of radio to that of television, where of a sudden the potential and demands of technology altogether outreached the simple if arduously acquired discipline of the written word. It became necessary in an instant, as the second hand swept past the hour, for him and a handful of other men like him to impose the standards of an older craft on the swirling, chaotic, unformed, and unfathomable phenomenon which technology had let loose upon an unsuspecting and too welcoming public. More specifically, a phenomenon which was to penetrate and reshape the innermost processes of democratic society, a phenomenon with the capacity to create and the capacity to destroy, and a destiny none knew and even now none knows."

In this technological revolution, the word—what is spoken—remains the best means devised for the communication of ideas, a statement so patently true that it has become trite. It is no denigration of the power of pictures to say that they show *what* better than they show *why*. In 1958, CBS put together a book called *Television News Reporting*. It said, in something of an understatement, that "one of the real needs of any successful television program is a man who can write. His role, his ability to write good, clean prose, his ingenuity, his education, his authority, his understanding of the medium, his thinking—all can make the difference between a good and a bad show."

One of the most ingenious, most erudite writers in broadcast journalism is Heywood Hale Broun, whose sports reporting has contributed to the success of "The CBS Saturday News." Broun recognizes the fleetingness of the broadcast word. He concedes with ingratiating immodesty, "Most of what I say goes by, and you just have the feeling something classy is happening." Broun borrows phrases from Shakespeare and refers continually to outsize characters like Paul Bunyan, D'Artagnan, and assorted Greek gods. Through this embroidery of language—this fancy name-dropping—he builds impressions. The listener does get "the feeling something classy is happening."

In hard news, you do not indulge in this kind of writing. When John Chancellor became an anchorman on "The NBC Nightly News," he said, "My objective is to say it and not to adorn it—to be limpidly clear."

If you report a sports event, your meaning still better be clear. Despite Broun's adorning phrases, there never is doubt about what is happening when he reports. Thus, broadcasting from Shea Stadium on the eve of a World Series, he can get away with a line like, "Not since the dancing madness of the fourteenth century has there been such unrestrained mirth and mania as can be invoked by the New York Mets." Not one listener in a million remembers the madness of five hundred years ago. But the meaning is clear. Broun sees to it that the listener gets the meaning by using the phrase "unstrained mirth and mania." It was wild.

Broun loves similes and metaphors—"Baltimore did get the tying run to the plate in the ninth, but the outfield cavalry was ready for the charge"—and they are effective in broadcast writing, SO LONG AS THEY EMERGE NATURALLY AND ARE NOT OBSCURE.

Here are examples of simile and metaphor employed effectively by other broadcast journalists:

After a heavy German raid on London, Ed Murrow wrote; "As I walked home at seven in the morning, the windows in the West End were red with reflected fire, and the raindrops were like blood on the panes." And when, in peacetime, Murrow approached the eye of a hurricane in an Air Weather Service plane, he said, "A big cloud seemed to summon its neighbors, and they built castles and lakes and cities on hillsides—all white against the blue sky." At another point in the same broadcast, he said, "The ocean was heaving about below as though a giant were shaking a rug."

When Carl Stokes was re-elected mayor of Cleveland, John Chancellor said: "In the months ahead he must struggle against the voices of fear that infect his city. He must grapple with the conflicts between blacks and whites. He must broker the demands of the poor upon the rich."

Perry Wolff, on the subject of the Acropolis: "For all who have known or remembered or longed for freedom, this temple is the Holy Grail they seek to build again, in their hearts and in their way of government. It was here in Athens, after millennia of dark and numb existence, for most men, that the sun of reason penetrated the human mind and ignited a fire. Here, in the city and the plain below, it burned briefly, died down, flickered. . . . It never went completely out. It still warms us, and by its light civilized men try to conduct their lives today."

And Eric Sevareid, after describing the nation's officially proclaimed mourning for Martin Luther King: "So the label on his life must not be a long day's journey into night. It must be a long night's journey into day."

Such figures of speech make communication easier. They complement —reinforce—the television picture. They create pictures in radio, where the listener's imagination is brought into greater play. John Hart of CBS says, "In radio, I find myself just naturally using more imagery, more allusions, more intracacies because, I guess, I sense without thinking that the listener is working with me on this idea." Hart believes that because of the radio listener's involvement, the writer can use a few—repeat *few*— more dependent clauses and interdependent ideas than he can in writing for television. "It should always be lucid," he says, "but I think you can deal with subtlety more easily on radio because the listener is working at it and he's not expected to be fed a finished *gateau glacé*."

Along with many newscasters, Hart finds writing for radio more fun. "You can get more in," he explains, "and you aren't limited by the requirements of using that extra dimension—visuals, production values, RP's and that kind of thing."

But lucidity first, last and always, "For ye shall speak into the air."

12

THE LEAD

The lead is your most important line. It says what listeners need to know to understand your story. And it sets the tone—whether a sense of urgency in late-breaking developments or the leisurely pace of human interest features.

Charles Kuralt has written many memorable features. He also can write a strong news lead, as demonstrated on August 30, 1968:

Hubert Humphrey set out today to pick up the pieces.

One brief sentence gives perspective and captures the flavor of the story. It avoids saying the obvious—that Humphrey won the presidential nomination in a tumultuous Democratic convention that ended the day before. Kuralt's lead moves the story ahead with the verb *set out*. It's a simple declarative sentence with no word over two syllables. The meaning is clear. And in broadcasting, clarity is essential.

Translate Wirese

Remember, listeners hear you only once. Don't keep them guessing. Get to the point of what you are talking about. One broadcaster who does this is

Neil Boggs of NBC. His adeptness at translating wirese into the spoken word was put to the test with this story:

WASHINGTON (UPI)–DESPITE AN IMPASSIONED PROTEST THAT HUGE SUBSIDY CHECKS ARE A NATIONAL SCANDAL, THE HOUSE REJECTED EFFORTS WEDNESDAY TO LIMIT FEDERAL FARM PAYMENTS TO LESS THAN $55,000 PER CROP PER YEAR FOR WHEAT, FEED GRAINS AND COTTON.
    IT TURNED DOWN AN AMENDMENT TO SET AN ANNUAL CEILING AT $20,000 PER CROP ON A NON-RECORD VOTE OF 161 TO 134 AND THEN APPROVED THE $55,000 PER CROP CEILING ON A VOICE VOTE.

For his newscast, Boggs rewrote:

The House today rejected efforts to make a major reduction in government price support payments to farmers. An annual ceiling of 55-thousand dollars per crop was approved. A 20-thousand-dollar limit had been proposed on grounds that huge subsidy checks are a national scandal.

The Boggs rewrite ran only 17 seconds, while telling the story clearly and accurately. It was able to do so because its lead quickly pinpointed the story's essential element in a way the UPI failed to do.

A writer for the Associated Press once tried to cram too much into his lead on an "A" wire story and thereby became the target of Harry Reasoner's wit on television:

One further note on Marina Oswald's remarriage. It produced, from the Dallas bureau of a major news service, a classic example of journalistic writing: an interesting attempt to get all the elements of a piece of news—romance, history and occupational data—into the first paragraph. The paragraph read as follows: "Marina Oswald, the pretty blonde Russian whose assassin husband died from a stripper club operator's bullet, was at a honeymoon hideaway today with a dashing electronics technician." All the writers around here said, "Boy, I wish I'd said that!"

What is terribly wrong with the AP lead requires no further analysis. (And, incidentally, in a matter of minutes it was revised.) Reasoner's own lead is worth noticing because of its brevity, in contrast to the AP lead, and because it contains no verb. His second sentence also is instructive. It demonstrates how, on occasion, you can get away with a long sentence (in this case, 38 words) IF you recognize the problem and structure the sentence accordingly.

Getting to the point usually means you avoid starting with a question. The question lead sounds too much like a commercial. Besides, journalism is the business of communicating fresh information. You may raise questions in preparing the news, but in your script you concentrate on answers.

The Five W's and H

Generations of journalists have abbreviated their six basic questions as "five W's and H." Only a few newspapers still insist on beginning a story by telling who, where, what, when, why, and how—all in one sentence. Most dailies long ago discarded that notion. Some editors advise their reporters to answer the five W's and H in the lead, then say the lead may encompass several sentences or even paragraphs. This compromise with tradition stems from a desire to make newspapers easier to read and understand.

Robert Garst and Theodore Bernstein helped pave the way to newspaper clarity in their book, *Headlines and Deadlines*. They show how good leads tend to emphasize one or another of the five W's and H, rather than wrapping up all six. They cite examples for each kind.

It is difficult to match good broadcast leads against two of the categories—"how" and "why." The best leads emphasize <u>where</u>, <u>when</u>, <u>who</u> and <u>what</u>, as in these samples by Ed Murrow:

WHERE: I'm standing again tonight on a rooftop looking out over London, feeling rather large and lonesome.

WHEN: Early this morning we heard the bombers going out. It was the sound of a giant factory in the sky.

WHO: General Eisenhower finished speaking here in Abilene about 15 minutes ago.

WHAT: There are no words to describe the thing that is happening. Today I talked with eight American correspondents in London. Six of them had been forced to move. All had stories of bombs, and all agreed that they were unable to convey through print or spoken word an accurate impression of what's happening in London these days and nights.

Murrow got to the point immediately. He rarely began with the "how" and "why" but dealt with those questions in the body of his reports.

Attempts to use the "how" and "why" in the lead result in more bad writing than good. Witness this example from a student:

After Maryland Governor Marvin Mandel agreed to give top priority to their demands, 500 students today surrendered the historic treasury building in Annapolis.

The sentence is awkward. You wouldn't say it that way, though a newspaper-man might write like that. It isn't conversational to begin with a long prepositional phrase. Change to a "where" lead:

In Annapolis, Maryland, 500 students today surrendered the historic treasury building after Governor Mandel agreed to give top priority to their demands.

We still begin with a prepositional phrase, but it is short and the story flows.

That student's problem is too common among professionals. Nick George of ABC tried to do something about it with this directive to his staff:

Let's go to the simple declarative sentence, shall we? No more stuff like "By a vote of two hundred and seventy-two to one hundred thirty-two, the House this afternoon approved. . . ."

He had caught a writer trying to explain how before telling who, where, when and what. And again it didn't work. Neither did it work for a radio station in Washington D.C. on September 1, 1970.

By a vote of 55 to 39, the Senate today defeated the McGovern-Hatfield amendment to cut off money for the Vietnam War by the end of next year.

In both cases, the numbers were meaningless at the time they hit the listener's ear. A frame of reference should precede the vote count in each story, and then the numbers would be retained by the mind. In the case of the McGovern-Hatfield amendment, the size of the vote was the only element of surprise. The writer may have thought he was leading with the most important part of the story, and he was. His lead would be good in print. But it was poor broadcast writing because the numbers were in limbo until the listener heard what the story was about. And by then they had been forgotten.

Unfamiliar names, like abstract numbers, may be missed unless the listener is prepared for them. They need to be teed up—put into place before being spoken. Don't write

Leon Panetta, chief of the Office of Civil Rights, has resigned from the Department of Health, Education and Welfare.

Write

The chief of the Office of Civil Rights, Leon Panetta, has resigned from the Department of Health, Education and Welfare.

Writers striving for straight declarative sentences may wish to eliminate the need for commas in this kind of lead. Here's how the problem was solved by a staffer at WCBS in New York:

A former aide of the late President Kennedy says he is considering running for the U.S. Senate from New York. That man is Theodore Sorensen.

The writer didn't make the mistake of beginning the second sentence, "Theodore Sorensen said today that. . . ." This would have left the listener wondering whether Sorensen was THAT man or only a spokesman for him.

Don't put tough names in the lead. Here's how Russ Ward handled a jaw-breaker in a newscast on NBC Radio:

A fire last night in the official summer residence has claimed the lives of Iceland's premier, his wife and one of their grandchildren. Sixty-two-year-old Bjarni Benediktsson became prime minister of Iceland in 1963.

Hardness and Softness

Broadcast news frequently is described as "hard" or "soft." The greater the urgency, the harder the lead. Thus this program interruption by Walter Cronkite on November 22, 1963:

Here is a bulletin from CBS News: In Dallas, Texas, three shots were fired at President Kennedy's motorcade in downtown Dallas. The first reports say that President Kennedy has been seriously wounded by this shooting.
    More details just arrived — these details about the same as previously reported: President Kennedy shot today just as his motorcade left downtown Dallas. Mrs. Kennedy reached up and grabbed President Kennedy. She shouted "Oh, no!" The motorcade sped on.
    Stay tuned to CBS for further details.

That was the lead on a newscast four days long. At 1:40 that Friday afternoon, it was urgent and immediate. Only the phrases, Here is a bulletin and In Dallas, Texas helped prepare listeners for shocking news. They heard but couldn't comprehend. So the basic information was repeated along with reinforcing detail.

Responsible broadcasters use bulletins only on stories of great magnitude. But important stories do break almost every day. Normally they call for hard leads, as in this David Brinkley report of July 10, 1970:

> The Nixon Administration has decided to deny tax exemptions to private schools, if they are segregated. Most affected will be the private academies recently set up in Southern states to avoid integration . . . .

Hard leads emphasize the newest element and are appropriate for first reports on major developments. Soft leads take the feature approach. They permit a writer to use his individual style. Maybe that is why Brinkley seems to prefer soft chronological leads when circumstances permit, as they did in another part of the broadcast quoted above:

> The Senate voted about a month ago to repeal the Tonkin Gulf resolution. That was what gave Lyndon Johnson power to carry on the war in Southeast Asia. He used it to send more than half a million men to Vietnam.
> Today, even though it's been repealed once, the Senate voted to repeal it again. Senator Fulbright said he didn't like the parliamentary manner in which it was done last time, and he wanted it for the record, done again, and done right.
> So they did, again.
> President Nixon, however, keeps saying that he doesn't need the resolution, and he can carry on the war without it.

Here Brinkley sacrificed brevity for the sake of historical perspective. He interpreted the Senate action while reporting it.

With a soft lead you can put a fresh angle on a story that has lost its immediacy. It worked for Walter Cronkite on a Sunday night in May of 1961:

> John Tower stands only five feet six, but tonight he is sitting tall in the saddle of Texas politics.

Some in Cronkite's audience had heard, hours earlier, that Tower was the winner in a special election to succeed Lyndon Johnson as U.S. senator. Yet the lead held their attention. Others were hearing the news for the first time. Fresh writing served both groups.

Where Do You Begin?

Herbert Bayard Swope said the best rule for telling a story was laid down by the Red Queen in *Alice in Wonderland*. When asked how to tell a story, she explained: "Begin at the beginning, go through to the end, and then stop." Some stories have to be told this way. They are just too complicated to summarize in a couple of sentences.

Newscasters who follow the Red Queen's advice on how to tell a story include David Brinkley of NBC and John Hart of CBS. Hart says the lead doesn't have to come at the top of the story. "I think it's useful sometimes to back into a story to get your listener's attention. Then when you deliver your message he'll be there and ready to receive it."

Hart recalls how he handled the obituary on Merriman Smith, White House correspondent for United Press International. "You start by talking about the man who got on the telephone first on President Kennedy's shooting, the man who always said, 'Thank you, Mr. President.' And there are a couple of other real great stories about Smitty that are just standard fare in the lore of the Washington press corps. In telling these stories you reveal this fascinating character, the last of the great hard-running newspaper reporters. And then you say, 'He died last night, apparently because he wanted to, of a gunshot wound.' I think that is a legitimate way of announcing the death of Smitty, and it certainly is as affectionate as any obituary could be."

Successful writers, including Hart, talk their stories into the typewriter. They may begin by asking themselves, "What is the lead?" More likely the question is phrased, "Hey, you know what happened?" Then the lead comes naturally, the story phrased as if it were being told to a friend over the dinner table. What makes broadcast writing more difficult than dinner conversation is the need for accuracy, brevity, and clarity—the A,B,C's. But the language is roughly the same.

Who Said That?

Victor Borge invented phonetic punctuation, translating into sound the comma, semicolon, period, and related symbols as part of his act. But the public never adopted Borge's system, and quotation marks still can't be heard. That's why attributions precede quoted material on radio and television. Without that attribution, listeners may think the broadcaster is making the statement on his own. A story from the newspaper wire might go like this:

WASHINGTON (AP)—PRESIDENT NIXON WILL SPEND THE CHRISTMAS HOLIDAYS AT KEY BISCAYNE, FLA., THE WHITE HOUSE ANNOUNCED THURSDAY.

The attribution dangles. For broadcast, you put it at the head of the sentence:

The White House says President Nixon will spend the Christmas holidays at Key Biscayne, Florida.

Now the listener knows who is making the statement at the time he hears it. The item could be shortened still more if there's no uncertainty about the White House announcement:

President Nixon plans to spend the Christmas holidays at Key Biscayne, Florida.

Note that the verb has been weakened from "will spend" to "plans to spend" because the writer wanted to avoid predicting the future. You can assume that the White House spokesman is a solid source of information about the President's plans. But if the announcement conflicts with previous reports about where the President might spend Christmas, we must keep the attribution.

Attributions should accompany all statements that imply blame, are of doubtful validity, and that may be disputed. Some of each was present in November 1969, when newspapers first reported that American soldiers had massacred Vietnamese civilians at My Lai, eighteen months earlier. Broadcasters protected their credibility by attributing reports about the massacre to other journalists. They continued to say "alleged massacre," implying doubt that it had happened, until evidence became strong enough to remove all reasonable doubt.

Alert writers occasionally question the validity of wire service stories. They try to nail down the facts on their own. If unsuccessful, they attribute the story to the agency. Here's how:

President Nixon reportedly plans to fire his education commissioner, James Allen, within the next week. United Press International quotes what it calls well-informed sources as saying. . . .

As we stressed in chapter 10, first reports of disasters normally need attribution. Who said the airliner crashed? Who said there was an earthquake? When corroborating reports remove your doubts, drop the attribution. But you do need to cite a source in the investigative follow-up which fixes blame.

Federal investigators said today that pilot error caused the crash of a Japan Air Lines plane in which 62 persons died. The pilot was among those killed when the airliner nose-dived into San Francisco Bay last November.

If the story goes on to say more about the FAA report, repeat the attribution. Listeners must always know whose conclusions they are hearing, and once at the top is not enough in a long story.

Reasonable doubts should be expressed about the guilt of accused persons until those doubts have been removed by the courts. Though the problem goes deeper than the mechanics of writing, proper use of attributions will help. Among journalists who have been seeking solutions is Jim Bormann, former news director of WCCO Radio in Minneapolis. He says: "In the streamlining process, there is a danger that necessary attributions may be shucked off or ignored. This is particularly dangerous in the field of crime reporting and court reportage. We also find that the average reporter does not come equipped with a full enough knowledge of the hazards of careless reporting about accused persons which emphasize that in those rare instances when the people's right to know conflicts with a defendant's right to a fair trial, the defendant's right must take precedence. For this reason," says Bormann, "we broadcast a confession or a prior criminal record only in exceptional circumstances."

Conscience and common sense should be the writer's guide for using attributions. They can be overdone. The story is told that when Mark Twain was a reporter, his editor instructed, "Never state anything as fact that you do not know of your own personal knowledge." The next day Twain submitted: "A woman giving the name of Mrs. James Jones, who is reported to be one of the society leaders of the city, is said to have given what purported to be a party yesterday to a number of alleged ladies. The hostess claims to be the wife of a reputed lawyer."

Setting the Tone

A good lead sets the tone of a story, helping the listener sense the substance of what you're about to tell him. Imagery can catch his attention, but to be effective it must be deft. It was in this lead written by Gerry Solomon of CBS Radio:

The Army's former top policeman stuck to his guns today, contending that some confiscated weapons he later sold actually belonged to him at the time he sold them.

"Stuck to his guns" ordinarily is a cliche. Here it is bright writing—a phrase with a double meaning, both of them appropriate to the story.

Music titles can sometimes be altered slightly to brighten your leads. Here's how Jack Perkins of NBC began a radio analysis during the college commencement season:

> On college campuses across the nation, the sounds of pomp and circumlocution are heard this week.

Just the right touch.

An Associated Press reporter, Harry Rosenthal, accurately captured the spirit of the event when Neil Armstrong and Buzz Aldrin landed on the moon in July, 1969. There was a long delay while the astronauts remained in their lunar module, putting on special space suits. Rosenthal wrote:

> They kept the whole world waiting while they dressed to go out.

Cronkite quoted that lead on television. He called it "perfect for the occasion."

Writing leads for stories with excitement and urgency comes naturally to most broadcast journalists. Usually, more thought must be given to composing the lead for a development that is important but entirely expected. That's the way it was for John Chancellor on "The NBC Nightly News," August 24, 1970:

> It's official. The long-awaited Middle East peace talks start tomorrow.

You knew it was coming. Now it's official. The long-awaited peace talks are about to start. Simple. Straightforward. Effective. A good approach for writing any story the listener knows is in the works.

Umbrellas, Shotguns, and Rifles

Most broadcast leads emphasize a single act. Others encompass several related developments. The difference has been likened to that between a rifle and a shotgun—a single bullet aimed at a pinpoint target contrasted with a spray of pellets directed toward a larger area.

The shotgun or summary lead is often called an "umbrella" lead and can be effective. For example, "A rash of strikes broke out today along the West Coast." Or, "This was another busy decision day for the Supreme Court."

Here's how Roger Mudd employed the umbrella technique on one of his Sunday evening broadcasts in the summer of 1970:

Several developments today indicated the gravity of the situation in the Middle East.

Assistant Secretary of State Joseph Sisco said the Soviet Union is sending Egypt amphibious landing craft that could be used in an attack against Israel. Appearing on NBC's "Meet the Press," Sisco said, "It doesn't look like defensive equipment to me."

In addition, the U.S. reportedly is acting quietly to replace F-4 Phantom fighter-bombers Israel has lost in combat. *Newsweek* said today President Nixon has ordered a rush shipment this month of eight planes with electronic gear, designed to jam Egyptian radar.

Israel said its planes again today attacked Egyptian army positions along the Suez Canal and Arab guerrilla installations in Jordan.

Prime Minister Golda Meir confirmed Israel proposed secret peace negotiations to Egypt two weeks ago, but said Israel received no answer.

It took less than one minute to report those four stories. Yet the details were clear to the television audience and, thanks to a good lead, so was the overall perspective.

Writing an umbrella calls for clear thinking and precision in language. In the example above, Mudd preserved accuracy with the verb <u>indicated</u>. A stronger verb might have made the story more exciting but probably would have distorted its meaning. A writer should always double-check for accuracy, being sure that the generalities in his lead are buttressed by specifics in the body of his story.

The first rule for the umbrella lead is that it should not be forced. It should come naturally. It will, if the items introduced belong together.

An umbrella lead should not be placed toward the end of any newscast that isn't carefully timed in advance. Otherwise the broadcaster may drop part of the material promised by the lead. In that Middle East wrap-up, Mudd would sound silly if he dropped all but the first or second paragraphs.

And individual items should be brief if the thought from an umbrella lead is to carry throughout the series. Experience indicates that the ideal length for each item is 10 to 20 seconds.

One final note about leads. On rare occasions, two extremely important stories break on the same day and both deserve to be at the top of a newscast. This calls for a double-barreled lead. It gives a quick headline on one story, promises "more on that in a few minutes," then proceeds to tell the second story before returning to the first.

13

LEAD-INS AND TRANSITIONS

Think of the lead-in as a tee setting up your film piece or audio report. It must provide all information essential for the listener's understanding of what follows. It tells where the event occurred—and usually when. In other words, it sets the scene. It identifies the reporter or speaker unless he identifies himself or a superimposed visual does it for him. And it should be written in such a way that, without oversimplification or exaggeration, it generates interest. The lead-in should take no more time than necessary to meet these requirements. This is the LAST place to be wordy.

Here's a typical lead-in:

At the White House today, President Nixon sat down with his advisers to review the Vietnamization program. Dan Rather reports.

Observe that the lead-in consists of two basic parts. The first tells when and where the event took place. It also suggests what happened. If the lead-in did more than suggest, there would be no need for the report that follows. The second part introduces the reporter. Here, the writer has succinctly described the subject and who will report it. Other lead-ins may have to be longer in order to "fill in" the listener so he can understand, and appreciate, what he's about to hear and see:

Nearly 300 years ago, forces of King William of Orange defeated Roman Catholics led by Britain's King James the Second. It was the Battle of the Boyne. And in Northern Ireland, Protestants today celebrated that anniversary. The biggest demonstrations are expected tomorrow. We have a report from Charles Collingwood in Belfast.

Collingwood told what had happened in the previous two days and about preparations for tomorrow. Viewers could understand why it was happening because of perspective provided by the lead-in.

There was no redundancy between lead-in and film report, and there shouldn't be any. Such duplication is scorned by broadcast journalists who sometimes call it "parroting" or "round-robin feedback." Emerson Stone refers to it as the "echo-chamber effect" and gives an example from a lead-in referring to President Nixon's proposal for anti-ballistic missiles:

[ANNOUNCER]: . . .He said he would fight for it as hard as he can:

[NIXON TAPE]: I'm going to fight for it as hard as I can. . . .

This sounds amateurish. Moreover, it takes up valuable time. One way to save that time—especially in radio—is to cut the lead sentence from the tape and use the information as a lead-in. Then pick up on the reporter's second sentence as in this instance from CBS:

[A nuclear submarine has run aground in one of the main channels of Charleston harbor.] The Navy and Coast Guard ordered the harbor closed to all sea-going traffic until further notice. The sub had been identified by Navy spokesmen at the base as the *Nathaniel Green*. . . .

The bracketed sentence was rephrased slightly to make it "the harbor of Charleston, South Carolina" and to include the name of the reporter. But it was worth the saving in air time.

In the early days of radio journalism it was commonplace to say, "For that story, we switch to Paris, David Schoenbrun reporting." Or, "We take you now to City Hall, Bob Trout reporting." Sometimes you still hear such introductions, but they are hackneyed and out of style. Anchormen don't "switch" and "take you" as often as they used to—that's left up to the engineers. Those phrases are now reserved for the few times when radio and television do switch live to the scene of an important story. Otherwise it's simply "Dan Rather reports" or "Greg Jackson tells what happened," or "For the story, Bob Green in Hong Kong."

Vary your introductions. Don't go through a whole broadcast repeating "X has the story," "Y has the story," "Z has the story." Mix it up. That's what Dallas Townsend has done in years of anchoring the World News Roundup on CBS Radio. He shuns pat formulas, using a variety of styles to develop this form of writing into a fine art, as on July 1, 1970:

This is New Year's Day—for fiscal 1971, that is—and that means that the 5 per cent federal income tax surcharge is no more. It expired at midnight. CBS News business reporter Mike Stanley examines the economic impact of the surtax and its demise.

Townsend caught the listener's attention with writing that was bright without being cute, with an opening phrase that was both imaginative and appropriate. From there the ideas progressed logically toward the report being introduced. Now examine another Townsend lead-in, also from July 1970:

President Nixon—his brief California holiday at an end—is back in Washington this morning. And CBS News White House Correspondent Robert Pierpoint notes that Mr. Nixon faces just the sort of situation in the Middle East that he had hoped to avoid.

This lead-in flowed logically out of the routine news that the President had returned from his Fourth of July weekend at San Clemente. By so doing, it subtly established where the reporter was. Then it identified the correspondent as it set the scene for Pierpoint's interpretive piece on a diplomatic dilemma facing the President. It all resulted in a lead-in that was both functional and listenable.

Other variations of the lead-in are possible with television, where essential information need not be spoken. It can be conveyed through words flashed on the screen. These "supers," meaning superimpositions of writing over picture, have been around as long as TV itself. They frequently reinforce identifications spoken by the broadcaster.

Only rarely, until 1969, did supers substitute for important parts of the scripted introduction. And then NBC adopted a new format for television lead-ins. No longer would anchormen introduce field reports by giving the name and location of correspondents. That job would be done by supers.

But sometimes the anchorman would establish the thought of the story, as Chet Huntley did in July 1970:

HUNTLEY (ON CAMERA):

Dollars deposited in ordinary bank savings accounts during this tight-money period have earned less than those invested in high-grade securities and bonds. So bankers have tried new ways to keep their depositors, and to lure new ones.

BRELIS (ON FILM):
SUPER:
REPORTING DEAN BRELIS,
NBC NEWS, NEW YORK.

All over the country, usually-conservative banks have been running ads, announcing massive give-away programs. In New York City, the papers have been flooded in this desperate attempt to get money flowing *into* savings accounts, not *out*. . . .

Thoughts voiced by Huntley flow directly into those spoken by Brelis without being interrupted for an oral introduction. The anchorman provides perspective for the ear but leaves it to the eye to catch the identification. "This gets you into the news faster," according to Wallace Westfeldt, executive producer of "The NBC Nightly News." He estimated a saving of five or ten seconds on most lead-ins. But this saving was not the main reason for adopting the new format.

"The idea," said Westfeldt, "is to get the anchorman as much as possible out of the role of master of ceremonies. It doesn't always work, obviously. But when it works, our anchorman is reporting news right up to the time the film rolls. Then a report from a correspondent in the field will be on a subject that fits, that's related. This strips away the ceremonial function that existed traditionally. We don't put our anchorman—either David Brinkley or John Chancellor or Frank McGee—in a position of saying, 'And now we have so-and-so with a report from such-and-such,' like, 'Here come the broads out on the stage.' "

Fifteen months after adopting this format, Westfeldt said it had become a permanent fixture but that his staff was still experimenting with refinements. "I don't like the supers, the type face and size of type, but I hope that'll improve."

Another difficulty involved the structure of film stories. "It's a murderous thing at times," Westfeldt said, "getting the reporter in the field to remember to report a self-contained story—a story that has a very specific beginning within itself, where you're not relying on your anchorman to tell part of it. It used to be a correspondent could start his report down around paragraph three or paragraph four, after the hard news. Now the correspondent has to do his story with a beginning, a middle, and an end. It can stand by itself."

Some of the NBC lead-ins are extremely brief, amounting to little more than a cue to roll film. David Brinkley introduced a report on an American Legion convention by saying simply, "In Portland, Oregon," and then the film came up. At other times a whole string of reports may be introduced in this manner. Westfeldt recalled an occasion when the anchorman said something like, "There are all sorts of reports on inflation," followed by three or four film reports back-to-back on various aspects of the story. Viewers had no warning what was going to happen.

This technique requires viewers to pay more attention to the picture on television. "We are asking the viewer to *look*, which I think is not a bad idea," said Westfeldt. "Maybe the problem we have with hearing is that often people hear things they think they didn't, or don't hear things they think they did. We hope we're getting people to watch for specifics, maybe a little more intently."

As this is being written, other network news organizations still regard the NBC format on lead-ins an experiment, with the outcome uncertain. So they continue to rely primarily on the spoken word to introduce film reports.

Take Your Choice

A lead-in can be written in hard news or feature style, but it should always be appropriate to the subject. A light-hearted film piece deserves a bright lead-in, as this one written for Walter Cronkite by Mervin Block on August 16, 1966:

Americans may think that the way British play croquet isn't cricket. But despite an ocean of difference between the two groups, they both play with English on the ball and mallets for all. Charles Collingwood reports from London.

For some stories, both the hard news and feature approach are suitable. You have a choice. For example, when former President Eisenhower was buried in Abilene, Kansas, on April 2, 1969, the evening newscasts of the major television networks used totally different kinds of lead-ins, illustrating the variety that is possible in writing introductions.

Frank Reynolds on ABC-TV used the feature approach. He backed into the film by saying:

The population of Abilene, Kansas, is 8-thousand. Today, 100-thousand persons crowded into the little town to say goodbye to a national hero who had been something more to many of them. He had been a neighbor, long ago, and a friend through the years.

Walter Cronkite, at CBS, had become a personal friend of the late President. As a war correspondent, he covered the D-Day landings in Normandy. He had frequently interviewed the general in the White House and in retirement. Cronkite knew how Eisenhower thought. So he was moved to compose this lead-in:

Once upon a time, as the nursery stories go, young Americans played hooky, rather than becoming dropouts. Once upon a time, an American boy was mischievous, rather than a delinquent. Once upon a time, few people doubted that defense of one's country was an honorable career. Once upon a time, you weren't square because you loved your wife, your children, your parents and your country. In Abilene, Kansas, today, America said goodbye to a man who represented that "once upon a time."

At NBC, Chet Huntley led into the story entirely differently. First he summarized the burial service.

The honors, the rites and the ceremonies were completed today, and the body of Dwight D. Eisenhower was interred in a small spired chapel in his hometown, Abilene, Kansas. As the body was committed to the chapel vault, a retired Army chaplain, Major General Luther Miller, intoned the words, "Unto God's gracious mercy we commend you, dear friend."

Only 300 people, including the still-living members of General Eisenhower's high-school graduating class, were invited to the ceremonies, but an estimated 100-thousand persons were on the streets of Abilene, whose population is about 8-thousand.

When the general's funeral train left New York, the family had hoped to keep its route secret. But it leaked out, and finally the family, recognizing the affection and admiration the American people had for Eisenhower, permitted it to be made public so that people could see the train as it passed through their cities. Today it stopped in St. Louis, and Mrs. Eisenhower came out and thanked the people gathered there for their tributes.

While the ABC and CBS programs went directly to a correspondent and film taken of the burial rites in Abilene, the NBC program switched to a videotape recording of Mamie Eisenhower thanking the crowd that met the train in St. Louis. The VTR ran 25 seconds. Only after that did Huntley go to the pre-taped report of the final rites, using this lead-in:

The train arrived in Abilene early this morning. Many of the dignitaries already were there. Many arrived shortly thereafter.

The NBC report from Abilene ran 4 minutes, 50 seconds. There was no reporter, only the actual sights and sounds from the scene.

By an unusual conincidence, all three networks omitted the names of their reporters from the scripted lead-ins. And they were similar in another, more important respect: they were all in good taste while providing information that helped viewers understand and appreciate the reports they introduced.

Lead-ins resemble leads in style but not in content. The differences become apparent when we compare two pieces of copy written by Neil Boggs for WRC-TV in Washington. The first is a self-contained story, broadcast on the early evening news of August 5, 1970:

There were two more motions for mistrial in the Charles Manson trial in Los Angeles today. The judge rejected both. President Nixon's remarks about the trial again were the basis for the defense action.

But Judge Charles Older said he is satisfied the jury could return an impartial verdict even though members now know about the President's comments.

That lead went straight to the most newsworthy aspect of the story, permitting Boggs to condense all the essentials into an item only 20 seconds long. Five hours later, Boggs wisely withheld some essentials when he introduced a report from the scene:

In Los Angeles, lawyers for Charles Manson are still trying for a mistrial. Today's developments, reported now by NBC News Correspondent Don Oliver:

Oliver's report ran about two minutes. It gave all the specifics, therefore Boggs limited his lead-in to generalities and let the reporter supply details.

A writer must know what is on the piece being introduced if he is to avoid redundancies and have his script flow logically into the film or tape. He must take special care when reports begin with natural sound rather than the correspondent's voice. A writer-broadcaster for WNEW in New York handled such a situation effectively when scripting into a radio report about a World Youth Assembly. The tape began with 15 seconds of off-mike voices, arguing angrily. The lead-in said:

Mike Eisgrau reports from the United Nations, where 600 delegates have been meeting.

This technique puts the reporter's name up in the sentence, not at the end. Thus the natural sound is identified immediately before it hits the listener's ear.

Frequently those sounds need a more exact description than in the example above. Such was the case on April 28, 1969, at CBS Radio News, as Richard C. Hottelet introduced a report from Paris about the resignation of President Charles de Gaulle. The tape began with ten seconds of natural sound in the clear, then the sound continued under the voice of Correspondent Peter Kalischer. Hottelet wrote:

Thousands of Frenchmen gathered in the streets and sang, "Adieu De Gaulle." Peter Kalischer stood and listened.

Those in the radio audience also listened and understood what they heard—even the singing. Hottelet had adroitly tuned their ears to receive those words set to music. He knew that phrases sung or chanted by a crowd frequently are less distinct than the same words spoken directly into the microphone. Listeners weren't distracted by uncertainty over the actuality and were able to appreciate Kalischer's report. It explained how the singing of "Adieu, De Gaulle" symbolized the mood of the French people, beset by a year of economic and social turmoil. De Gaulle seemed to want a vote of confidence when he called a national referendum on a minor proposal that didn't have to be submitted to the people. He threatened to resign if voters rejected it. They did and De Gaulle quit the same day, causing Kalischer to report:

The issue was important to no one but De Gaulle. He's like a man who could stride across mountains but stumbled on a pebble. . . . It's as if someone able to walk on water drowned in a puddle.

This graphic and thought-provoking assessment made its mark in the listener's mind. And a good lead-in had helped guide it there, by answering in advance any questions that might have derailed the listener's train of thought.

Natural sounds may sound unnatural unless listeners understand the setting. Lead-ins should provide this understanding. Tell listeners that an interview was conducted in a politician's office or campaign headquarters and they'll be less distracted by noises such as ringing telephones and background voices. Airplane engine sounds may intrude on reports about arrivals and departures, so be sure to set the scene at the airport. An extreme form of that problem was solved by this lead-in, used on an all-news station in New York:

WINS Newsman Allen Shaw had to put cotton in his ears during part of his research for the following report about jet noise on Long Island.

Experienced writers sometimes forget that there can be, in a sense, no nonsequitors in broadcast news. It happened in a film report on July 24, 1970, when the president of the Coca-Cola Company appeared before a Senate committee investigating the plight of migrant workers. Neither the writer nor the correspondent in Washington explained the presence of the Coca-Cola executive. The news editor corrected the oversight by referring in the lead-in to Coca-Cola's ownership of Minute Maid. This served the purpose because Senator Walter Mondale was questioning the Coca-Cola president about orange pickers. The association between orange pickers, Minute Maid, and Coca-Cola was thus established. The viewer understood.

Lead-outs and Transitions

You can call them lead-outs or tag lines or caps, they all mean the same thing—that piece of copy which comes immediately after tape or film. They're a stylistic luxury in television but a necessity in radio. Their basic function is to re-identify an actuality so listeners will know whose voice they just heard. Television has visuals to do this job.

There's no more reason for repetitiveness in lead-outs than in lead-ins. Yet it's not uncommon to hear a string of actualities in a newscast with lead-outs no more varied than "That was Governor Reagan," "That was Senator Cranston," and "That was Mayor Yorty." This is stilted writing. It reveals laziness in the writer.

Ideally, the lead-out does more than re-identify. It adds something to the story or provides a bridge to the next item, or both. Some instructive examples come from the broadcasts of Dallas Townsend:

[TOWNSEND (lead-in)]: A strong comment on the Con Son affair has been made by Democratic Representative Lee Hamilton of Indiana. Hamilton was a member of a special House committee that went to southeast Asia on an inspection trip last month.

[HAMILTON (on tape)]: I think it's an exceedingly serious matter. . . .etc.

[TOWNSEND]: Congressman Hamilton's remarks about the Con Son prison camp have been followed by even stronger ones from Senator Robert Byrd of West Virginia. [Goes on to quote a speech Byrd planned to give that day.]

That was from the CBS World News Roundup of July 10, 1970. So is this next example, which demonstrates an effective way of handling two pieces of actuality on the same subject:

[TOWNSEND]: Last night on CBS News, this country's just-concluded intervention in Cambodia drew contrasting remarks from Secretary of Defense Melvin Laird and Clark Clifford, his immediate predecessor in the Johnson Administration. Laird was all for it.

[LAIRD (tape)]: I think the most important thing about the operation. . . etc.

[TOWNSEND]: Taking sharp issue with Secretary Laird, *former* Secretary Clifford stated his case *against* the Cambodian operation in strong terms.

[CLIFFORD (tape)]: If I've ever had a deep conviction in my life. . . .etc.

[TOWNSEND]: Clifford also said the cost of the Cambodian operation was infinitely greater than he thinks this country realized when the decision was made.

Thus Dallas Townsend told the story of the Laird-Clifford debate with grace, brevity, and clarity. He never left doubt about whose voice was being heard. Neither did he insult the intelligence of his listeners with simplistic statements.

Our third and final excerpt from a World News Roundup was broadcast on July 16, 1970:

[TOWNSEND]: Roman Catholic Bishop James Walsh met with reporters today in Hong Kong, making his first public appearance since Communist China released him last week from twelve years imprisonment. The 79-year-old American prelate, speaking in a rather weak voice, described his treatment in captivity.

[WALSH (tape):] I was treated very well, apart from the grueling interrogation process. . . . etc.

[TOWNSEND:] Bishop Walsh, who sat in a wheel chair during the news conference, added that he could never be angry with any Chinese. [Townsend then described the bishop's plans for visiting the Vatican and returning home.]

Note how the lead-out, by referring to the wheel chair, subtly explained again the weak voice of Bishop Walsh. This combination of lead-in, actuality, and lead-out comes close to being a classic example of "Tell them what you're going to tell them, then tell them, then tell them what you told them." Not all actualities need or deserve this treatment. This one did.

We've already discussed how a radio lead-out can be a transition into the next story. Television also uses the technique. But transitions aren't effective in either medium unless they come naturally. A writer shouldn't strain for connective phrases. Connectives usually are not necessary if the script is properly organized. The flow is in related stories—one story flowing into another on a kindred subject. The stories are connected, not by artificial word combinations, but by subject. Forcing transitions can lead to absurdities such as, "In a totally unrelated development. . ." A writer really did include that phrase in his script!

14

VOICE OVER FILM: IMAGE AND WORD

Whether you write news for radio or television, the style is much the same. The writing must be concise and so highly readable as to be conversational. Facts must be selected so that the story will be truthfully represented. And these facts — these words — must be arranged in such a way that they are supremely comprehendible. Without clarity and sound editorial judgment, all the truthful representation in the world is wasted. The listener (and the viewer of television is also a listener) must know what you are saying, or the whole complicated, expensive, important electronic news process is for naught.

So the news written for both media have this most basic common denominator — style. But television journalism sometimes requires the writer to perform functions alien to radio reporting. We refer to the matching of word with picture — writing scripts to be voiced over maps, charts, still photographs, film, and video tape recordings. This is writing voice-over (V/O). In it, words and pictures should complement each other.

Beginners tend to overwrite V/O. They state the obvious, telling the viewer what he can see for himself, and thus create redundancies. Or they pack too many words into a script. This causes a broadcaster to race his reading to keep pace with the film.

Seasoned practitioners of television news know when to shut up and let the picture carry the story. "Writing a silence," says John Hart of CBS, "is as important as writing words, particularly when you have film that carries. I personally don't think we rely on that enough." Hart and other broadcasters want scripts they can read at a natural pace, scripts with fewer words than the maximum that could be spoken in the allotted time. They want writers who are sensitive to the interplay between words and picture, who produce narration that reinforces or explains but that also contains pauses for those places where the picture needs no words—pauses of three seconds, five seconds, ten seconds, or more.

Writing news for television is communicating to the viewer what he doesn't see or understand. "Things have changed in the last twenty years," says Fred Friendly. "We are a verbal society. We're also a picture society. People are much more experienced at seeing things on films than they ever were before. They seek out elements. They fasten onto little facts out there. They may know more from looking at that picture than the reporter knows, especially if they're brighter, more perceptive. So for the writer just to recite the obvious is what our young people call 'Dullsville.' " And, Friendly adds, "The writer has got to understand more about his subject, he's got to tell the viewer something that he doesn't know."

If that sounds elementary, it is. If it sounds like needless advice, it is not, as a viewer can see for himself by watching almost any action story on television, especially sports.

Some film stories need no narration. Such was the case on June 18, 1970 when, by coincidence, both David Brinkley on NBC and Walter Cronkite on CBS ended their programs with film features over which not a word of narration was spoken.

Brinkley used a humorous piece, filmed in New York, on the controversy over women's skirts. The derrières of girls swinging down Fifth Avenue wearing minis were intercut with footage taken at a high fashion salon where models were showing buyers, who looked ever so bored, the calf-length midi styles for fall. No narration—only, throughout the montage, the music of "Ain't She Sweet, Comin' Down the Street." Picture and music carried it.

Cronkite's closing feature came from Rome. It showed a crowd of Italian youths going mad with joy because their soccer team had defeated West Germany in the semi-finals of international competition. The sound track was full of whooping and hollering and honking of automobile horns, and Cronkite didn't say anything until it came back to him. Then he said, "Italy meets Brazil for the world championship on Sunday in Mexico City. Brace yourselves. And that's the way it is, Thursday, June 18, 1970. This is Walter Cronkite, CBS News. Goodnight."

Both pieces were delightful. Each needed only the sentence or two of background that was supplied by the lead-in and tag-line. One used the cinema verité technique of natural sound from the scene. The other reinforced the light-heartedness of the pictures with music from a phonograph record—a "show biz" practice that's not permitted by some news organizations. But the effect in both cases was that film and sound carried the story, and those responsible for the broadcasts wisely refrained from adding narration that might have been obvious and intrusive.

Scripting in the Field

Film stories without narration are rarities. Most newsfilm on television needs some accompanying words—to identify people and places, to explain what is happening and why, to provide perspective by telling how the picture story relates to events not being shown.

As with all good journalists, the competent writer of newsfilm narration first learns as much as he can about his story. A reporter in the field does so in the normal course of his duties. For TV, the reporter does more than gather facts and write a story. He also works with his cameraman to be sure all important visual elements are covered on film and he usually films at least part of his narration—the open and the close—on the scene.

If circumstances permit, the reporter returns to the shop with his film. After it's processed he'll screen it and probably decide how it should be cut. Then he'll write and record any additional narration that's needed.

All of this film and narration will be edited for showing as a double projector piece. This technique was developed in the 1950s by Don Hewitt, a producer at CBS News, and is now in general use by television news organizations. It involves the editing of a single news story onto two reels, usually designated "A" and "B". The A-Reel may contain most of the sound, including narration. On the B-Reel may be silent footage, containing pictures synchronized with narration on the A-Reel, plus track of natural sound. The reels are put on separate projectors and both start running simultaneously. Only one of the pictures goes out to the TV audience and the director of the broadcast decides which it will be. He may begin with the A-Reel supplying both video and audio of the reporter's opening at the scene of the story. Then, after ten seconds, the director may cut to video from the B-Reel while holding the audio on "A" and, at the end, return both video and audio to the A-Reel for the reporter's closing.

It sounds complicated and it is, even in this simplest of examples. Stations and networks have tried to reduce the chance of error by transferring double projector pieces to video tape, in advance of air time. This eliminates the cutting back and forth while the broadcast is on the air and also eliminates the chance that film on one of the reels may break at an embarrassing moment.

Despite its complexity, the double projector technique has been mastered by hundreds of television reporters. Many never see their uncut film because they're on assignment far from the home office. These reporters must work closely with their camera crews — words and pictures should meld into a cohesive story in the editing room back home. So they talk about their story, establishing rapport and being sure each understands what the other is doing. They keep notes on all film that's shot, and take care to label every can of film as it is removed from the camera. The shot lists help the reporter write narration, and the narration helps the cameraman be sure he has all necessary covering shots. The shot list, narration, and any additional notes on the story — called a "dope sheet" — are shipped with the film. They are extremely useful when producers and film editors try to assemble the components into one story.

Some dope sheets are lengthier than others because a correspondent in the field often acts as his own producer and wants to let others know what was in his mind as the story was being shot. So he'll give a detailed set of recommendations on which part of the film should be used, and in what sequence. Producers almost always give these suggestions careful consideration, as in dope sheets that Russ Bensley receives from Charles Kuralt. Bensley is the producer who handles Kuralt's "On the Road" pieces for "The CBS Evening News with Walter Cronkite." Kuralt says he and Bensley have established an ideal relationship, wherein both agree on the concept of stories being covered and almost never disagree on the best way of covering them.

The "On the Road" reports are notable for two other reasons: their cinematography and their voice-over narration, written by Kuralt. In a style reminiscent of John Steinbeck's *Travels with Charley*, Kuralt and his film crew (cameraman, soundman, and electrician) roam the country in a camper. They visit such out-of-the-way places as the ranch of the last horse trader in Texas, the Bucket of Blood Saloon in Virginia City, and a small, white-steepled community in Vermont, simply because the community is lovely and they want to shoot a low-keyed story on the delights of autumn. Kuralt is directly involved in the filming, so that he "builds" the story as they go along. He says, "I seem to write the pieces in my head. By the time I start typing, they're pretty much done."

Often, while filming one story, they run into leads for others, perhaps in the next town. Suggestions also come in the mail. Nostalgia runs through most of the stories, as in this report on the demise of the famous Cannonball Express:

CRONKITE (ON CAMERA):

Charles Kuralt, who's been on the road reporting Americana for this program, rode the rails on his latest assignment, and that's not easy in this day of disappearing passenger trains—even those once famed in story and song.

BARROOM SCENE: BOB WALLER SINGING "WABASH CANNONBALL" TO BANJO ACCOMPANIMENT. SONG CONTINUES OVER AERIAL SHOTS OF TRAIN PASSING THROUGH COUNTRYSIDE.

KURALT (ON CAMERA):

In a bar near Bloomington, Indiana, Bob Waller and Wayne Schuman are asked to do the song almost every night. The Wabash Cannonball is as much a part of Indiana as the small towns and the rivers and the cornfields.

CUT TO CLOSE–UP OF TRAIN

"Listen to the jingle and the rumble and the roar."

CUT TO INTERIOR OF DINING CAR

You can still ride the Wabash Cannonball, but you'd better hurry. It's all going, all this—the gleaming white tablecloth with the single red carnation facing you, the sound of the great train rushing through the morning from St. Louis to Detroit. The day of the passenger train is nearly over, and this sound is nearly an echo now.

RECEDING SOUND OF TRAIN'S WHISTLE

INTERCUT OF EXTERIOR AND INTERIOR OF TRAIN TO MATCH NARRATION

The Norfolk and Western Railroad is asking the Interstate Commerce Commission to permit this train to be discontinued. A year from now, the Wabash Cannonball will very likely have passed into history. The first Cannonball went roaring down the tracks in 1884, the yellow light of its oil lamps in its elegant smokers and parlor coaches flashing through the cornfields. But that's all over now. The people go by car and stay at Howard Johnson motor lodges, and the Cannonball's seats are empty. It has shrunk to a pitiful short train, passing the silos of Illinois, whistling mournfully for the country crossroads of Indiana almost by force of habit now.

INTERCUTS (Cont'd.)

This is a part of America we knew as children, and our children will never really know. They will never hear the jingle of the couplings, the squeal of the wheels on the curves. They will never hear the conductor's song.

CLOSE-UP OF COUPLINGS

CONDUCTOR SEEN AND HEARD CALLING OUT NEXT STOP

Wabash is the next station stop. Wabash. This way out!

FOOTAGE OF TRAIN PASSING THROUGH

The Cannonball still stops at Wabash, also at Granite City, Mount Olive, Stonington, Decatur, Lafayette. Night overtakes the train at Delphi, and it goes on to Peru, Fort Wayne, Montpelier, but hardly anybody ever gets on or off. Once this was the way young men left Wabash or Milan or Edwardsville to seek their fortunes in the big cities. Those are old men now

CUT TO CLEMENT SILENT

and Norfolk and Western Vice President Walter Clement says not enough of them ride the Cannonball to make the train pay its way.

CLEMENT:

You won't believe this. The latest figures show 24 people a day in the entire state of Indiana have used the Wabash Cannonball. Twenty-four a day.

AERIALS OF TRAIN

So this train, like so many others, is about to die. Set your watch by the Cannonball while you may. Pause at the crossroads to let her pass. Take one last look. Tomorrow, the

Wabash Cannonball won't be a train at all,
only a banjo tune.

CUT TO WALLER SINGING MORE OF "WABASH

CANNONBALL" BALLAD

CUT TO KURALT RIDING ON TRAIN   Charles Kuralt, CBS News, aboard the
KURALT: Wabash Cannonball.

In telling this story, Kuralt had a wonderful time with the names of towns. He played on them, almost like musical notes. He milked the nostalgia in the story, which he recognized as its strongest element. He made expert use of alliteration, which is to say he used the device without beating the listener over the head with it. For example, the succession of "L" sounds in "the yellow light of the oil lamps in its elegant smokers and parlor coaches flashing through the cornfields." He may not have done it consciously, but the effect is there, working for him. His craftsmanship also shows in his selection of specific detail—the flower on the table is a <u>single red carnation</u>, the light is <u>yellow</u>, the farms are <u>fields of corn</u>, the motorists stay at <u>Howard Johnson motor lodges</u>. The train doesn't just pass through Illinois; it passes the <u>silos</u> of Illinois. It is the <u>couplings</u> of the train that jingle. The young ambitious men boarded the express at specific places: Wabash, Milan, Edwardsville. And certainly a factor in the good writing is that Kuralt felt the story. It meant something to him.

Unlike field reporters, some writers must remain at home base to help prepare news programs for broadcast. They rarely get firsthand knowledge of the film stories they write. Their information comes from such secondary sources as wire services, newspapers, and reference books. Occasionally a writer's personal experience or specialized knowledge may provide background for the story he is writing. Perhaps a phone call will permit him to consult with someone who has such knowledge, or help him learn about the latest developments in a film story that was shot some time earlier.

In all instances, the writer should try to look at the film itself and at notes that accompany it. Then, with a broad understanding of the story and specific data on this piece of film, he is ready to begin writing narration.

The specifics, known as a "spot sheet," tell him how the film has been edited—the sequence of scenes and length of each. This information goes into the video column of his script—usually the left hand side of the page—alongside the accompanying narration.

Here's an example of film narration, written and voiced by Alexander Kendrick for the "CBS Evening News" on November 1, 1966. It demonstrates how V/O can explain what is happening on the film without stating the obvious and, at the same time, tell how this event relates to other developments in the world:

LS CELEBRATION :05	Communist China's latest atomic achievement—the firing of a nuclear warhead on a guided missile, with a claimed
MS CELEBRATION :08 PAPERS HANDED OUT :06	hit—touched off jubilant celebration in Peking by the militant youthful Red Guards. Special editions of newspapers were handed out free to expectant crowds.
STREET DANCING :16	And there was dancing in the streets, all day and into the night. The significance of the timing—a sort of exclamation point to the Manila conference—was not overlooked in the official announcement, which said the new missile would greatly encourage the Communists in Vietnam.
MS MAO PIX :09	The portrait of Mao Tse-tung was displayed in the celebration, and Mao's thought, as it is called, was given credit for the Chinese success. Farmers from the countryside also
MORE CELEBRATING :16	took part in the celebration, filmed by Japanese cameramen. However, details of the size and range of the missile are still unknown to the West. Alexander Kendrick,
TOTAL FILM TIME: 60 SECS.	CBS News, reporting.

Kendrick wrote this narration for his own reading pace, without silences but with pauses that fit comfortably at dashes, commas, periods and paragraphs. The whole script is slightly underwritten, being about four seconds shorter than the running time of the film.

Note how each piece of identification told something that viewers couldn't see for themselves. The celebrants were militant Red Guards in one sequence and farmers in another. The newspapers were special editions, distributed without charge. We learn not only whose portrait is being displayed, but also why. The dope sheet told Kendrick that the film originated with the Japanese news agency Denpa, and his script specified that it wasn't shot by CBS staffers, because some viewers might have wondered whether CBS News now had cameramen in Peking.

This narration failed to say that Kendrick was in New York, not Peking or Tokyo. Viewers could have been misled, a point recognized in 1967 when CBS News adopted a policy eliminating the correspondent's final self-identification from narration on silent film received from outside sources. Under the same policy, writers were urged to have their lead-in for such film make clear that the narrator was not on the scene by the use of phrases such as "John Doe now describes . . ." or "John Doe now explains . . ." or "John Doe now narrates . . ." rather than "John Doe reports . . ." Three years later, the policy was tightened still further and CBS News began having the anchorman read narration for nearly all silent footage used in his broadcast. This made it doubly clear that the voice-over was coming from the studio, not the scene where the film was shot.

Not only ethics but good business demands that journalists avoid deceiving their audiences. This became apparent when the Federal Communications Commission threatened a New York station, WPIX-TV, with loss of its license over charges that it distorted the news. In one instance, the station was accused of showing twelve-year-old film of Soviet tanks in Budapest over the news reports about the 1968 Russian invasion of Czechoslovakia.

Film Over Voice

Most narration is written to go with film that's already shot. But sometimes it's the other was around, and the script gets written first. Such scripts frequently are carefully constructed essays, developing a thought through the combined use of un-photographable abstracts and concrete examples that can be portrayed visually.

A number of these essays were televised during the thirty-one hours of continuous coverage of man's first landing on the moon. They were needed to complement the central action and to fill those time periods when Astronauts Aldrin, Armstrong, and Lovell would either be out of touch or have nothing to report. One of these essays, dealing with the moon and tides, was written for CBS News by Jeff Gralnick and narrated by Charles Kuralt. Here is part of that script, showing how, in such a production, pictures are used to cover words.

VARIOUS SHOTS OF SEACOAST,

TIDES MOVING IN AND OUT

:35
                              The seas have rolled for millions of years,
                          swirling around the continents, pulled in ebbs

and flows, responsible to nothing except the moon, a quarter million miles away. Twice each day, as the earth revolves, it presents first one face, then the other, to the moon. And as it does, that heavenly body so far away pulls and tugs at the seas of the earth, causing the waters to roll in dramatically, sweeping all before them in a majestic rush for shore, whipping up waves as the moon seemingly tries to drag the oceans from their floors.

QUIET, EMPTY BEACHES
:15

And then the tide recedes as the moon moves away. The seas fall back, leaving bare the strands of glistening sands, which would have remained covered forever were it not for the inexorable pull of the moon riding silently out in space.

PEACEFUL BEACH
:05

The tide can drift in easily, kissing the shore, or it can be whipped in mightily in great, crashing, storm-driven waves that force people from the beaches.

STORM
:05

PEOPLE STANDING ON BULKHEADS,
WATCHING THE SEA
:15

But never too far, because there seems nothing so majestic as the sea enraged, driven by the wind, pulled by the moon. So inexorable is the tide, so relentless, that across a span of several centuries—a drop in the bucket of time—the tide turned the French abbey Mont St. Michel from a tree-surrounded refuge near the coast to an island outpost, a fortress protected by high walls. And, once a day, by high tide. Tide that is tugged by the moon until it surrounds the old fort with waters more than 60 feet deep, covering the road that leads to it, protecting it completely in a way no knight of old could have hoped, or planned his castle to make it safe.

SHOTS OF ABBEY OF
MONT ST. MICHEL
:25

LS FORTRESS :03	Man couldn't protect this fortress as well as the moon.
DISSOLVE TO SEAGULL SUPERED OVER FULL MOON :15	One myth-maker once likened the moon to a great silver bird circling above the earth, lighting the earth, brushing the sea with its wing-tips, piling up the oceans' waters as it flew overhead.
LOSE THE SEAGULL, SEE ONLY FULL MOON :10	Now two men sit on the moon, looking down at the blue earth, at the waters of earth, controlled so long by the moon and still answering only to it.

This piece of voice-over was aired on July 20, 1969. The astronauts had reached the moon, but Armstrong still had not taken his first step. There was a wait of more than three hours between the landing and the historic first walk, which explains use of the verb *sit*—"Now two men sit on the moon." Neither Armstrong nor Aldrin had emerged from the lunar module.

When Gralnick furnished the authors with this script, he remarked in an accompanying letter: "While it is a good illustration of words and pictures matching, it strikes me that it also shows how a writer in television, or radio, has as a prime responsibility the job of making words sound as though the man speaking had written them for himself. I think only Kuralt could have delivered that piece. Had I written it for anyone else, it would have been done differently."

A Final Important Point

We've saved a cardinal rule for the concluding paragraph of this chapter on voice-over: Don't let the words fight the picture. Make one match the other. Remember that your narration should explain and identify what a viewer can't see for himself, always reinforcing and elaborating on what can be seen. Sometimes counterpoint between image and words can be effective, with the right material and an expert writer. But most voice-over needs to have a relationship to the picture. Conflict between words and picture confuses the viewer, causing a piece of television journalism to fail in its primary goal of informing those who watch and listen.

15

WRITING FOR THE TV DOCUMENTARY

There are two kinds of documentaries—news documentary dealing with current issues and the cultural documentary, which deals with man's life style—his mores, institutions, and art.

The two forms differ in content but are alike in requiring close coordination between writing and production. So close, in the view of Fred Friendly, that they are one and the same. "We are all writers," says Friendly, "the editor who selects the film, the guy who writes the copy, who plans the broadcast, they are all the writers. Writing is really only the final act of what you do in a documentary. If you do your work well, most of the writing is done by the people in the program and by the sequence of scenes."

Other documentarians concur. "The more the pictures can tell by themselves, the better it is," says Richard Hanser, chief writer for the Project XX series on NBC. This does not mean eliminating narration. It does mean "compression and placement," a phrase Hanser first used in 1957. Fourteen years later he thought there had been no basic change in writing for the documentary: "I still work with the rule, 'The less narration the better.' But there is always the delicate point of whether you are saying too much or too little. On many occasions the pictures themselves do not give their own meaning, or not enough of it, and then a paragraph of narration is required to point it up and give it its full impact."

Though used sparingly in the documentary, words are no less important here than in the reporting of hard news. We think of the introduction to NBC's extraordinary two-and-a-half-hour broadcast, "From Here to the Seventies," narrated by Paul Newman:

We will see a great many pictures, many of them familiar, many of them painfully familiar. And there will be sounds. But mostly there will be words. The words that tell our past and portend our future. Words about ideas and feelings and events which have brought us to this day. Words to help us interpret where we are tonight and affect where we may be going tomorrow.

Words. Ubiquitously important. Words in television documentaries chosen as painstakingly as pictures. Andrew Rooney, who produced many documentaries for CBS, says the writing is the hardest. He says, "It's putting down on paper for the world to read and reread where you make a fool of yourself. If a producer or a director makes a movie or a television broadcast with pictures and few words and some arty editing and far-out sound effects, he can convey the impression that there is a great deal he isn't saying. I firmly believe that if you can't say it, it isn't a thought. When you leave the onus of completing the thought to the viewer, it is easier to gain the reputation of genius without ever having to finish the idea in your own mind."

Ed Murrow composed almost nothing for print. However in an article co-authored with Friendly, he once wrote, "Writing for television is not unlike writing for radio. It must be the language of speech, lean copy, sparing of adjectives, letting the picture and the action and the indigenous sound create the mood, and then maybe a few words—the fewer the better."

Murrow and Friendly believed that most of the good writing in the "See It Now" series was done in the field by non-professionals ad-libbing what they knew and believed, by those who, "under the pressure of the moment and armed with a conviction born of conflict," spoke compellingly.

And both believed in restraint in the use of their own language. As Jack Gould of the *New York Times* said of Murrow's style, "If one uses the right words, there is no occasion to raise one's voice."

Get Immersed

Reporting and writing are interdependent functions, perhaps inseparable. So if Fred Friendly is correct in saying that everyone who helps make a documentary is a writer—and we think he is—then it is equally true that all are reporters. They may not have that label, they may not go out with the film crew, but they should be gathering facts and digging up details that help make the documentary accurate, complete, and absorbing. Each should "immerse himself in the subject," as Richard Hanser says he does when preparing to write a script.

"What we don't know can kill us" is a quote from Friendly's past that he rarely uses any more because others have overused it. But he still believes it, and its philosophy runs through the advice he gives those who would write news documentaries:

A journalist today is an interpreter, an explainer of complex issues. You can't write that documentary unless you understand the issue. You've got to know more about your subject than the viewer knows, though maybe not as much as the expert who spends his whole life on it.

Look at Walter Cronkite, one of the profession's most lucid ad-libbers. He's not really ad-libbing. He has written that copy over and over—while he shaved, while he ate, while he did his homework.

You've got to do your homework. Before you write you've got to understand. And before you understand you've got to dig and be informed.

When Friendly was producing documentaries at CBS, a visitor to his office would find books piled all over his desk. Browsing through them gave a preview of subjects to be covered in forthcoming broadcasts. He was immersing himself in his subject, reading books and whatever else he could find, at the office and away. He did his homework and encouraged his staff to do theirs. The object was to have all who were working on the story to know it, to understand it.

This behind-the-camera effort—combined with first-rate reporting from men such as Murrow, Sevareid, and Cronkite—contributed to the unsurpassed excellence of "See It Now" and "CBS Reports." Those broadcasts, through the understanding that comes from knowledge, explained complex issues with great clarity. And millions of viewers learned some things they didn't know before.

Give It a Name

Documentaries have titles. Even some news specials—that is, programs pegged to news events—have titles. When a spacecraft carried Astronauts Neil Armstrong and "Buzz" Aldrin to man's first landing on the moon, CBS News titled its special coverage "The Epic Journey of Apollo Eleven." Documentaries were given titles as early as 1922, when Robert Flaherty made his classic film study of Eskimo life and called it *Nanook of the North*.

The criteria for selecting documentary titles are the same as for titles of magazine articles and books. The title must be pertinent. It must provoke interest. And generally it is brief. And it may reveal a point of view, as did "The Twisted Cross." Seeing that title superimposed on a swastika, you knew that the documentary was the story of nazism in Germany, told from a definite point of view.

As in all writing, attention is paid to sound. Sometimes this results in alliteration: "Our Durable Diplomats" on ABC; "Christmas in Korea" on CBS; "The Battle of Newburgh" on NBC.

Some titles are simplicity itself: "The Vatican" (ABC); "The Italians" (CBS); "The Tunnel" (NBC).

In 1958, a popular novel was *The Ugly American*, co-authored by Eugene Burdick and William Lederer. Its title lent itself to adaptation, and American television audiences soon were treated to two documentary programs titled "The Flabby American" (ABC) and "The Fat American" (CBS).

These imitating Americans!

Getting It Started

The documentary consists, as every good work should, of a beginning, a middle, and an end. Friendly calls the beginning, paradoxically, the "shirt-tail," because he hates the word "tease." This is the opening where the producer through engrossing pictures or words—usually pictures AND words—seeks to capture the viewer's attention while indicating what lies ahead. Friendly paid special attention to shirt-tails during his years as executive producer of "See It Now" and "CBS Reports," and told about it in 1970 from his professor's chair at Columbia University:

Sometimes we would have a hundred thousand feet of film in, and I would say, "Let's write the shirt-tail, let's write the prologue."

And we would try to say what the program was going to be about, in that first two or three minutes before the opening credits. Then we would come in with that title—"Biography of a Bookie Joint," "Population Explosion," "Return to Normandy," "Argument in Indianapolis," "The Case of Milo Rudolovich."

If you can compress your idea into a foreword that says to the viewer, "This is what we're trying to do, this is what we call our program," it not only helps the viewer to understand it, but I think it helps you to form the broadcast.

It's very important, in a television or radio documentary, to know where you're going. That's why I like the self-generating story.

We can say, "We're going to show them how to build a Polaris missile. We're going to take a piece of paper with some lines drawn on it—a blueprint on the drawing board. And we're going to build until that rocket is fired from a hundred feet down in the ocean off Cape Kennedy or San Clemente Island, and until it breaks through the surface of the water and fires 15-hundred miles downrange." That story is written for me.

If your story isn't self-generating—and 90 percent of them aren't—then you've got to make sure you have a road map. That's the phrase—"road map." The self-generating story gives you a road map, an outline ready-made. For other stories you've got to figure one out. You need to know where you're going with that broadcast, and your viewer should know, too.

Stories told in news documentaries, whether self-generating or issue-oriented, are more than mere narrative. They are interpretive reporting on important human problems, through what Reuven Frank calls "transmitting experience." In 1963—five years before becoming president of NBC News—Frank explained the concept in a memo:

I do not mean that we transmit to the viewer one participant's impression of what it was like to undergo the experience, but that we ourselves transmit to him the essence of the experience itself. Ideally we should make him smile and sweat, fear and exult. We want him to feel that he is crossing the Vietnamese marsh under fire, that it is he who has just been elected, that it is he who faces the problem of learning a new trade and moving his family to a new city.

Frank practiced what he preached. In 1962 he produced "The Tunnel," a documentary which shed light on human problems of East Berlin by transmitting the experience of some who escaped by digging under the wall that had been built to keep them in.

The Body of the Broadcast

The problem being explored—whether that of East Berliners or hungry Americans or migrant workers—is presented in the middle, or body, of the broadcast. It is examined from a definite point of view. It is structured for examination of the issue in the most compelling terms.

For the writer, that means moving the story forward with but a minimum of narration, just enough to fill those holes of ignorance that the picture automatically carries with it. Friendly says some of the best copy can be heard when the reporter sits in a screening room with co-workers to watch rough cuts of film from his story:

He doesn't say, "There's a guy picking grapes." You *see* there's a man picking grapes. He says, in effect, "The son of a bitch who runs that farm is paying that guy 12 dollars a week for doing that. . . . " He says what the screen doesn't show.

There is no known rule, according to Richard Hanser, for gauging when enough words have been written:

Too little commentary can leave the pictures a confused jumble, with the viewer asking, "What the hell is going on here?" Too much narration can be distracting and irritating. It is a matter of feeling and instinct, as with practically everything else in writing. Sometimes we hit it just right, and sometimes we sin with too much, at other times with too little.

"Feeling and instinct" mean sensitivity. It is clearly present in Hanser's scripts for a long list of NBC cultural documentaries, beginning with "Victory at Sea" in 1952, through "The Twisted Cross," "Meet Mr. Lincoln," and, in 1971, "Meet Ben Franklin." Most of them reveal Hanser's preference for the historical over the contemporary.

Hanser shies away from current controversy without getting into fiction. He agrees with Donald Hyatt, the producer of the Project XX series, that their documentaries are "drama rooted in reality." "We don't distort anything for dramatic impact," says Hanser, "but we do try to make it as dramatic as the facts and situations warrant." He and Hyatt do not regard their work as news and, in fact, are not part of the NBC News division. Their purposes, says Hanser, are "entertainment, enlightenment, and enlarging the viewer's vision of the world."

Sensitivity in writing helped bring acclaim to the 1969 documentary, "Down to the Sea in Ships," produced by Hyatt and narrated by Burgess Meredith. Here is an excerpt from Hanser's script:

PAN BACKLIT SEA & ROCKY COASTLINE	What pulls men to the sea is something elemental, ageless. It is the pull of his origins, the origin of life itself. For life first came from the sea.
LONE MAN WALKING EDGE OF SEA	Even the landsman who ventures no farther than the water's edge feels that eternal tug. It is in the blood, literally. For the composition of human blood is strangely similar to that of sea water. There is sea-salt in the veins of all of us.
MOOD SILHOUETTE SHOTS OF MAN WALKING ALONG WATER'S EDGE	We are all islanders, inhabitants of the only water planet in the solar system. The sea surrounds all the continents, making them islands in one huge ocean.

LIGHTHOUSE, WRECK OF SHIP IN FOREGROUND

RIDGWAY, BLYTH AND *ENGLISH ROSE*

MCU RIDGEWAY & BLYTH, CROWD IN BACKGROUND

CU RIDGWAY AS HE ROWS

LS *ENGLISH ROSE* BEING ROWED OUT TO SEA

SURGING SEA AS SEEN FROM INSIDE A ROWBOAT

HEAVY, ROLLING SEAS TOSSING ROWBOAT, SHOT
FROM BOAT'S GUNWALE

OFF-SHORE LIGHTHOUSE

ROCKY COAST, OMINOUS WEATHER

We live on the land, but our world is a water world. (PAUSE) We are all children of "that great mother of life, the sea."

And she calls us in different ways.

It was a strange sea-call, one of the oddest ever heard, that brought a pair of adventurers to the New England coast in the summer of '66 for an incredible voyage. Two British paratroopers proposed to row across the Atlantic in a 20-foot dory.

Captain John Ridgway and Sergant Chay Blyth wanted to prove something to the world but mostly to themselves: that sheer human endurance could, and would, beat the Atlantic Ocean.

"I was always looking for ways to test myself, to see what I could stand up to," Captain Ridgway said. It was the same for Blyth, who had never been to sea before: the physical challenge was what drove him to tempt the Atlantic in an open boat—3,000 miles, endless and perilous, from Cape Cod to the coast of England.

"You only get to know the sea when you're right *on* the sea," Ridgway said. "There are incredible forces out there that you never feel on a ship.

"You have to be within a few inches of the sea to come to know it."

They came to know it, with all the terrifying intimacy of mere inches, through two hurricanes and storm after storm.

"I pray quite a lot now," Blyth recorded in his mid-Atlantic log. "It is all rather fearful."

But they proved what they set out to prove. They endured. On the 92nd day of their impossible voyage, they sighted the English coast.

Afterwards they said: "We didn't really beat the Atlantic. It let us go."

LS CAPE HATTERAS LIGHTHOUSE

The sea is whimsical.
It will let a rowboat go, but cannot be trusted to spare the biggest ship. And nowhere is the ocean more unpredictable than off Cape Hatteras, whose lighthouse is the tallest in the United States.
With reason. . .

LS BEACH & SEA FROM TOP OF LIGHT

For here, on North Carolina's Outer Banks, the cape bulges into the Atlantic toward the dread Diamond Shoals, where the warm Gulf Stream meets the cold current of the North Atlantic.

FURIOUS WATERS WHERE THE TWO CURRENTS CLASH

And here, as was said in the Book of Job, "the Lord maketh the deep to boil like a pot."

PAN FROM SHORE TO WRECK

Shoals and storms and currents all combine to make Hatteras "the graveyard of the Atlantic," a cemetery for ships like the *Laura Barnes* of Norfolk, a proud four-masted schooner before Hatteras destroyed her.

PLANKING OF ANOTHER WRECK

Sailing ships, steamships, pleasure craft, freighters, tankers—over the years the sea has cast them up indifferently, hundreds and hundreds of them.

MORE WRECKAGE HALF BURIED IN SAND

Mute warnings that say: "Sailor beware of Hatteras!"

LS: PAN TO WATER & STEEL WRECKAGE

And not only Hatteras. . .
The cape is roughly the middle point of the Outer Banks. But the graveyard stretches the whole length of this fatal coast, where anonymous tombstones of ships whose names have long been forgotten still stand forlornly in the sea that killed them.

The poetry of the broadcast was composed by the cinematographers, film editors, and writer, working together. About his part–the writing– Hanser says:

I can only say that I immersed myself in sea literature and made extensive notes and then classified them—STORMS, SHIPS, SAYINGS, DISASTERS, and so on. It sounds a pedantic way of working with such poetic materials, but as the footage came in I could see just where particular quotes, or facts, or comment, would fit. When the final cut was ready, I had a fairly clear idea of what I was going to say for all major passages (allowing, of course, for the agony of that stop-watch writing necessary to make the words fit the footage exactly, whenever that was required).

You will note that there are a great many quotations in the script. I was naturally awed by the subject, and whenever I could make Melville, Conrad, Whitman, or an eloquent sea-dog speak to our picutres, I did so. As Montaigne says somewhere, "I quote others only in order to express myself."

A point which is not obvious from the script is the amount of "open space" in the narration. That is, the script says nothing and lets the music take over, whenever possible for as long as possible.

Again the lesson: Don't talk when the picture says it better.

Friendly says of Murrow, "Ed was always good at knowing when to shut up." Then Friendly goes on to blame his own over-use of words for the dullness of "The Water Famine," a documentary on the worldwide shortage of water:

We tried to get in so much information about water that we made it more of an encyclopedia than a documentary. My colleagues and I wrote so much copy that Howard Smith was talking for almost sixty minutes. The viewer can't absorb that much. You can't just keep pitching information in there, bang-bang-bang. You've got to let it sink in.

It's very improtant to leave some little silence here and there, to let natural sound from the film track carry for five or ten seconds, so the listener has time to digest and think about what is happening. Some moments are so dramatic that if you step on that scene, you wreck it. Sometimes the most effective thing a writer can learn is when to shut up.

The drama of those moments may come from someone who speaks with "fire in his belly" (Friendly's phrase) or through television's "transmitting of experience" (Reuven Frank's). Either can be an effective way of presenting an issue. Both call for lean prose, and a minimum of it, in the body of the documentary. At the end, in the summation, there may be room for a small essay to wrap up the whole meaning of the program.

Writing the Ending

Robert Lewis Shayon, the documentarian-turned-critic, has called the summary the toughest thing about documentary. "It can not merely be a reprise," he said, "or a tacked-on exhortation. It must be an explosion whose fuse is buried in the body of the program itself."

The most celebrated summary in the first two decades of television documentary was written by Murrow for the famous broadcast on Senator Joseph

McCarthy, which he and Friendly produced in 1954. Friendly tells how he felt uncertain about the program, not sure it was ready, but fearful history would pass them by before they were fully prepared. It was then that Murrow said he would undertake to write a summary that would sharpen the focus and make apparent its purpose.

No one familiar with the history of this country can deny that congressional committees are useful. It is necessary to investigate before legislating. But the line between investigation and persecution is a very fine one, and the junior senator from Wisconsin has stepped over it repeatedly. His primary achievement has been in confusing the public mind as between the internal and external threat of Communism. We must not confuse dissent with disloyalty. We must remember always that accusation is not proof and that conviction depends upon evidence and due process of law. We will not walk in fear, one of another. We will not be driven by fear into an age of unreason if we dig deep in our history and our doctrine and remember that we are not descended from fearful men, not from men who feared to write, to speak, to associate and to defend causes which were for the moment unpopular.

This is no time for men who oppose Senator McCarthy's methods to keep silent, or for those who approve. We can deny our heritage and our history, but we cannot escape responsibility for the result. As a nation we have come into our full inheritance at a tender age. We proclaim ourselves, as indeed we are, the defenders of freedom—what's left of it—but we cannot defend freedom abroad by deserting it at home. The actions of the junior senator from Wisconsin have caused alarm and dismay amongst our allies abroad and given considerable comfort to our enemies. And whose fault is that? Not really his; he didn't create this situation of fear, he merely exploited it and rather successfully.

Cassius was right. "The fault, dear Brutus, is not in our stars but in ourselves."

That broadcast was almost as controversial as McCarthy himself. Jack Gould of the *New York Times* called it "crusading journalism of high responsibility," but it was described as a "smear" by Jack O'Brian, the radio-TV columnist of Hearst's *New York Journal-American*.

Another end-piece from the same series in the same era was just as strong but attracted less attention. Here's how Friendly tells the story, and relates its significance to documentaries in general:

I remember in the early days of the Murrow–Friendly coverage of McCarthy, we did an interview with Harry Truman shortly after he left the White House. It was right after McCarthy had attacked George Marshall. And Joe Wershba, the reporter, asked Harry Truman in Independence about the attack. Truman's answer was, "I wouldn't let the senator who said that, shine my shoes." We ran that and afterward Ed said,

"The editors of this program and Mr. Truman agree on some things, differ on many. On his choice of shoe-shine men, we are in agreement."

That gave the report a piece of punctuation, a piece of meaning.

Now I'm not for editorializing, although that comes very close to being editorial. I think it is interpretive reporting where you have a point of view, not an editorial point.

Point of view as far as making up the listener's or viewer's mind, that's a completely different thing. And I would think the good documentary wouldn't do that. A good documentary would have the point of view of saying "We're going to show you how migrant farmers may be exploited. We're not going to show you the beauty of the orange groves of Florida, or the sex life of the crocodiles in the Everglades. We're going to show you how the migrants get exploited." And that is point of view. We're not telling the viewer, though, what he ought to do about that. There's the difference between point of view and editorializing.

The summation on a good documentary is often provocative, though rarely to the extent of those two examples from 1954. Its function is partly stylistic—a "piece of punctuation," as Friendly put it. And partly it is pragmatic, to jog the viewer's mind into thinking about the facts and ideas that have been presented in the broadcast. In the words of Robert Lewis Shayon, "Emotion is but one half of the pure coin of documentary creativity. Intellect is the other half."

A popular documentary series of the early 1960s was "David Brinkley's Journal." On May 9, 1962, it explored the relationship between magazines and the deficit being piled up by the Post Office which, at that time, was handling more than 8 billion newspapers and magazines a year. For this service in 1961, the Post Office collected about a hundred million dollars. The service COST the Post Office 445 million dollars.

In the course of the program, Brinkley used on-camera opinions of officials of the Post Office, members of Congress, and magazine publishers.

How did Brinkley end the broadcast? Simply by saying:

No doubt each side has a persuasive case, and maybe they are both right. But what is the issue? The Post Office spends more than it gets. Its answer is to raise the rates. Raising the magazines would cut its losses about 10 percent. But even allowing for some publishers' exaggerations, many magazines are in trouble, competing with television and dealing with printers and papermakers, not making any money, and some good ones are dead already.

They do some things better than any other medium, introducing new writers, discoursing on specialized and complex ideas, and the need for that never was greater.

If I may express an opinion here, it is this. The Post Office loses money, but to some extent it is supposed to. Raising the rates very likely would kill off more of the good magazines a literary society needs, while leaving the trash to thrive and prosper. So I think if the Post Office needs money, this is the wrong place to get it.

Here, Brinkley's analytical approach led him to a specific conclusion. Seven years later, he was more contemplative as he extracted generalities from a mass of detail at the end of an evening-long documentary, "From Here to the 70's." That summation is instructive for what Brinkley says as well as for the way he says it:

There was a new way to hear the words and see the events of the 60's—television. And sometimes the meaning of the word or the meaning of the event is changed by the manner in which it is heard or seen. What television did in the 60's was to show the American people to the American people. Until then, we did not truly know much about each other. We knew only what we had seen, which was very little, and what we had read, which was even less. As to what we had seen, very few Americans had personally inspected Watts, California. Few had seen those psycho-dramas acted out in the committees of Congress or seen the political conventions, the Dallas jail, the New York welfare office. As for what we had read, we are not the world's most avid readers. There are those among us who never read beyond the sports pages or the grocery ads.

Television did a lot else, good and bad, but it *did* show the people places and things they had not seen before. Some they liked and some they did not. It was not that television produced or created any of it. It was not only a new message but a new medium, and it spread the message more widely and vividly than ever before. It was a new delivery system, efficient and effective. Old information is new information to those who didn't know it. An audience becomes an audience only when it is assembled and its attention is held.

Television assembled the biggest audience in the history of the world. And the information it delivered showed a society that was in many ways working better than any other, but in other ways was not working at all. It showed the need for change, and it showed the change was not being made. It showed public institutions were preventing change, more intent on their own purposes than on the public's needs. These institutions included various elements of federal, state and local government, colleges, business and labor unions.

The effects of seeing and hearing all this in a way it had never been seen or heard before can only be guessed at. But there certainly is a general restiveness and dissatisfaction among Americans, white and black, young and old—a feeling that the more taxes we paid the less we got, that the glittering new public programs usually turned out to cost a great deal and not to work very well.

Through history, when public institutions resisted giving the people what they wanted, when they resisted peaceful change, they had it forced on them. Violently. Indeed, that is almost the unbroken history of human society. Public institutions not meeting the people's needs, continuing to serve only themselves, until violence destroys them. After a decade in which the American people saw and heard more than ever before, it is clear they are dissatisfied. But this time, unlike Louis XVI and history's other losers—*this* time we know it. We also know we have the resources and the ability to do what needs to be done. But we *don't* know how much time we have.

That documentary took a broad view of society. Most are sharply focused and, in the opinion of Charles Kuralt, the sharper the focus, the better. "The most important thing you can say about producing a documentary," Kuralt told a meeting of news directors, "is that a show about China fails. You have to tell the story of a *Chinese*. We have to narrow our focus to find truth."

In June 1969, ABC News focused on the issue of abortion. The network's advance publicity said the program would "not offer a judgment for or against abolition of existing abortion statutes." But it did, when Frank Reynolds ended the broadcast with a pair of questions:

The central question is a simple one: Is abortion the business of the state or of the individual? If indeed abortion is a matter of faith and conscience, has anyone the right, in a pluralistic society, to legislate a question of conscience for anyone?

Reynolds took a stand by implying an answer to his first question in the way he asked the second. His phrasing of the central issue left out an important argument used by those who oppose abortion—that a fetus has a right to life, even in the early stages of pregnancy. Through omission, Reynolds indicated he thought the argument either irrelevant or wrong, or both. Yet the technique of questioning injected a subtlety which softened the conclusion, making it less likely to arouse resentment among those who disagreed than would a forthright statement.

At other times, a set of questions in the summation permits the writer to suggest courses of action while avoiding the exhortations of an editorialist. A good example came at the end of "Pollution is a Matter of Choice," produced by Fred Freed and presented on NBC in 1970:

What quality of life is possible in an industrial society? Do our institutions, created for simple times, have the vision, the power to control technology?

What are we willing to give up to clean up our environment? Are we willing to drive fewer or smaller cars? Have fewer television sets, fewer air conditioners? Have fewer comforts?

Are we willing to pay for the cost of cleaning up our air and water? Are we consumers willing to pay higher prices for cleaner engines and those who produce them, to take lower profits? Are we willing to have fewer babies, accept more rigid government controls? Would we dare set limits on our scientific and technological development?

We know that a species survives only as it adapts to its environment.

We know that unless we adapt, we may disappear from this earth like the dinosaurs before us.

Those questions make an appropriate ending for a documentary on a problem that has no clear-cut solution. They stimulate thought that could lead to solutions.

Some summations do recommend specific action to alleviate the problem under discussion, especially if research for the broadcast uncovered potential solutions that haven't been tried. Such was the case with "Hunger in America," a 1968 winner of the Peabody Award. The script was written in straight declarative sentences by Martin Carr, Peter Davis, and the reporter, Charles Kuralt. Their summation described the magnitude of the problem that had been graphically portrayed in microcosm during the body of the broadcast, then it recommended what should be done:

The families we have visited tonight are, sadly, more typical than unique. Hunger can be found in many places in the United States—too many places. Ten million Americans don't know where their next meal is coming from. Sometimes it doesn't come at all.

More than one thousand counties in need of food programs have no program whatsoever. States and counties often keep out federal food programs. Surplus commodities mean less food purchased in local stores. And states and counties must share in the cost of food stamps. There is also the failure of these programs themselves. Surplus commodities are free but do not contain the right foods. Food stamps are not free and too often the people who need them most can't afford them.

The Department of Agriculture has emergency power to bring food to hungry people in any county in the United States. So far, it has been reluctant to exercise this power. In the last two years, the Department of Agriculture has quietly turned back to the Treasury 408-million dollars that could have been used to feed hungry Americans. CBS News has learned that this year the Department plans to turn back to the Treasury another 227-million dollars, more money than ever before. According to the Department of Agriculture, the existing food programs are run as efficiently as possible without this money.

Meantime, American farmers, in recent weeks, have slaughtered and buried 14-thousand hogs because, they say, there is no market for them. The Department of

Agriculture protects farmers, not consumers—especially not destitute consumers. The federal food programs might be better administered by the Department of Health, Education and Welfare, or by a special commission whose only concern would be to see that hungry Americans are fed.

We are talking about 10-million Americans. In this country the most basic human need must become a human right.

This is Charles Kuralt for CBS REPORTS.

[ANNOUNCER:] Today in Washington the House Committee on Education and Labor began hearings on the problem of hunger. On Thursday the Senate Subcommittee on Employment, Manpower and Poverty will also begin an investigation of hunger in America.

Though "Hunger in America" had been in preparation many months, it had a direct relationship to the news of the day it was first broadcast—May 21, 1968. It was even more newsworthy when rebroadcast a month later, because by that time it had been attacked by the Secretary of Agriculture and spokesmen for farming interests. Some congressmen demanded that the Federal Communications Commission look into the accuracy of what had been said and shown on the program. CBS resisted and the FCC, after some months delay, refused to investigate.

The lesson for writers and others who help make hard-hitting documentaries: Expect a counterattack when your broadcast assigns blame for a problem to specific individuals or groups. Prepare for it by writing as cautiously or boldly as the facts dictate. Be sure every statement—whether factual or interpretative—is supported by solid investigative reporting. Where such support is lacking, let qualifiers in the copy show it.

In short, don't be afraid to say what you know is right. Just be sure you are right. In a documentary, *document*.

Is the Documentary Dying?

Documentaries have almost vanished from network radio, largely because affiliated stations don't want to carry them. In the late '60s, there were those who thought the species was in danger of disappearing from television, too.

In his book, *The People Machine*, Robert MacNeil claimed that documentary production reached its peak of excellence in 1963. "Since then," he said, "it has lapsed into a period of commercialized timidity." David Brinkley seemed to concur. "Television," he said, "is lacking in excitement these days. We lean toward soft, pastel programs—trips through the Louvre, or up the

Nile with gun and camera." To Brinkley, such broadcasts are irrelevant to these times.

These views appeared justified. In the 1969-1970 television season, the Nielsen service rated 176 prime-time specials on the networks. Only 18 of these could be considered in the news category. A CBS broadcast on the draft lottery was the highest-rated news special—55th on the list. An ABC documentary on ethics in government landed in last place.

As in radio, television networks have difficulty getting affiliates to carry news documentaries. In the fall of 1968, *Broadcasting* reported that NBC had 222 clearances for "Bonanza," 201 for its evening news and only 171 for the documentary series NBC White Paper. And it is true that the commercial networks have cut back on production of traditional documentaries.

The cut-backs were due partly to reduced network income and partly to the emergence of magazing-format broadcasts. "First Tuesday" on NBC and "60 Minutes" on CBS used air time and personnel previously assigned to documentaries. They also took over the documentary form, shortening it to fit their own requirements.

Similar developments were noticeable on television's expanded news programs, network and local. They regularly presented investigatory reports, four to seven minutes in length, on serious social problems such as environment, poverty, racial discrimination and drugs. These reports began appearing in 1963, when CBS and NBC expanded their early evening news programs from fifteen minutes to half an hour. Not long after that, Cronkite coined the phrase "pocket documentary." Other broadcasters refer to these longer film pieces as "mini-documentaries" and are only partly jesting in likening them to a woman's skirt: "Long enough to cover the subject but short enough to be interesting."

At the same time some important, socially relevant documentaries continued to be produced. Among them were ABC's two-hour study, "The American Adventure," examining the state of American society, and NBC's "Cry Help," a 90-minute report on mental illness among adolescents.

Perhaps the most interesting documentary of 1970 from a historical point of view was the NBC White Paper on the plight of migrant workers, which was a sequel to "Harvest of Shame," produced ten years earlier by Friendly and Murrow for CBS—both highly controversial programs.

Public television, at the start of the '70s, increased its output of documentaries. Among these, "Banks and the Poor," "Hiroshima-Nagasaki: 25 Years Ago," "Hospital," and the Black Journal series are notable. Allan Levin's "Who Invited US?" received the George Polk Memorial Award from Long Island University in 1971. And "The Great American Dream Machine" became public television's magazine, a counterpart to "First Tuesday" and "60 Minutes."

It was a full-length CBS Reports, "The Selling of the Pentagon," that rekindled excitement in 1971 about the documentary as a journalistic instrument. It reported how the Defense Department spends up to $190 million a year trying to win public support for its policies and practices. The agency's wide-ranging operations in the areas of radio, television, motion pictures, newspapers and exhibits were shown in detail. The documentary included film clips of TV stars giving the standard Pentagon line. One film, made years earlier and still in circulation, featured CBS's own Walter Cronkite. At another point a former Air Force major told how a CBS crew in Vietnam had been duped into conducting interviews with pilots who had been carefully screened and briefed beforehand so that they would speak "in a one-voice concept," as the ex-major put it.

"The Selling of the Pentagon" was written and produced by Peter Davis and narrated by Roger Mudd. In summary, Mudd said:

On this broadcast we have seen violence made glamorous, expensive weapons advertised as if they were automobiles, biased opinions presented as straight facts. Defending the country not just with arms but also with ideology, Pentagon propaganda insists on America's role as the cop on every beat in the world. Not only the public but the press as well has been beguiled, including at times, ourselves at CBS News. This propaganda barrage is the creation of a runaway bureaucracy that frustrates attempts to control it.

The next few days were reminiscent of the aftermath of a Murrow-Friendly documentary. Representative F. Edward Hébert, chairman of the House Armed Services Committee, didn't see the broadcast but secondhand reports were enough to convince him it was "the most misleading and damaging attack on our people over there that I have ever heard of." (In 1971, "over there" meant Vietnam.) But newspaper critics raved about "The Selling of the Pentagon." Jack Gould of the *New York Times* called it "brilliant" and Bob Williams of the *New York Post* said it "smacked of the old, bold energetic style of network journalism so desperately needed now."

So the television documentary is alive, perhaps getting healthier. And writers are needed.

16

"IT SEEMS TO THIS REPORTER"

Walter Duranty, the famous Moscow correspondent for the *New York Times*, wrote a book titled *I Write As I Please*. The first "big names" in broadcast journalism wrote pretty much as they pleased. They raised storms. Sometimes their programs were dropped, or they went to another network. But there was relatively little editing of Gabriel Heatter, Elmer Davis, H. V. Kaltenborn, and Boake Carter. In fact, Boake Carter wrote a book called *I Talk As I Like* and proved it by campaigning on the air against Prohibition, naval power—an ex-RAF flier, he championed air power—American involvement abroad, and the New Deal. Harold Ickes called him "Croak" Carter. His isolationist views became increasingly unpopular with the advent of World War II, and his career declined during the war, just as many new careers in broadcast journalism were beginning.

H. V. Kaltenborn's series of broadcasts over WEAF, New York, was canceled in the early 1920s because of the displeasure of the American Telephone and Telegraph Company. Kaltenborn, an associate editor of the *Brooklyn Eagle,* had dared in one of his broadcasts to criticize Secretary of State Hughes for what seemed to him to be an out-of-hand rejection of Soviet Russia's bid for diplomatic recognition. Hughes took umbrage at the criticism and, according to the part-time commentator, expressed the view that "this fellow Kaltenborn should not be allowed to criticize a cabinet member over the facilities of the New York Telephone Company."

In his excellent history of broadcasting in the United States, Erik Barnouw quotes a former AT&T official as saying that at that time the company had a "fundamental policy of constant and complete cooperation with every government institution that was concerned with communications." As a result of this government interference, and mistaken policy, Kaltenborn was no longer heard on WEAF. Later, broadcasting over WOR, Newark, he repeatedly attacked New York City's playboy mayor, Jimmy Walker, and the station supported him. His voice was heard.

Throughout this period, Kaltenborn served as an editor of the *Eagle*. He was, in fact, the highest paid member of the staff, and in 1930, when the Depression brought a severe loss in advertising, he was let go. CBS, which had long admired his perceptive mind and gift of speech, promptly hired him to do two analyses a week—at $50 each! Fortunately, most of his income came from talks given from lecture platforms.

It was on CBS—a national platform—that Kaltenborn ultimately achieved fame. In 1936, during the Spanish Civil War, he made the first broadcast of actual battle sounds in radio history. Americans, in their homes, could hear shells bursting and the rattle of machine gun fire. More important than the actuality was Kaltenborn's commentary on the civil war. He called the nonintervention agreement among the Western Powers a mockery. He correctly saw the war as "part of the Fascist international drive for power." As nearly as anyone, he recognized it as the curtain-raiser to a second world war.

Kaltenborn performed his greatest tour de force as a news analyst in 1938 when, during the Munich crisis, he maintained a marathon, round-the-clock schedule, catching only catnaps on the big leather couch in CBS' Studio 9. It is almost no exaggeration to say that he held the whole country spellbound. In those eighteen days when Hitler threatened war with Czechoslovakia, Kaltenborn followed the peregrinations of Neville Chamberlain over the face of Europe—from No. 10 Downing Street, to Berchtesgaden, to Godesberg, to Munich, where the treaty securing the nonexistent peace in their time finally was signed.

Throughout the eighteen days, CBS' pioneering director of news, Paul White, remained at Kaltenborn's side, feeding him the latest bulletin copy from the wires of AP, UP, and INS and cueing him for the short-wave reports of William L. Shirer, Edward R. Murrow, and others from abroad. White recalled in his *News on the Air*: "The foreign correspondents would report and Kaltenborn would then analyze. He analyzed everything. The height of something or other was reached one afternoon when, in a fervor of commentation, he analyzed a prayer by the Archbishop of Canterbury! But the public loved it. We began to get so many telegrams, so much mail, that we had to hire three girls to handle the influx."

In his history, Barnouw calls Kaltenborn's performance "the greatest show yet heard on American radio." But it was more than a "show." Through the efforts of Kaltenborn and the news teams of all three networks—CBS, NBC, and MBS—the American people finally were exposed to Hitler. They had heard his voice by short-wave; they had followed his power plays. They were made aware of his ruthlessness. And, as Paul White said, "If any man contributed most to this awareness, it was the redoubtable Kaltenborn." Kaltenborn had interpreted the melodrama. It was his interpretation that most Americans heard.

But CBS and the commentator, at the height of his popularity, would soon part. And it is because of this parting, due to honest differences over the role of interpreter, that we have related the story of H. V. Kaltenborn in this detail. (It's too good a story to pass up anyway.) Kaltenborn was prone to express his opinion. CBS insisted that its newsmen refrain from expressing personal opinion. A clash was inevitable. Here are excerpts of a memorandum on the subject issued by Ed Klauber, executive vice president of CBS, to the network's news staff upon the outbreak of war in 1939:

Columbia's announced policy of having no editorial views of its own and not seeking to maintain or advance the views of others will be rigidly continued.

In being fair and factual, those who present the news for Columbia must not only refrain from personal opinions, but must refrain from microphone manner designed to cast doubt, suspicion, sarcasm, ridicule, or anything of that sort on the matter they are presenting.

What news analysts are entitled to do and should do is to elucidate and illuminate the news out of common knowledge or special knowledge possessed by them or made available to them by this organization through its news sources. They should point out the facts on both sides, show contradictions with the known record, and so on. They should bear in mind that in a democracy it is important that people not only should know but should understand and it is the analyst's function to help the listener to understand, to weigh, and to judge, but not to do the judging for him.

It is impossible, within any reasonable limits, to define completely this last-mentioned aspect of news analysis. Fairness and temperateness are of its essence.

CBS insisted that its explainers of news developments were analysts and not commentators. The term *news analyst* described its concept of objectivity. Kaltenborn said that for the life of him he could see no difference between a commentator and a news analyst—they were doing the same job. He called it nonsensical to pretend that opinion could be excluded from any evaluation of events. In 1940, he went to NBC.

Ironically, not long after Kaltenborn switched networks, NBC joined the Mutual Broadcasting System in declaring that "no news analyst or news broadcaster of any kind is to be allowed to express personal editorial judgment." There was that phrase "news analyst" again, and the National Association of Broadcasters itself had said, "Elucidation of the news should be free of bias."

It was against this background that Kaltenborn in 1941 played a leading role in founding the Association of Radio News Analysts, later known as the Association of Radio and Television News Analysts. In a speech, Kaltenborn said: "No news analyst worth his salt could, or would, be completely neutral or objective. He shows his editorial bias by every act of selection or rejection from the vast mass of news material placed before him. . . . Every exercise of his editorial judgment constitutes an expression of opinion."

But Kaltenborn made a concession. "The radio news analyst," he said, "cannot, and should not, function night after night as preacher or soap-box orator. He cannot constantly make himself the medium for passionate expression of personal or minority opinions." Paul White, in rebuttal, said: "The key to Kaltenborn's argument would seem to concern only the frequency with which the news analyst becomes a pulpiteer. In other words, he apparently agreed with me in the main but felt that if a radio analyst wanted to get passionate about something occasionally, then a network should throw its policies out the studio window and dust off the soap box."

White got into a radio discussion of the subject with John W. Vandercook of NBC. Vandercook was speaking for the Association of Radio News Analysts. He said:

Perhaps the kindest interpretation of the policy of prohibiting news analysts from expressing their opinion over the air is that CBS desires to air only the truth, and that, as I see it, is the basic fallacy. Columbia infers that it is competent to judge what is fact and what is opinion. That's an extraordinary assertion. Man has been seeking to distinguish between truth and untruth ever since he began to talk. Only self-appointed censors and only those of a dictatorial trend of mind have ever been so vain as even to claim that they could make that fine distinction. . . . We news analysts insist upon our right to speak as individuals to the American people as individuals. In short, we trust our fellow Americans, as they've always been trusted, as they must always *be* trusted, if the democratic system is to endure. We don't believe, as does Mr. White, in measuring or selecting the doses of opinions and points of view which we present. We think it's for the listener to decide what he shall choose to hear. . . . We do not believe in corporate control.

Throughout the 1940's, Paul White tried to hold the line at CBS against the expression of personal opinion on the air. In 1943, he said, "Ideally, in the case of controversial issues, the audience should be left with no impression as to which side the analyst himself actually favors."

Later, White abandoned this position. He had left CBS News when *Newsweek* quoted his statement of 1943 on how analytical reports should be completely impartial. White sent *Newsweek* this telegram, dated April 8, 1954:

AN ELEVEN-YEAR-OLD QUOTATION ON THE EMASCULATION OF COMMENTATOR'S OPINIONS ON RADIO OR TELEVISION HAS RETURNED TO HAUNT ME. I HAVE SINCE CHANGED MY MIND AND HAVE RECANTED PUBLICLY ON SEVERAL OCCASIONS. MY NIGHTLY BROADCAST IS PROOF THAT I NO LONGER SUBSCRIBE TO THAT 1943 VIEWPOINT. IN THAT YEAR I ALSO THOUGHT THAT SOVIET RUSSIA WAS A VALUABLE ALLY, THAT NUCLEAR FISSION WAS IMPOSSIBLE AND THAT, AFTER THE WAR AND WITH RATIONING AND CONTROLS REMOVED, STEAKS WOULD BE PLENTIFUL AND CHEAP. I AM PERTURBED ONLY BECAUSE SOME READERS MAY THINK I AM NOW IN DISAGREEMENT WITH ED MURROW. I AM NOT. HE IS STILL MY FAVORITE BLEEDING HEAD IF NOT BLEEDING HEART. DURING THE WAR A BRITISH CENSOR ONCE ADVISED ME FROM LONDON THAT MURROW WAS NOT IMMEDIATELY AVAILABLE TO ANSWER A QUESTION I WANTED TO PUT TO HIM. "HE'S ABOUT SOMEWHERE," SAID THE CENSOR, "WEARING HIS CUSTOMARY CROWN OF THORNS."

> PAUL WHITE
> EXECUTIVE EDITOR
> KFMB AM-TV
> SAN DIEGO, CALIF

The *Newsweek* quote and White's telegram were timely because, just a week earlier, Murrow and Fred W. Friendly had broadcast their now historic exposé of Senator Joseph R. McCarthy. That broadcast had left an indelible impression "as to which side the analyst himself actually favors."

One searches in vain in Ed Murrow's analyses for naiveté. After Army Counsel Joseph Welch's celebrated denunciation of McCarthy in the Army-McCarthy hearings—a denunciation triggered by McCarthy's attack on Welch's young associate, Fred Fisher—we find Murrow saying:

It is safe to assume, I think, that had Mr. Welch never heard of Mr. Fisher, his emotion, his anger would have been considerably less. It seems to this reporter that there is a widespread tendency on the part of all human beings to believe that because a thing happens to a stranger, or to someone far away, it doesn't happen at all. The muscles of moral indignation become flabby when those who are being damaged, either in their bodies or in their reputations, are remote or unknown.

Many of Murrow's wartime broadcasts were written for a 15-minute program heard in the United States on Sunday afternoons. These broadcasts dealt in editorial opinion in a way which Alexander Kendrick, who became Murrow's biographer, has accurately—if somewhat confusingly—described as "subjectively objective." Here is a sample. Murrow reports from London on December 27, 1942:

As the year ends, more people are thinking about the future. The governments in exile are making estimates of the food, medicine and raw material required to rehabilitate their countries. Some of them, but not all, may be hoping to ride back to power on Allied food trains. What happens in the liberated countries will be largely decided by the United States. Many of the weapons and men that free them will be American; most of the merchantmen carrying the stuff will fly the Stars and Stripes.

I believe that any American who watched the first year of global war from London would have at the end of it one dominant impression, and that would be the power and responsibility of his own country. It is fashionable, and probably true, to speak of this war as a revolution. When the French made their revolution more than a hundred years ago, they hoped to regulate the destiny of nations and found the liberty of the world. That is the task that now confronts America and her allies.

A little more than a year ago I stood in that crowded room under the big dome in Washington and heard the President ask for a declaration of war. And as I watched those men and women, as I had watched other men and women in London more than two years before trying so hard to be casual while making history, I realized that Congress had decreed the freedom of the world. We are yet far from achieving it. On occasion we have done less than our allies expected. But we have done more than our enemies believed possible. . . .

We see in this commentary, written three years before the end of the war, Murrow already probing for answers to postwar problems. It was like him to see news in terms of history.

In his biography, Kendrick said—again accurately—that in this series of Sunday programs "the Murrow style of broadcasting—temperate yet crisp, dignified yet informal, understated and never condescending, and always probing behind the news—set the pattern for what had become in effect a CBS style." Kendrick reported Murrow's instructions to his European staff of correspondents: "Never sound excited. Imagine yourself at a dinner table back in the United States, with the local editor, a banker, and a professor, talking over coffee. You try to tell what it was like, while the maid's boyfriend, a truck driver, listens from the kitchen. Talk to be understood by the truck driver while not insulting the professor's intelligence."

Still good advice.

The Perennial Argument

One of the longest-running arguments in journalism is this argument over objective versus subjective reporting. The lines are not always laid down clearly. Today some newsmen say: "Forget objective reporting—it's impossible. Just try to be fair." Other newsmen say: "A better term than subjective reporting is the New Journalism, the journalism of involvement. As a reporter, be involved. Get your message across."

In broadcasting, as in other media, this issue is very real. Reuven Frank, president of NBC News, says: "Today in the United States, facing a jigsaw of crises for which we are unprepared, many people seem to think that American journalism and, above all, American television journalism, should be governed by ennobling purposes. We are castigated for not promoting unity, for not opening channels of interracial communication, for not building an edifice of support for our fighting men, for not ignoring dissent, for not showing good news.

"Our system does not now provide for working toward social good. Let us even postulate that there is a unanimously accepted social good which television journalism should set itself to achieve or promote, and the decision would be made by five Albert Schweitzers sitting around a table. Whoever put them there could in time—perhaps far, far off in the future—replace them with five Joseph Goebbelses or five Joseph Stalins, or five George Lincoln Rockwells. You see, it's not the five Albert Schweitzers who are important but the table.

"I say the table itself is evil. To those who worry about television, or television news, being too powerful I say there is no doubt that there is great potential power here, but only if used. The only safeguard is free journalism, journalism without directed purpose, because whether that purpose represents good or evil depends on who you are."

Jim Bormann of WCCO, Minneapolis, says: "It is our feeling that if the advocacy syndrome takes hold, we shall have lost the thing that is most precious to any news operation—our credibility. I know there are those who believe journalism would be answering a higher call if it employed the news media as a weapon for social change. I totally disagree. If social change is desirable, it will come with or without help from the news media. But if the media become populated with ax-grinders clamoring for a cause, then we are in trouble. The people no longer will trust their newspapers and broadcast stations, and the role of the media in the democratic process will be so weakened that the process itself may collapse. This is why we must continue to strive for objectivity, even though we know that absolute objectivity is humanly unobtainable."

The bearing of all this on writing news for broadcast is obvious. Journalists of these two schools write differently, though the requirement for clarity remains the same. The Pacifica stations (WBAI in New York, KPFA in Berkeley, KPFK in Los Angeles, and KPFT in Houston) practice advocacy in some of their news reports. They look upon their public affairs broadcasts as complementing, rather than competing with, other broadcast services.

Most stations, like WCCO in Minneapolis, belong to the objective school. We have already quoted James E. Mays of WTAR, Norfolk. Mays goes on to say: "I have heard network reporters use 'editorial' words which would never have gotten on our air. You can gather—correctly—from this that I am not an admirer of advocacy journalism. And if that marks me as old-fashioned, then I cheerfully plead guilty."

One of the dividends accruing from "telling it straight" is that when you do make your views known, they carry an impact which otherwise would be impossible. Because of Cronkite's reputation as an objective reporter, any editorial comment by him stands out. Thus his comment on "The CBS Evening News" of May 21, 1970, carried extraordinary weight.

An informal White House memorandum leaked to the press had charged CBS News with faking the fatal stabbing of a captured Viet Cong soldier by a noncommissioned South Vietnamese officer. The memo had been circulated by Clark Mollenhoff, a newspaperman who at that time was serving as a presidential assistant. Cronkite reran the film of the stabbing, which took place in the presence of U.S. personnel. The program also ran an interview with the South Vietnamese officer, who claimed he acted in self-defense.

After showing this documentation, Cronkite told his viewers:

We broadcast the original story in the belief it told something about the nature of the war in Vietnam. What has happened since tells something about the Government and its relations with news media which carry stories the Government finds disagreeable.

It was perhaps the strongest premeditated language Cronkite had ever used on the air. The White House disclaimed responsibility for the memorandum. News Secretary Ron Ziegler said Mollenhoff's duties "do not include the investigation of news agencies."

Jack Gould of the *New York Times* has remarked that in their radio pieces, broadcast journalists are more outspoken than they are on television. And it is true. Here, for example, is Cronkite's "Dimension" report of August 4, 1970:

The old children's saying—"Sticks and stones can break my bones, but words can never hurt me"—is being tested anew by the Nixon Administration. A look in a moment.

PENNZOIL COMMERCIAL :60

When top Nixon Administration officials informally urged Washington newsmen to judge them not by what they *say* but what they *do*, they evidently weren't kidding. At least so far as the words are concerned. Here are recent examples:

Item One: In mid-July the Justice Department announced it would send 100 lawyers and other federal officials to five regional offices in the South this month—to anticipate any problems before the Supreme Court's ordered end to legalized school segregation this September. The lawyers from Washington would be on hand to smooth things over as much as enforce the law, it was explained. Nevertheless, Southern politicians complained. Whereupon President Nixon reversed field—announcing that the number of officials sent south would depend on whether states or localities with problems *asked* for them. Yet the very night he spoke, his top domestic advisers were telling newsmen he was wrong. And the next day, presidential News Secretary Ron Ziegler announced the officials already were in place, ready to enforce the law, if necessary, this fall. There the matter stands. In limbo.

Item Two: In a written report to the nation, at the conclusion of the U-S incursion into Cambodia, President Nixon said U-S planes would continue to bomb Communist infiltrators moving *toward* South Vietnam. He declared, "We do this to protect our forces in South Vietnam." Now it has become evident that U-S bombers are also flying missions in Cambodia to protect the regime of General Lon Nol, despite earlier denials from the brass. In Washington, CBS Newsman Bob Schieffer reports Pentagon officials were quite candid about this duplicity—in private.

Item Three consists of President Nixon's remarks yesterday on the Sharon Tate murder trial. First, in Denver, while speaking from notes, saying that Charles Manson is guilty of eight murders—a statement so clearly prejudicial that not even a high-school student could miss it, much less an experienced lawyer like the President. Then, in Washington, denying he meant to speculate on the defendants' guilt or innocence—or prejudice their legal rights. In the meantime, the entire case may have been gravely jeopardized.

Maybe mere words can't hurt after all. The only trouble is that one day the President could say something he really means, unequivocally, and possibly nobody will believe it until News Secretary Ziegler appears for a clarification.

This is Walter Cronkite. Good day.

PENNZOIL CLOSE

On the evening of July 1, 1970, the three commercial networks carried an hour-long interview with President Nixon called "A Conversation with the President." Howard K. Smith represented ABC, Eric Sevareid represented CBS, and John Chancellor represented NBC. Two days after the broadcast, Sevareid made the interview the subject for his commentary, which is as instructive for what it says about the difficulty of interviewing such a figure as it is for the language employed—analogy, adjectives, clarity, conversational tone.

Interviewing the world's most powerful leader on live television, in front of half the world, is a test of the adrenalin. For interviewer and interviewee it is a bit like crossing above Niagara Falls on a tightwire.

The President can't be sure he's anticipated your questions in advance, however thoroughly his advisers brief him. You don't know what his replies are going to be, and you don't even know what questions the other interviewers are going to put to him. You do know that if you don't press for relevant answers, the eagle-eyed and elephant-eared printed press will accuse you of not doing your job and that if you press one degree too hard, 10-thousand letter-writing citizens will accuse you of discourtesy to the President of the country.

And when it's all over, you have to sit down and read the transcript or listen to a recording to know exactly what the President said and exactly what you said. The slightly embarrassing truth is that the citizen relaxed at home absorbs the President's statements more clearly than the interviewer, who can listen with only part of his mind. Another part is racing to adjust his line of forthcoming questions on the basis of what the interviewee has seemed to say and what another interviewer has just asked, which is often enough just what you were about to ask.

The opening analogy should be expanded—it is like crossing Niagara on a tightwire while doing a juggling act.

It can't be a debate because the audience wants the President's views, not yours, and it can't really be a conversation, whatever the advance advertising has said. With the enormous exception that any mistake the President makes can affect the fate of nations, the advantage in this kind of transaction is all with the President. He can control if not the kind of questions, the quantity of questions simply by responding with a chapter when a verse would do. That eats up the minutes. Mr. Nixon did this at various points on Wednesday night, and he did it—if this interviewer's antenna was properly sensitive—because two or three of the opening questions surprised him, and he decided then that he must control the hour as much as possible.

The demonstration of what he thinks was absorbing. So was the demonstration of *how* he thinks. He is fascinated by the convoluted complexities of events, and he does not always simplify them by any means. He thinks, not like a philosopher or a moralist, but like a lawyer, analytically, and with each question the brief instantly begins to take form in his mind and continues to form even as he talks.

Sevareid almost never uses the first personal pronoun. Instead, he says "this interviewer" and, in other commentaries, "this observer" and "this correspondent," recalling how Ed Murrow, expressing opinion, used to say, "It seems to this reporter. . . ." Sometimes Sevareid leaves out reference to himself entirely. Other writers of commentary do not hesitate to use the first person.

Howard K. Smith of ABC News did this interpretative piece, an outgrowth of the same televised conversation with the President.

The other night, when our one-hour television interview with President Nixon was over, I expressed regret to him that we had no more time because I had a lot more questions. Since he didn't say it was off the record, I might as well repeat what transpired.

He said, "What did you want to ask?" and I said this, "With Russia and China on the outs, should we not have regular diplomatic relations with China to gain the utmost information and diplomatic leverage from the situation?"

His answer was short and unequivocal. He said, "Yes, we should have those relations." And he indicated that he hoped it would happen.

Well, the urgency of such an action increases. Russia is engaged in a puzzling and dangerous strategy. She is, as Secretary Laird said yesterday, pushing missile production to catch and pass us while we hesitate.

A German white paper recently said that Russia is at what it called "flood tide" in expanding the biggest peacetime army Europe has ever seen. In the Mediterranean, she has reached into new areas with her brand-new fleet and her pilots flying combat patrols in Egypt.

The one weakness in that strategy—reach into the West—is that Russia at the same time has felt it necessary to put 45 divisions—that is, nine armies—into the East on Red China's border. Nobody here has a good explanation of why, in a time of bland peace with the United States, Russia is pushing so hard. But she is visibly doing it, and it endangers the world balance which keeps the peace.

One countermeasure would be to regularize relations with her neighboring opponent. No one knows what information and advantage might come, once channels have been opened.

Smith's piece is a combination of hard news and commentary. He used the opportunity of speaking informally with the President to get a story. He then used that story as a peg for analyzing Soviet strategy and suggesting that a countermeasure would be to "regularize" relations with Red China. Both commentators take you behind the scenes—Sevareid on how it feels to question the President "live" before an audience of millions and Smith on a further conversation he had with the President after the television cameras were turned off. It's interesting that though both scripts read easily, Sevareid's sentences, on the average, run half again longer than Smith's—25 words a sentence to 17.

Two Views

On November 13, 1969, Vice-President Agnew made a speech in Des Moines, Iowa, in which he attacked the television networks. Specifically, he objected to the networks' "instant analysis" of President Nixon's Vietnam policy speech of the preceding week. Mr. Agnew said that "a small band of querulous men" had, in a few minutes, sabotaged what the President said. A week later, Mr. Agnew attacked the Eastern Establishment press in general and the *New York Times* and the *Washington Post* in particular for what he said was their prejudiced reporting of the Nixon Administration.

Network commentators defended the news media's right to criticize the actions of government, including statements made by the President. The commentaries carried by ABC-TV are of special interest because their authors, Frank Reynolds and Howard K. Smith, then frequently offered contrasting views*—Reynolds generally was more critical of the Administration than Smith—and because they spoke over the same network. Responding to the Vice-President's attack, Smith said on November 18:

Agreeing with Mr. Agnew about the dangers of instant comment, I have waited a few days. But now—speaking for myself alone—I would like to say a few words about some points in his famous speech.

It is true that TV news has greater impact than other kinds. We did not arrange that. Technology did, making our form of reporting more vivid. We are few in numbers. But we did not plan that. Circumstance simply provided space for only three networks, so far. Anyhow, you have a wider choice in networks than you do in newsmagazines, of which there are but two. Or of newspapers, of which most communities have but one.

*Reynolds has since been reassigned and no longer co-anchors the ABC evening news program.

We do make mistakes, sharing that fault with quarterbacks and most others, including Vice-Presidents. However, we do not do it deliberately. And I think we make fewer than, for example, *Time*, which this week called me a conservative. We are not elected. But neither is Joe Namath or, for that matter, a Vice-President. He is chosen solely by a presidential candidate who goes on to win.

For the rest, I agree with much of what Mr. Agnew said. In fact, I said some of it before he did. We must continue to discipline ourselves to fairness. We must do something to change the negative tradition of all American journalism, reporting mainly what goes wrong in a nation where much goes right.

We will continue to try. But I suspect we shall also continue, occasionally, to make mistakes.

Reynolds' commentary came three days later.

Although Vice-President Agnew has broadened his discussion to include certain newspapers, I want to talk tonight only about his first speech—the one devoted exclusively to network television news. I am the anchorman the Vice-President twice quoted but did not identify. He quoted me correctly, but I think in a misleading way. However, that is not important.

The Vice-President proclaims his opposition to any form of censorship, and I agree with him, but I think he disagrees with himself. For what he wants is not independent analysis but collaboration. Mr. Agnew confuses commentators with cheerleaders. Do you? I think not, and that raises a point that is important. Ask yourself whether the nation is ever well served when honest men withhold honest opinions, for fear of an angry reaction from the government or the public. Are we to say not what we believe but what we think most people want to hear? Again, Mr. Agnew seems to confuse commentators with certain politicians. Do you? I think not, and that raises perhaps the most important point of all.

There is something much worse than a public official attempting to frighten a broadcaster. And that is a broadcaster who allows himself to be frightened. Put us to the test. Watch us. If on your television set you see timidity disguised as objectivity, fear masquerading as fairness, then we will deserve Mr. Agnew's contempt—and yours.

Finally, I would like to suggest a word of encouragement to the Vice-President. Let him be of good cheer. The people are wise. They are not as easily misled as he seems to fear. In fact, I dare to suggest that they do not need him to protect them from us. The position of a commentator's eyebrow will not determine their position on really important matters. I have never been under the illusion that I could fool anybody, and despite the Vice-President's bombardment of the moment, I am enormously encouraged by the firm conviction that, in the long run, neither can he.

The Reynolds piece is "stronger" than Smith's. Smith agrees with Mr. Agnew on the dangers inherent in instant analysis, on the need for self-discipline and on the desirability of breaking away from journalism's "negative tradition." He says the editorial decision-making by a relatively few people in television is no plot—"we did not plan that." The networks are not the public's only news source. And although network newsmen, as well as Vice-Presidents, do make mistakes, the mistakes are not deliberate. The tone of Smith's piece is sympathetic. He does point out misconception on the part of the Vice-President. But nowhere does he suggest an effort by Mr. Agnew to intimidate the news media in order to get a better press.

Reynolds, on the other hand, sees the Des Moines speech as a clear attempt to squelch commentary that is critical of the Administration—"What he wants is not independent analysis but collaboration." He sees an attempt to frighten broadcasters into becoming cheerleaders and, using strong language, he says that broadcasters who are intimidated deserve everyone's contempt. And, reserving the strongest language for the last, he expresses faith that Mr. Agnew, in the long run, will fool nobody by the charges he has made.

Both Reynolds and Smith have, naturally, written commentaries which are readable. What they are saying, in each case, is "limpidly clear." Both start their pieces with a fairly long dependent clause—something which, structurally, is less than ideal. Still, these clauses do not confuse the listener. In fact, the "ramblingness" of these lead sentences helps signal to the listener that he is about to hear commentary and not hard news. There is a real change of pace.

Note the short sentences and the device of starting new sentences simply by putting in periods before the conjunction *and, for,* and *but.* The careful organization of Reynolds' piece bears study—the flow from "not important" to "important" to "most important" in what he has to say.

An Agnew Proposal

At the height of the 1970 Congressional campaign, Vice-President Agnew proposed the introduction of TV panel shows in reverse, with public figures such as governors and members of Congress questioning newsmen like Eric Sevareid and Howard K. Smith. He asked, "Don't you think it would be beneficial for the viewing audience to know what they believe so that when they characterize certain things, that there be some understanding of what their underlying philosophy is?"

Eric Sevareid replied to the Vice-President's suggestion with what probably was the most publicized commentary of the year.

The Vice-President proposes that network commentators, like this one and brothers Smith and Reynolds down the street at ABC—people of that type, he says—be publicly examined by government personnel. The public has a right to know, he says, our opinions and prejudices.

The phrase, "people of that type" hurts a bit; we certainly don't think of Mr. Agnew as a type; we think he's an original.

What really hurts is the thought that maybe nobody's been listening all this time. If, after some thirty years and thousands of broadcasts, hundreds of articles and a few books, one's general cast of mind, warts and all, remains a mystery, then we're licked and we fail to see how a few more minutes of examination by government types would solve the supposed riddle.

Mr. Agnew wants to know where we stand. We stand—or rather sit—right here, in the full glare. At a disadvantage as against politicians; we can't cast one vote in committee, an opposite vote on the floor; can't say one thing in the North, an opposite thing in the South; we hold no tenure, four years or otherwise, and can be voted out with a twist of the dial.

We can't use invective and epithets, can't even dream of impugning the patriotism of leading citizens, can't reduce every complicated issue to yes or no, black or white, and would rather go to jail than do bodily injury to the English language.

We can't come down on this side or that side of each disputed public issue because we're trying to explain far more than advocate and because some issues don't have two sides; some have three, four or half a dozen, and in these matters we're damned if we know the right answer. This may be why most of us look a bit frazzled while Mr. Agnew looks so serene.

Another reason may be that we have to think our own thoughts and write our own phrases. Unlike the Vice-President, we don't possess a stable of ghost writers. Come to think of it, if there are mysteries around, unseen spirits motivating the public dialogue, maybe that's the place that could use the glare of public scrutiny—that stable of anonymity.

Finally, at the risk of sounding a bit stuffy, we might say two things. One, that nobody in this business expects for a moment that the full truth of anything will be contained in any one account or commentary, but that through free reporting and discussion, as Mr. Walter Lippmann put it, the truth will emerge.

Second, that the central point about the free press is not that it be accurate, though it must try to be; not that it even be fair, though it must try to be that, but that it be free. And that means, in the first instance, freedom from any and all attempts by the power of government to coerce it or intimidate it or police it in any way.

A year after Mr. Agnew's Des Moines speech, the networks were not sounding intimidated.

Perhaps the most popular commentator in America today is Paul Harvey, whose "Hello, Americans. This is Paul Harvey" is a trademark known to millions of listeners. Harvey began his career as a radio announcer in Tulsa, Oklahoma, and has been a commentator for the American Broadcasting Company since 1944. A conservative on most issues, *Esquire* once called him "the voice of the silent majority," but Harvey disputes this. He calls them as he sees them, he says, and he isn't sure there IS a silent majority anyway. He cites his disagreement with the Nixon Administration's Southeast Asia policy. The day after Mr. Nixon announced the U.S. invasion of Cambodia, his lead was: "Mr. President, I love you, but you are wrong."

Here is a Paul Harvey script, written for radio shortly after the near-disastrous Apollo 13 flight. Notice the short paragraphs AND the short sentences. There is spice to his language. "You've got to get people to listen," he says. "The cold, hard facts have to be salted and peppered." He coins phrases like "salvation by legislation" and "warless war." But he is not above returning to that much-used methaphor of Earth as a ship in space.

You are on a spaceship. You had intended to leave the hazardous early exploration of space to others less timid, more skilled. Sorry about that.

This minute you are on an orbiting satellite, spinning in space.

Watch over there to the East, the sun appears to rise. The sun is not rising. You, on your spaceship, are rotating forward toward the sun.

At twilight the sun will appear to be descending into the western horizon. That's you, on your spaceship, rolling away from the sun—and orbiting around it.

You are on a spaceship and your spaceship is in trouble. An oxygen tank short-circuited. Your residual life support systems are limited. Recirculating water is becoming toxic.

And there is mutiny among the crew.

What went wrong? How did we get off course? Check the computers, back-track, trace the trouble.

Seven years ago, a civil court overruled the Builder of your spaceship, required modifications. Those modifications constituted sabotage.

A rumor spread, gaining credibility with repetition, that God had died. That meant our inertial guidance system no longer could be trusted. In our frantic effort to improvise another, we turned Earth upside down.

We piled laws on laws seeking salvation by legislation.

Crime was pyramiding 12 times faster than our population, so we passed gun laws—taking guns away—from people who obey laws.

Last year, Ground Control spent 350-thousand of the taxpayers' dollars to try to discourage people from smoking—and 30-million taxpayers' dollars to subsidize the growing of more tobacco.

With right and wrong indicators inverted, we applauded filth in the name of free speech.

Your parked car is stolen, the thief may go free. But you will be punished for leaving the keys where they belong.

An intruder breaks into your house, you shoot him. He can sue you.

When we had a fixed star to steer by, we could stray off course and yet find our way back. Now the stars are an oblong blur.

We sentence American sons to fight a warless war. If they destroy enemy villages and villagers with bombs, we decorate them. If they do it with guns, we courtmartial them.

When there is more compassion for the rapist than for his victim. . .

When we reward the loafer with more after-taxes dollars than the worker. . .

When the policeman who risks his life in a shootout with a felon subsequently finds himself on trial. . .

Then the inversion of right and wrong has resulted in a perversion of justice.

You start a business. The Government says how you run it. The law says whom you hire. The union says what you pay. And it's called "free enterprise."

And trouble always starts out being fun. Women started with immodesty—ended up topless, then bottomless. Then popping pills for the sheer boredom of it all.

How can we turn the world right-side-up again? Only thing I know to do is to get back in contact with the Builder of our spaceship and re-read his directions.

A lesser-known writer of commentary whose work bears the mark of thoughtfulness and craftsmanship is Rod MacLeish, aired in 1970, of the Westinghouse (Group W) stations. Here is one of his radio pieces:

To the hesitant pleasure of its critics and to some puzzlement among the large corps of people in the capital classified as Administration-watchers, the Nixon team has suddenly and publicly switched the tone of its rhetoric and the emphasis of issues it has chosen to deal with. Suddenly it's Tone Down, Be Positive and Forgiving Week in Washington.

The latest presidential picture shows Mr. Nixon talking to a group of Talos Pueblo Indians, and right there in the picture with him is Interior Secretary Walter Hickel. The Indians are there because the Administration has just come out with a proposal to give American Indians more independence within the ward relationship to the Federal Government. Mr. Hickel is there, partly one suspects, to display a beatific spirit within which the White House feels forgiveness for its most prodigal cabinet officer. Mr. Hickel wrote the famous letter urging the President to open up his administration a bit more and to listen to people who don't agree with all of its policies. He had been less than wildly welcome at the White House ever since.

Meanwhile, Attorney General Mitchell, the house law-and-order man, took himself off to Texas a few days ago, where he got a damp reception for an excellent speech praising the vast majority of American dissenters. Mr. Mitchell reminded his listeners that their right of expression is protected under the First Amendment. And the Attorney General praised the art forms, marches and speeches of most of the dissenters.

While all of this was going on, Vice-President Agnew was, and is, out on the stump accentuating an extraordinary positive. He gave an interesting speech on education and has addressed himself to the plight of Indians and Mexican-Americans. Hardly a word of attack on his critics.

All of this is, of course, most welcome because it is part of the stitching together process. Those things which the Administration has done so far this week won't alienate anyone except the harshest reactionaries. And it all will surely come as a pleasing surprise to many of the disenchanted, the critical and the unbelieving.

The weather is hot and stormy in Washington, but the highest rhetoric is calm and cool and constructive.

This is Rod MacLeish in Washington.

MacLeish begins with a prepositional phrase of 23 words, but because he is writing a "think piece," and because of the structure of the phrase—there are two good places where he can pause—it comes off. But it is more than the pauses which make the phrase readily understandable to the listener. An additional factor is that the phrase breaks up into two easily comprehended units which are parallel: To the hesitant pleasure of its critics and to some puzzlement among the large corps of people in the capital classified as administration-watchers. You can get away with this in commentary. Don't try it when you are writing hard news.

The Group W commentator creates interest with language like "prodigal cabinet officer," "house law-and-order man" and "beatific spirit." The establishment of Tone Down, Be Positive and Forgiving Week makes a point in an entertaining way. Instead of using such routine phrases as "to the pleasure of its critics" and "less than welcome," MacLeish writes "to the hesitant pleasure of its critics" and "less than wildly welcome." Instead of using a worn-out phrase like "got a luke-warm reception," he writes "got a damp reception." In writing commentary, as well as hard news, refuse to be trite.

The Assessment

Not all commentaries on television are identified visually as commentaries. That is, the word commentary does not always appear as an identifying label on the television screen. At CBS, it is assumed that when Eric Sevareid speaks, the viewer understands that he is listening to news analysis, which is, inevitably, a personal interpretation of events. The name of Sevareid, and his earnest, almost stern visage, have come to stand for most of the commentary heard on CBS Television. Moreover, on the Cronkite evening news he usually is introduced as someone who will give his "thoughts" or "observations" on a given subject. Any serious listener knows that he is hearing an essay.

Even at ABC, where the label *commentary* does appear when either Howard Smith or Harry Reasoner engage in comment, there is visually unlabeled commentary. For example, during the Jordanian crisis of 1970, Smith's lead-in to John Scali in Washington after an overseas report read, "For an American assessment, here is ABC's State Department correspondent, John Scali."

Isn't *assessment* by a newsman really commentary? Analysis? This is what Scali said:

A bitter civil war now seems inevitable in Jordan, and officials here believe the outcome will determine not only the fate of the cease-fire [between the Arab states and Israel] but whether Hussein becomes an exiled king who lost control of his country to Arab fanatics who are determined to destroy Israel. As authorities here see it, Hussein, after months of stalling, finally has turned his army loose to smash the commandos in an all-out battle for survival.

The little king had virtually no choice. His army of Bedouin tribesmen was in virtual mutiny, demanding that it be allowed to make clear who it is that rules Jordan. Hussein can win this battle, it's believed, if Iraqi army troops stationed in Jordon do not intervene on the side of the guerrillas. If they do, it's almost certain that Israeli troops will enter the battle. And there will be chaos of the kind that will trigger a renewal of the war on all fronts.

This is John Scali, ABC News, at the State Department.

This is definitely analysis. The attribution given Washington sources and use of the phrase "it's believed" do not alter the fact that Scali is analyzing —interpreting—developments in the dangerous Middle East situation. The statement that civil war "now seems inevitable" is a view, one gathers, which Scali shares with State Department officials. He goes on to say, with regard to Hussein's decision to make all-out war on the commandos, "The little king had virtually no choice." It is not clear whether this is a conclusion arrived at by John Scali or is the informed opinion of people at the State Department. Again, one is led to believe that the correspondent concurs in the judgment of State Department experts. Concurrence is, itself, subjective. Nothing in Scali's script connotes skepticism regarding what he has been told. He buys it.

And most commentary includes source material, reinforcing the views expressed.

Less than a year after making that broadcast, Scali became a White House aide specializing in information about foreign affairs.

Interpretative reports like the Scali piece are not restricted to ABC; they often show up on CBS and NBC. Coming as they usually do from some of the most experienced, most knowledgeable reporters in broadcasting, they contribute to the public understanding of issues.

Commentary—or, to use the term favored by Ed Klauber, news analysis—is the most difficult and perhaps the most significant writing for broadcast you can do. When you do it, be sure you have done your homework. If you do not know the facts, and lack perspective, you will be a broadcaster without honor in your own shop and, very soon, in every place you may be heard.

17

SPORTS, CRITICISM, AND SELF-CRITIQUE

Most good journalists begin as generalists but not all stay that way. Many become specialists—either out of the news beats they cover, or from interests that occupy their leisure time. This second group includes sports commentators and critics of the theater, movies, and journalism. Their work deserves special attention because it differs from other forms of news writing and, for many journalists, affords a desirable freedom to express personal opinions.

A critic's right to comment does not relieve him of responsibility for adhering to high journalistic standards. Those who do their job properly are accurate in their reporting and fair in their criticism, yet write with the zest and zing of a lively discussion. Each is aware that his topic—whether sports, culture, or journalistic performance—may be less momentous than the significant problems of politics and economics. And he uses this greater freedom for expressing reasoned opinion through individualistic style.

Sports for the Fan and the Non-Fan

Summaries of sports news are rare on network television and infrequent on network radio. Networks do broadcast many live sports events, but these are handled through separate sports departments rather than the news divisions. Some reasons for the separation involve journalistic ethics, others relate to business aspects of broadcasting and of big-time sports. Though the ethical and professional considerations are substantive enough to fill a book, they are not germane to this one about the writing of news.

Sports news is covered regularly on most local stations but written poorly on too many of them. The offending writers rely heavily on hackneyed jargon picked up from sports pages, other broadcasters, or the wire services. Listeners are submerged in a stream of dull sentences, polluted with clichés, when they should be experiencing writing as refreshing as a run in the rain.

Bright writing comes from thinking through what you are going to say and how you are going to say it. It need not always be put on paper. One who prefers to write in his head, then talk from notes, is Warner Wolf of WTOP in Washington. Wolf says he ad-libs because "People like it when I talk to them with eye-to-eye contact as in normal conversation, rather than reading." He goes over his piece at least three times before saying it into the microphone. The result is a relaxed and thoughtful commentary, such as this one on February 26, 1971:

For the last three baseball seasons, the owners have had more rain-outs than in any other three years combined. And the reason was, they started the season early.

So what did they do this year? They started the season earlier than ever before, on April 5th, which is only five weeks away.

It seems to me the answer is obvious—they should have fewer games.

Here they're starting the season April 5th. Have you ever been in Minneapolis or Chicago on April 5th? It's freezing—30 degrees. In fact, there's ten feet of snow on the ground right now in Montreal.

It just doesn't make sense to start the season this early. At least the players will tell you that the season is so long—they'll tell you off the record, they won't say it on the air—but off the record they'll tell you that because the season is so long that, come August or September, they're really not giving you 100 percent performance. The fan is being cheated because the player is tired.

The answer is, to me, start the season May first. Then you have less rain-outs. Secondly, the player is not as tired.

And there might be more of a premium on the ball games. Now, let's see, the Senators play Cleveland 18 times a year. So why should a fan rush out to the park and see the Senators play Cleveland, when he knows they're going to play 17 other times?

So I say, start the season May first and have fewer games.

On paper, Wolf's syntax is less than ideal. But the sentences are effective when spoken out loud. His entire set of notes consisted of four phrases of two words each:

1. Rain outs
2. Players tired
3. May first
4. Fewer games

As for the structure of the commentaries, Wolf favors stating his position as soon as possible: "Say you favor a shorter season, then tell why. Maybe you can sway them. But they want to know what your point of view is, right away."

And he has this advice for others who would specialize in broadcasting sports news or commentary:

Every sports fan thinks he knows more than you, and he's waiting out there for you to make a mistake. The worst thing you can do is mispronounce a ball player's name. He'll put you on the bottom of his list. Don't say the name if you can't pronounce it.

Next-worst is using fancy words. The sports fan wants it simple, he doesn't want to have to go to a dictionary, he wants to understand. You can turn an audience off, if you talk over their heads.

That advice runs counter to the style and philosophy of Heywood Hale Broun, who says:

I'm very aware of the sound of words. If a big word sounds good and has the right rhythm, I use it. You may not understand that word. You'll understand what I'm getting at. And you may even be pleased to hear the word, thinking, "Well, I'll go and look that up sometime."

Broun entered television in 1966, after seventeen years as an actor. Before that he was a sports writer for a newspaper. The combination seemed ideal to Gordon Manning, a vice-president of CBS News, and he invited Broun to try out. The experiment worked and Woody Broun became a fixture on "The CBS Saturday News with Roger Mudd." Here's how Broun describes what he does and how it evolved:

Originally, they billed me as a kind of sporting Sevareid. I would just write a little column and speak it on camera. That didn't seem to set the world on fire, so they started sending me out on the road. These pieces started out being three minutes, now they run about six minutes.

Bud Lamoreaux has been the producer of them right along. And between us, like some old double-play combination, we have just kind of evolved it out of our personalities.

I don't consider myself an expert. Experts tell you the inside view. I'm trying to do sport for everybody.

I have always described what I do rather awkwardly as a "sports essay." By the time you see what I have, you already know the score, or you didn't want to know the score. I have to tell you something other than who won.

What interests me is, why people play, or why people watch, or what is it that people want to get out of watching.

As to the writing, I try to give the words a gallop, as it were, so that you may even enjoy the shape of that, along with the shape of the game. People have told me they saw a show of mine and didn't know what all the words meant, but they enjoyed it. It's like watching a flock of geese go overhead. You don't know how they do it, but they're pretty.

The critics have been kind to Broun. The *New York Times* said he brings to the television screen "not only a fabulously impressive moustache but also a refreshingly detached attitude and delightful way with words."

Newsweek called Broun "television's most literate sports commentator." Then it went on to ask rhetorically, in a parody of the Broun style, "Who else but this superb athlete of images could vault so high on a poetic flourish, could race so swiftly with a fragment of fancy, could so surely snatch from the afternoon sky bits and scraps of Charles Dickens, George Meredith and Alexandre Dumas?" Obviously no one, in the opinion of *Newsweek*, which was describing how Broun covered the 1970 Super Bowl football game between Kansas City and Minnesota. Broun rarely relies as heavily on writers of the past as he did that day. He usually prefers to create his own metaphors and similes, as when he reported the victory of the New York Mets in the 1969 World Series of baseball:

BROUN (off camera):	Early in today's game, the Orioles seemed to have found a way of thwarting the Met
LONG SHOT OF SHEA STADIUM MCNALLY HITS, BALL SOARS OVER FENCE	miracle men as Pitcher Dave McNally hit one where outfielders aren't allowed—over the fence. The day got darker.
CLOSE-UP KOOSMAN	With the previously baffling Jerry Koosman on the mound, Frank Robinson followed his
ROBINSON HITS	two-run sock with a drive which would have been hard for parking lot attendants to catch.
MET FAN RAISES SIGN: "WHO'S PERFECT?"	The crowd feared that the lovable, laughable '62 Mets had returned. These are Mets of a different mettle, however, and

SWOBODA FALLS, LOSES CAP

LONG SHOT ACTION IN STADIUM

MEDIUM SHOT OF STANDS

JONES & UMPIRE

CLENDENON HITS

WEIS HITS

BALL GOES OVER FENCE

JONES HITS, BALL BOUNCES OFF WALL

SWOBODA HITS, FAN RAISES SIGN: "BELIEVE IN MIRACLES"

ACTION IN STADIUM

CROWD SHOT

SWOBODA BEING MOBBED

losing their caps instead of their cool, they kept on arriving at the right moment, even when, as it so often was, it was the last moment.

Now to Baltimore fans the fates appeared to be walking across the skies carrying a Met banner.

The Met rocket rose slowly from the pad in the 6th when Cleon Jones won an argument about being hit by a pitch.

And then Met power made its first appearance as Donn Clendenon hit his third home run of the series, a blow which later won him the car which goes to the Series star.

In the 7th, Met power made an unexpected appearance as Al Weis hit his third home run of the year to tie the game and tighten everyone's strings to E above high C.

An inning later, the strings began to tune up for the Met victory song. Cleon Jones struck the drum of the center field wall for a double. When Swoboda followed with another double, everyone but the Orioles knew that Shea Stadium, of all places, was the home of the world's baseball champions.

Baltimore did get the tying run to the plate in the 9th, but the outfield cavalry was ready for the final charge, which cut 'em off at the pass, ended a 5–3 ball game and started the leaping, cascading fires and fun of celebration.

Suddenly 57-thousand fans seemed to have made their way from stands to field—all of them were determined to show as much dash as had their heroes, and they swirled and zig-zagged with ecstatic revelry. Ike

PAPPAS ON CAMERA IN CROWD

Pappas barely raised his head above the maelstrom.

PAPPAS (AMID PANDEMONIUM):

And so, as the turf gets pulled out of Shea Stadium, this place goes absolutely crazy. They obviously won't play another ball game here this year, but who cares, because the Mets are the champs of the world.

BROUN:

CHAMPAGNE BEING SPLASHED ABOUT, PLAYERS HUGGING EACH OTHER

In the club house, the Mets flung aloft the symbols of their new eminence. And then it was time for champagne, the liquid that nobody ever drinks on these occasions. For the Mets, it was the shower of champions.

MARCIANO AND SWOBODA IN CLUB HOUSE

Sal Marciano, combining the qualities of skin diver and eel in arriving at the side of Ron Swoboda.

MARCIANO:

How you feel?

SWOBODA (ON CAMERA):

We've come so far so fast that, that—it's just so exciting. I want to say, I think we should say, that this is a sweet one. This is the first one, and I don't think it will ever be this nice again.

MARCIANO:

You weren't supposed to win it.

SWOBODA:

We weren't supposed to do anything this year, but we did it all. Did it all!

BROUN:

PAPER DRIFTING DOWN FROM OFFICE WINDOWS

CROWD WAVING, CHEERING

Wall Street, ever glad to get rid of read-out paper and warmed by averages, went mad for the Mets in a most unbusinesslike way. It would have been a poor time to call your broker.

NEWS OF MET VICTORY IN ELECTRIC LIGHTS ON SIDE OF ALLIED CHEMICAL BUILDING IN TIMES SQUARE. LIGHTS SAY, "METS WIN WORLD SERIES."

It usually takes the end of a year or the end of a war to rouse this old town, but the Mets did it today by ending victoriously the 1969 World Series.

BROUN (ENDS OFF-CAMERA):

This is Heywood Hale Broun in New York.

Others share credit with Broun for that piece. First, those who participated—especially the Mets—for an exciting event. Second, the cameramen who captured it on film. And third, credit the producer, Bud Lamoureaux, for selecting the film and arranging the sequences to convey the ebb and flow of the drama. But Broun's writing is what brought enjoyment, over and above the story of the game, to fans and non-fans alike.

Criticism and Reviewing

Cultural reviewing for print and for broadcast differ in two important respects: One is for the ear, the other for the eye; and the one for the ear is much the shorter of the two. The reviewer for radio or TV normally must limit his piece to a maximum of 200 words, about one-fifth the space allotted to a similar effort in newspapers and magazines.

This contraction leads to all kinds of things. "The main one is an inability to develop an idea," says Clive Barnes, who, as dance and drama critic for the *New York Times*, broadcasts reviews on the radio station owned by the *Times*. On the night of a Broadway opening, Barnes will first write a lengthy review in time for the paper's 11:30 deadline, then write a shorter and totally different one for the midnight news on WQXR. He can do the one-minute radio piece in about five minutes—without duplication in phrasing—because he has already worked it out in his mind. As for other differences, Barnes says:

The broadcast review is almost entirely an expression of opinion, rather than the development of any critical analysis. One of the best things you can do in a written review is to get someone to say, "Well, *he* didn't like it but I think *I* would." I don't think you can do that in a broadcast review, because you can't show the workings of your mind. The good broadcast reviewer knows exactly why he arrived at a certain conclusion, but he only has time for the conclusion itself.

Barnes was talking in relative terms. His radio pieces do reveal some of the workings of his mind, though not nearly as much so as his printed reviews. He understands the necessity for brevity and explains it this way:

If you find a newspaper review and you don't like it you turn the page, but you don't throw the newspaper away until you've read it. But if you find a broadcast review you don't like, you may very well switch stations.

Even with its limitations, the broadcast review should fulfill the same three obligations as good critical writing in print. The first is to report on the work, to identify it, to put it in perspective so that your listeners will understand where it fits in relation to other things they know about. A critic's second obligation is to explain what the author, the producer, or the artist was trying to do. And the third is to evaluate the work, to express opinion by saying whether you thought it succeeded in its purpose, and to say why you reached that conclusion.

Notice that we are using the words "review," "criticism," and "critique" interchangeably. If there is a difference, it is one of degree more than substance. Criticism may be a separate species when it deals with a trend or a broad array of cultural events. But in the context we are using it—that of a detailed examination of one event—it is a critique and amounts to high quality reviewing. The distinction may lie more in the mind of the person using the words than in the words themselves, and critics who write for print are likely to continue thinking that the very brevity of the broadcast review automatically precludes it from achieving the level of criticism.

There are some knowledgeable and articulate reviewers on the air. One of them, Edwin Newman, covers the theater for WNBC-TV in New York. He says a great many people have told him they are glad he is reviewing plays, even when they disagree with his opinions. Newman thinks he knows why they are pleased:

I think that a lot of people enjoy reviews and I don't mean that they enjoy only my reviews.

I think they enjoy reviews on television for a number of reasons that are worth considering. One of them is that the review is quite definite. You get on, you tell them that the play has opened, and you tell them what you think about it. And that's the end of it.

And that's fairly unusual on television, to have someone get up and give a flat opinion and walk away. It's fairly unusual in the news business anyway to have a story that has a beginning, middle and end all on the same night.

The beginning and end of a television review, according to Newman, should tell what the reviewer thought of the play. That's fairly easy. The middle is the difficult part of the one-minute review, where you must write briefly about what Newman calls "the interplay of ideas." Here is how Newman reviewed a familiar play that returned to Broadway on October 18, 1969:

NEWMAN (ON CAMERA):

This is essentially the same revival of *The Front Page* that we saw last season. It was a great show then, and it is a great show now.

There are a couple of cast changes.

VIZMO: HAYES & RYAN

One of them brings in Helen Hayes in what, in today's jargon, is called a cameo role, and she seems to enjoy doing it very much. That is Robert Ryan with her, as the evil editor, Walter Burns.

NEWMAN:

I had reservations about him last time, but by now Ryan has polished his interpretation to perfection, a marvelous portrayal of happy malevolence.

VIZMO: CONVY

Bert Convy is back as Hildy Johnson, the star reporter, not tough enough, but working on it.

NEWMAN:

John McGiver is again the mayor and Charles White the sheriff, and as before, they are superbly funny.

The Front Page is about a subject—cynical political corruption—that in our times is not amusing. And the hard-boiled reporter is passé. But Hecht and MacArthur wrote their play with such brazen assurance, and such comic flair, that now, forty-one years later, we see it as a classic of its kind.

Edwin Newman, NBC News.

Newman did not emphasize the play because it was familiar to many of his listeners. This approach—concentrating on the cast and the staging—is appropriate in criticism where the play itself is well known.

For a new play, the approach is different, as we see in another review by Ed Newman. This was broadcast October 21, 1969:

NEWMAN:

Butterflies Are Free is a strange little comedy about a blind young man, living away from his mother for two months to see whether he can get by on his own. Into his life comes an improbably perky girl, nineteen years old and divorced. Every joke imaginable about blindness is made, love bursts forth, the solicitous mother intervenes, and everybody lives happily ever after.

There was no point at which I believed any of it, and the girl is one of the most inconsistent character creations in years, knowing but naive, and sounding like the mouthpiece of a professional gag writer.

VIZMO: DULLEA AND DANNER

But Keir Dullea is good as the blind man, Blythe Danner does everything that can be

VIZMO: HECKERT

done as the girl, and Eileen Heckart, as always, is a tower of strength as the mother.

NEWMAN:

Butterflies Are Free is a contrived play, at times nothing more than a fusillade of gags tossed in for their own sake and of uneven quality. It is obvious and sentimentally tough,with more surface skill than genuine merit. But for what it is, it works.
Edwin Newman, NBC News.

In both reviews, Newman fulfilled a critic's duties and did it concisely. He says it is not always easy to write briefly when plays need a lot of explanation, as in the work of Harold Pinter. But most plays, in Newman's opinion, can easily be reviewed in less than a minute.

There is agreement on that point from Judith Crist, who has become one of the best-known movie critics through her work on the NBC-TV "Today" show. She felt differently about it when she started in broadcasting. That was 1962, and a strike had shut down all daily newspapers in New York. Dozens of reporters—Mrs. Crist among them—found temporary work by contributing to the suddenly expanded news coverage on radio and television.

She was on WABC-TV where, she recalls, she "fumed and complained" that you couldn't do justice to an important new play in a one-minute review. But in doing as required, she discovered "You really can get to the essentials without wasting time." Reviewing for broadcast taught her to condense, says Mrs. Crist, and helps her to be more concise in print.

On the "Today" show, Judith Crist is allotted nine and a half minutes, once a week. In this time she critiques an average of seven movies and one or two plays. It is all ad-lib, a feat made possible because she has already written criticism for *New York* magazine of the movies she is reviewing on television. Mrs. Crist says the technique of "just talking" helped her adapt to the oral medium:

Because broadcast journalism had not been my profession, I ran into difficulty by writing very good readable sentences that were not sayable sentences. I have a great affection for the compound-complex sentence. Well, that simply will not do on the old tube. And I've found that spoken language was the one solution.

I suppose there is some repetition on television of certain phrases I have written, especially the witty ones. You never forget your own witticisms. And they spring most readily and liltingly to the tongue.

Mrs. Crist keeps a list to be sure she talks about movies in the right order to coincide with vizmos—the visuals on the screen behind her. But she uses no script. She just talks, sometimes as long as two or three minutes on a movie she considers significant. Other films get brushed off quickly, as in this review from December 1967:

Well, there's usually lots that's good and lots that's clean in an Elvis Presley movie. *Clambake* is clean.

Or this one, from 1971:

Rio Lobo is a lousy Western but it has John Wayne. So you John Wayne fans will go regardless of what I say.

Sometimes a second-rate movie deserves a critique instead of a brush-off because its arrival has been preceded by a big publicity buildup. Here is how Mrs. Crist handled one of them:

Well, there's sad news for the smuts today: *Valley of the Dolls* has finally arrived on the screen and it's not a dirty movie. And alas, once you take out the prurience of the book, you're left with a mawkish, trite, cheap story that only smut could sell. It did. But the bowdlerized screen version goes on to be badly acted, badly photographed and sleazily made, with a cheapjack production underlining the near-idiot literacy level of the script.

The author of *Valley of the Dolls*, Miss Jacqueline Susann, makes her debut in this film as a newspaper reporter; she acts about as well as she writes. Perhaps Patty Duke, who scores high in the repulsive bracket, and Susan Hayward, who can count this as HER horror movie (all middle-aged stars have their monster roles these days), will live down their appearances herein. Perhaps not. Let's just hope that they will escape the sequel. Lord knows we will.

Reviews such as that cause Judith Crist to call herself "a severe critic" and others to use stronger descriptions. She says her "most glorious epithet" came from a film industry man who gave her the triple-S rating of "snide, sarcastic, supercilious bitch."

Being a severe critic doesn't mean she hates movies. Rather, she proves her love by seeing 500 of them a year. And when one of the 500 meets her critical standards, Judy Crist expresses her love in glowing detail:

In the Heat of the Night is an American movie of great distinction. This goes beyond its being a very good who-done-it story with social significance about a murder in a small town in Mississippi.

A Philadelphia policeman, played by Sidney Poitier, happens to be in town. He's picked up initially as a suspect because he's a transient Negro and he stays on to help the local police solve the crime. But it's the local police embodied by Rod Steiger that gives this movie distinction.

We've known Rod Steiger. We've always thought of him as a good actor. The subtlety of his portrait of the heretofore cliched redneck, the authority with which he molds the many moods of character are remarkable.

Sidney Poitier adds a new dimension to the "noble Negro" he has been portraying recently, providing a streak of bigotry and tension that gives superb complement to Steiger. Theirs is a remarkable duet. There are other excellent performances, outstanding ones by Warren Oates and Lee Grant, and Norman Jewison's direction is beautiful and at times brilliant. But the film is Steiger's from beginning to end.

In the Heat of the Night is really a memorable movie because of that.

Others agreed with Mrs. Crist's judgment. *In the Heat of the Night* won the Academy Award as Best Motion Picture of 1967, and Rod Steiger was named Best Actor of the year.

Critiques of Journalism

In 1946, when he was a CBS vice-president, Ed Murrow conceived the radio program "CBS Views the Press," to scrutinize performance of the print media. Newspapers and magazines were not accustomed to being criticized by broadcasters. There was excitement. Here was a case of man bites dog. But Murrow said, "We believe freedom of the press and freedom of radio are inseparable, and that mutual criticism will help both."

The program disappeared as television arrived and radio changed. It has reappeared periodically in New York and other cities, on both radio and TV, but not at the network level. The current variation in New York is a miniature of Murrow's program and is part of all-news radio on WCBS. The subject matter includes broadcast journalism in addition to print. And the critiquer no longer is a staff newsman but a journalism professor, William A. Wood of Columbia. He calls his pieces "Report on the Press" and does about four of them a week, each running two and a half minutes. Wood's favorite approach is to compare and analyze the handling of one story by two or more papers. We get the flavor in this excerpt dealing with the student occupation of a Columbia University building in March 1970:

The *News* gave it top billing . . . banner head with pictures and caption on page one, story on page three with another picture. The *Times* gave it story space and a picture, but they were on page 40.

What accounts for the difference? Well, the *News* sells papers with the sensational story. The *Times* does not. The *Times* is inclined to be sympathetic or at least lenient with student dissent; the *News* takes a hard line. The story-play may be related to the degree of indignation felt by the editor.

Wood also appraises the performance of broadcast journalism, a practice that could present conflicts of interest. But the CBS-owned station was willing to have him say that NBC-TV did a better job than CBS-TV on covering an eclipse of the sun in 1970:

In this case, the simple approach proved to be the best one. ABC and CBS—in addition to their airborne coverage—deployed men and equipment from Mexico all the way to Halifax, Nova Scotia. And they did switch to Mexico for the aftermath of the eclipse and pictures taped earlier. But NBC, with a much less complicated technical array, took the honors with its "Darkness at Noon," the coverage of the 1970 eclipse of the sun.

The electronic media also get covered in media commentaries that are broadcast on WTOP in Washington. The critiquer, Edwin Diamond, is a former senior editor of *Newsweek* who often writes magazine articles about journalism and its role in American life. Here is one of his radio scripts that deals mostly with newspapers:

One extra advantage of running your own newspaper or radio-TV station is that you can keep news about yourself quiet. Consider the best-kept journalistic secret around these days—the revolt of the reporters. In a score of cities newsmen—usually young and mildly militant—have made demands on their bosses ranging from improved racial coverage to a say in electing their editors.

At the Minneapolis *Tribune*, city room dissidents have announced that they want to "advise and consent" to management's choice for two assistant editor vacancies. In San Francisco, reporters at the *Chronicle* have been talking to management about playing a more direct part in news decisions. And at the *New York Times*, some of the brightest bylines have broached similar ideas.

None of the readers of the *Tribune*, the *Chronicle* or the *Times* have been told of these developments—or of the *Tribune's* decision to go along with the reporters' request. Of course, readers have been told about student demands to take part in faculty tenure decisions and about black demands for community school control. And it is easy to imagine the splashy coverage these same papers would give the story that the San Francisco Giants had held clubhouse meetings to elect their starting line-up.

But it is also news when reporters raise the cry of participatory democracy and collective action. The media, like the universities and the phone company, are semi-public institutions. Their affairs should be everybody's business, especially if the balance of news power is changing. Right now, the media are under the siege of Vice-President Agnew. Like a ham-handed dentist drilling without novocaine, Agnew has hit his most sensitive nerve of media objectivity. It is a subject that demands discussion. Will newsroom democracy lead to a more balanced coverage? Will elected editors produce better news reports than the present appointees? These are hard questions. It would help if the media proprietors—so quick to play up the troubles of the Harvards and the Harlems—shed some light on the revolt in their own house.

This is Edwin Diamond and this has been another commentary on the media.

Many have seen the need for constantly assessing the quality of journalism, both print and broadcast. Few have expressed it as clearly as Eric Sevareid when he helped dedicate the Klauber Broadcast Lab at the Columbia University Graduate School of Journalism in 1968. Sevareid also spoke of a related need on that occasion:

I believe there are two practical steps broadcast news and public affairs programers should take. Both have been tried in the past but only spasmodically.

One is to allow listeners and viewers to answer back. I am not speaking of the so-called "personal attack" rule, but of the public generally. This ought to be done on a regular and continuing basis. Particularly is this needed where the big networks are concerned. We are, with our blanketing news and documentary programs, a quasi-monopoly. We have a simple public duty to do this and it would be an act of institutional common sense.

It is the people who have the right to monitor and correct our efforts, not the government. Those publications and individual critics in the press now so casually discussing the alleged need of governmental controls of one kind or another over broadcast content will fall into their own ambush if they persuade the country that the First Amendment is divisible. It is not.

The other step is for broadcast news people to regularly monitor and assay the press, as the press monitors and assays broadcasting. It would be as healthy for the press as their attentions are, in the main, healthy for us. And it is required because American newspapers, by and large, lost, long ago, the lusty old tradition of taking issue with one another.

Sevareid stated the need, but in the ensuing three years there wasn't much evidence on the air that programers had responded.

Of the television networks, only CBS provided time for viewers to "answer back"—and that in very brief segments of the "60 Minutes" programs.

Although many local stations put listeners' opinions on the air during telephone call-in shows, only a few stations answer their mail publicly. One that does is WTOP in Washington. James L. Snyder, a company vice-president, handles these "Letters to the Editor" on radio. He quotes what listeners have written and adds his own comment. "People get the feeling you care," says Snyder. "They find out you really do read their mail."

Here's a typical column, written with a conversational, semifolksy approach:

Not all the letters we receive are concerned with praising or damning the performance of WTOP Radio. We also receive very thoughtful letters from listeners who are prompted to write to us by some thought-provoking news or feature they have just heard on the air. A fifth-grade teacher in Montgomery County wrote to talk about the need to somehow stop the polarization of the American people. A Washington man wrote to us to urge a more active role for black people in the anti-war movement. "Having been a black man over half a century," he wrote, "I am much disturbed. It will be tragic in a national sense if Negroes fail or refuse to contribute their energies to this development."

A Silver Spring man's letter is an expression of concern that "youth as youth is worshiped today as never before. Most of our youth," he wrote, "are sensitive, groping young people, but let's not put rock-throwing down as an expression of sensitivity."

As our regular listeners know, we have been getting a lot of mail from listeners about our sports director, Warner Wolf. My favorite pro-Warner Wolf letter this week came from a grandmother in Falls Church. "Fire Wolf?" she writes. "Never! In this blasé world Warner Wolf is a phenomenon, a reaffirmation of the essential value of life. Don't you dare take him away from us."

Finally, there was the letter from the lady in Washington who thinks our non-stop news girl promotion announcements are an affront. Our non-stop news girl suggests that ladies who keep informed by listening to WTOP Radio will dazzle their husbands with their knowledge of current events, and so their husbands will find them irresistible. The lady from Washington thinks such messages are a put-down to womanhood. "Don't you have any more respect for womanhood than to define them as stupid broads that need keeping up with their husbands?" The lady does us an injustice. We define womanhood only in the most glowing terms. Our policy is to do everything possible to be their humble obedient news broadcasting servants.

Here's a case where the broadcaster gets writing help from his listeners. He is also being helped with the process of constant self-criticism that every journalist should practice if he is to progress through the degrees of competence and on to excellence.

18

SO WHAT ELSE?

Now and then, a student will ask, "Are there any tricks?" Explaining what they mean, they say, "In writing for big name broadcasters, what do you do you don't talk about? What little things do you do to make them like what you write?"

What these students really are asking for are trade secrets. They want the inside information—not what everyone knows—on how a news writer in an extremely competitive business succeeds. What sets him apart? Because this is a recurring question—and a good one—we'll try to answer it. The answer is based on firsthand experience. This isn't theory—it's what works.

Remember, we are assuming you know all the rules. So what we are talking about here are the extras, those additional, unprescribed things you do that make for a good script. Often the broadcaster is not aware of these "extras." He doesn't know exactly why he prefers your writing. He just knows, as one broadcaster expressed it, "It's good on the tongue."

One of the first "tricks" is to adapt your writing to the style of the broadcaster. Write the way he likes to read. Nearly all broadcasters write some of their stories. Notice how your broadcaster writes for himself. Some broadcasters are more formal in their news presentation than others. Some go in for adjectives, more color. Some like their stories to flow from one to the next with the help of transitional phrases. Some broadcasters don't mind long sentences, IF the sentences are constructed for easy reading and easy comprehension. Some find it almost impossible to pronounce foreign names, so keep them to a minimum. (Tell them, in writing, how to pronounce them.)

So tip No. 1 is: Adapt your writing to the personality of the man (or woman) you are writing for. It's his (or her) show. Sometimes this means giving broadcasters the kind of story they like—Lowell Thomas likes stories about exotic places, like Tibet; Walter Cronkite is especially interested in stories about space. This should not be done at the expense of other, more important news. No responsible broadcaster wants it that way, and neither do you.

Tip No. 2: Be aware. A good news writer knows what is happening in the city where he works and in the world. He reads the newspapers and the newsmagazines. He listens to the news when he gets up in the morning. He listens to the news in the car, and he listens to the news when he gets home at night. He listens to the news just before he goes to bed. He reads all the wire copy he can get hold of while on the job.

The news writer keeps informed. If he cannot stand the steady diet of news—if he isn't willing to prepare himself for news writing, or reporting, to that extent—he should find other work. Top newsmen brief themselves in this way as a matter of course. When they report for work they are ready for the "new" news of the day.

The writing staff of a station, or network, should be aware of the content of preceding newscasts. Often the writer can monitor programs by listening to a loudspeaker in the newsroom. If this is not possible, he should read over the copy of the last broadcast to see which stories were used and how they were handled. In some newsrooms, the news editor decides what the lead story will be and what other stories should be reported. All this is necessary to avoid tiresome repetition, contradiction, and embarrassment in presenting news which listeners already have heard as though it were brand new.

The treatment of "old" news as though it were "new" news is something newscasters at network affiliates especially must guard against. It is easy for a local broadcaster to repeat a news item which has just been read by the network newsman. (If he does, he should make reference to that fact.) We recall an instance in which the network correspondent read a bulletin on an increase in the rate of unemployment, only to hear the local newscaster, taking over less than a minute later, read the same bulletin, which he said was "just in." He was not aware.

It is also to your advantage to listen to the reports of network correspondents if you are writing for a local station, because the correspondent reporting from London, Tel Aviv, or Saigon often has fresh information which you can incorporate in your script. If you are writing for an affiliate of that network, or for the network itself, there is, of course, no problem about quoting the correspondent or taping him for rebroadcast. If the correspondent works for the "other" network, the story has to be important for you to quote him. In any case, the exclusive story—and be sure it *is* exclusive—must be attributed.

Tip No. 3: Don't waste time. Broadcasting is serious business (though it can be fun, too), and the writer who feels so confident of his ability that he kids around with the secretaries for an hour, or spends the hour in the cafeteria, because his broadcast isn't scheduled for another three hours, is guilty of overconfidence. Normally, a five-minute newscast (which actually varies anywhere from three minutes to four and a half minutes, depending on commercials) requires an hour to write. As explained earlier, most news directors allow the writer an additional hour for reading the wires. Before he begins to write, a writer has to be "read in."

A few experienced professionals can write a five-minute newscast in 25 minutes. Others have trouble meeting the one-hour deadline. But the trick is to employ, usefully, *all* the time available. The writer cannot know what will happen to complicate his writing assignment. A late bulletin, some new leads, a story telephoned in by a reporter on the scene, or a call for help in editing a piece of audio tape or film—any number of things—can throw a writer off schedule. The time suddenly is gone. Earlier stories, no less important, are not written. News coverage suffers. Remember the fable of the tortoise and the hare. Don't dally. Stay on the job.

Tip No. 4 for success in news writing is related to the second. Get your copy up early. The broadcaster will want to look over the script, and time it, before going on the air. Give him ample time to do this. A conscientious broadcaster values this opportunity to rehearse. He'll be grateful to you for it. (So will the director!)

The fifth tip, or trick, is less obvious. Don't end a typewritten line in a way which may cause the broadcaster to stumble. You can confuse the broadcaster by separating two words which normally appear together, placing the first word at the end of the line and the second word at the start of the next line. Here's an example:

Brown announced it was the last speech he would make before election
day. . . when, he said, the people will decide.

A broadcaster reading this sentence, especially if he is reading it on sight, is apt to read the word <u>election</u> as if it were the last word in the sentence. After all, the sentence would make perfect sense if it did end there. The broadcaster who, if he is any good, is thinking in terms of the SENSE of what he is saying—as well as trying, if he is on television, to look as much as possible into the camera—may mistakenly assume that <u>election</u> does mark the end of the sentence. Though he does not see a period, he must make a decision. Sometimes he makes the wrong decision. Then he immediately comes upon the word <u>day</u>, and there is an awkward pause as he realizes his mistake.

So if you can help it—and you have time to think about such things—avoid splitting such "married" words as <u>election day</u>, <u>Memorial Day</u>, <u>Thanksgiving Day</u>, <u>Christmas Day</u>, <u>boat ride</u>, <u>jury trial</u>, <u>fire engine</u>, <u>paddy wagon</u>, <u>tuna boat</u>, <u>air fare</u>, <u>holiday trip</u>, <u>tree surgeon</u>, <u>horse chestnut</u>, <u>light bulb</u> and <u>body politic</u>.

The list can be expanded, but you get the idea. No one says you HAVE to type a word like *horse chestnut* on the same line. It's just that, for maximum ease in reading, all these words should appear in your script, like the animals entering Noah's Ark, side by side.

And here's another trick. We don't know how prevalent it is, but we have used it. And it seems to work. What it amounts to is "tying" the end of one line to the start of the next by ending the first line with a word which strongly suggests continuity. For example, *the* is a good word to end a line with. It sends the reader chasing down to the next line for the word it modifies. The article *a* is just as good for the same reason. Prepositions and adjectives are useful, too, in this regard. So are conjunctions. But nouns are bad. They don't link. They do nothing to improve the flow of one line of copy to the next. You may think this is pretty fancy. It is. But it's a trick one of the highest paid writers in the business has used. We'll call it tip No. 6.

Tip No. 7: Don't underestimate the importance of choosing the right word and spelling it correctly. This can affect pronunciation and the meaning of what you say—for example, *effect* and *affect*. Often pronunciation is not affected, as in the case of words like *separate* and *receive*, which frequently are spelled *seperate* and *recieve*. The listener is none the wiser. But a script replete with these so-called "harmless" misspellings still says something unfavorable about the writer. The broadcaster begins to wonder how far he can trust the writer who is careless in his spelling. Will he be careless, too, with facts? So keep a dictionary handy. If you are in doubt about the spelling of a word, look it up.

Finally, broadcasters are grateful for typewriter ribbons that make words that are black. Not words that are pale on paper. Words that are deep black. Words that are easy to read. No broadcaster enjoys reminding the writer to change his ribbon. Elementary? Yes. But it's one of the little important things a lot of writers forget.

An overused typewriter ribbon caused embarrassment to one of the authors of this book when he was his own writer for a television newscast in Roanoke,

Virginia. The story concerned a drought and the effect it was having on grain prices. Unfortunately, the *o* in *oats* was light. While his mind was distracted by a time cue from the studio floor manager, his mouth spoke what his eyes saw on paper: "Prices are expected to continue to rise on wheat, barley, and cats." *Cats!* A fluff quickly corrected but an embarrassing and unnecessary one—all because of failure to use a typewriter ribbon that was fresh.

You might call these tricks of the trade, though most of them are not really tricks, only common sense. What these tricks add up to, what the guidelines of all the previous chapters add up to, is good practice. We have sought, piecemeal, to explain the art of achieving clarity in news broadcasts. For clarity and communication ARE the goals. The late Carl E. Lindstrom, who taught journalism at the University of Michigan, once said: "The news writer is an artist. In its simplest terms, art is the business of selecting for effect—plus skill. The writer is the creative manipulator of the most plastic, the most resistant, the most mercurial and yet the stickiest substance known to man—the written word." Ah, you say, that sounds like a professor. But before Lindstrom went into teaching he was executive editor of the *Hartford Times*. He knew that art is not alien to news writing, that the good news writer is an artist.

The Extra Ingredient

Here we would add a postscript. It is that artistry—skill—is not enough. Good news writing, good reporting, is an amalgam of artistry and commitment. It takes both.

It has been said of James Gordon Bennett, and Ralph McGill, and Ed Murrow, that they were vivid writers, that they had a penetrating eye for the follies of politicians, and that they had a conscience. They had skill. And they cared.

Of McGill, the *New York Times* said, "He understood that the highest act of love toward any region or people was to speak the truth." J.B. Priestley wrote, regarding his work as a broadcaster during World War II, "This . . . is the final and important point: I never tried to cheat the microphone. I mean by this that I spoke on the air with as much sincerity as my personality allows me to have. I spoke what I believed to be the truth." When a student asked Eric Sevareid what it was, more than anything else, which moved him in his lifetime of reporting, he said, "I wanted always to find out the truth of things."

Skill is not enough. The responsible news writer asks everlastingly: Is what I am saying really true?

Frank H. Bartholomew, who went—not rose—from reporter to chairman of the board of UPI, has warned that fantastic improvements in news transmission must not blind journalists to the fact that human skills and integrity remain paramount. Murrow saw the first communications satellites, and marveled. Then he raised the fundamental question: "What shall we SAY to one another?"

Media are wondrously improved. What about the message?

Speaking of Ed Klauber, one of the founders of CBS News, Eric Sevareid said: "He hated humbug and pretense, private or public, and he could strip it naked with a phrase. I think he was in love with reality and found it far more exciting and portentous than wishes and dreams." Sevareid said, "I suspect that must be the core quality of anyone worth his salt in journalism."

The responsible news writer asks himself, "What is humbug here? What is real?"

George Polk was killed while on assignment in Greece. In a nationwide broadcast, Murrow spoke of Polk's reverence for fact. He said: "His stories stood up—every last one of them. He spared neither the corruption, inefficiency and petty political maneuvering of the Greek government, nor the vacillation of American policy, nor the atrocities committed by the Communists. What happened he reported, without fear and in language that all could understand."

The extra ingredient is integrity. It is honesty in seeking out and reporting the truth. And in radio and television especially, this must be done in language that all can understand.

19

THE EVENING NEWS: March 19, 1971

Let's look at one day of network evening news — March 19, 1971. For an examination of how ABC, CBS, and NBC handled the news that night, here are transcripts of their half-hour programs. They will enable you to compare these programs for format, use of film and graphic art, selection of stories and the time given to those stories — in other words, to compare news judgments.

But this is also an opportunity to compare styles of writing. Each writer reports the news in his own way. And the way he writes knowing that the viewer will be looking at a map — say, of Laos — is not the same way he writes a story to be read over silent film.

The accompanying photographs show relationships between audio and video. Notice how ABC's use of graphics differs from that of the other two networks. The NBC script provides examples of the lead-in policy discussed on pages 140–142. And the Cronkite broadcast shows how CBS reported a controversy over its own coverage of the news.*

It is for making such discoveries that these scripts are reproduced.

*For permission to use these pictures and transcripts, we thank producers Avram Westin of ABC, Leslie Midgley of CBS, and Wallace Westfeldt of NBC. The network news divisions provided photographers who took pictures from TV screens. ABC photos by Frank Santoro, CBS photos by William Warnercke, NBC photos by Fred Hermansky.

ABC EVENING NEWS WITH
HOWARD K. SMITH AND HARRY REASONER
March 19, 1971

OPEN WITH SMITH AND REASONER ON CAMERA

SMITH:

Good evening from ABC News headquarters in Washington. I'm Howard K. Smith

REASONER:

I'm Harry Reasoner in New York. These are tonight's headlines.

REASONER (AND VIZMO):

Egyptians fire at Israeli jets intruding into Egyptian air space over the Suez Canal, the first such incident since the cease-fire expired on March 7th.

CHANGE VIZMO

Enemy shelling of Khe Sanh is now so heavy at times that American pilots have to be withdrawn.

CHANGE VIZMO

The Administration reports that the cost-of-living rose again last month but is "encouraged" by the *small* increase.

CHANGE VIZMO

And a Senate committee *approves* funding of the S–S–T, setting the groundwork for a bitter battle in the full Senate next week. Howard?

CLICKER*

SMITH (ON CAMERA):

Reports tonight from:
Stephen Geer on Abba Eban discussing Israel's stand here in Washington. . .
Jim Giggans on the massive withdrawal of troops from Laos. . .
Kenneth Gale on the missing boxcar caper . . .
Ted Koppel on the growing split between West and East Pakistan . . .
Tom Jarriel with President Nixon at the funeral of Thomas E. Dewey . . .
And tonight's comment on cutbacks in Space and Defense and what that does to the spin-offs.

*Note: both ABC and CBS refer to this opening billboard as a "clicker." It begins with one entry. Other bylines and story slugs are added, one at a time, to match the copy being read.

SMITH (AND VIZMO):

The first Suez shooting incident in nearly eight months took place over Port Fuad at the northern end of the Suez Canal today.

ADD SPLAT AND PLANES TO VIZMO

Egyptian anti-aircraft batteries opened up on two Israeli Phantoms. They missed. The Cairo version is that this was strictly a military response to a violation of Egypt's air space. But ABC's Peter Jennings in Tel Aviv reports that the intent was political — to alarm the U–S, to press Israel for concessions.

CHANGE VIZMO

Here in Washington the Israeli position was aired in three places today. Israeli foreign minister Abba Eban talked to 40 senators on Capitol Hill for an hour. Then, before visiting Henry Kissinger at the White House, he spent two hours with Secretary of State Rogers. Here is a report from ABC's Stephen Geer:

FILM: GEER V/O ROGERS AND EBAN SHAKE
:07

[GEER]: Secretary Rogers, at his news conference this week, increased U–S pressure on Israel to accept guarantees of security and withdraw to pre-1967 boundaries with Egypt. Israel has insisted that guarantees are no substitute for secure boundaries.

CUTAWAY. ROGERS AND EBAN SIT
:08

NEWS CNF. SCENE

:06

At an afternoon news conference, Eban — in response to a question — made it clear today's talks did not change Israel's stand:

EBAN (SOF, MS):

:35

We are dealing now with an undertaking to change our viewpoint. I came here in the hope that I would be able to explain what our viewpoint is, to enumerate its justifications, to state why there are, in the Israeli position, certain points which engage the national welfare, the national security, and the national survival, to the extent that we ought to be free to seek those objectives in a negotiation. It is part of a continuing process whereby the United States and Israel explain their policies, each to the other.

CUTAWAY

:03

EBAN, MS

:07

GEER V/O EBAN LS

:07

[GEER]: Although Eban described the talks as "good and useful," he re-emphasized Israel's position on withdrawals:

EBAN (SOF, MS):

:31

There is no way of insuring Israel's security except by a peace agreement which includes the necessary establishment of secure and recognized boundaries. In other words, boundaries different from the previous armistice lines. We do not believe or admit that there is any substitute for a rational and new boundary settlement as part of the transition to peace.

GEER V/O LS, EBAN AND CROWD

:12

[GEER]: State Department officials are pleased at the tenor of today's talks, if not at the results. The U–S and Israel remain far apart, but it is hoped that further discussions will be fruitful.

Stephen Geer, ABC News, Washington.

SMITH (AND VIZMO):

Reports circulated today in the Middle East that Israel and Egypt recently waged a submarine battle in the Mediterranean, and that Israel was the loser.

Officially, Cairo refused to confirm that, and Tel Aviv called the story "nonsense." Whether the report is true or not, the potential is building for warfare at sea, as ABC's Bill Seamans reported recently from Haifa:

FILM: SEAMANS V/O WIDE SHOT, SUB

:04

[SEAMANS]: This is the submarine *Leviathan*, part of the Israeli navy you hear very little, if anything, about. The Israelis won't tell us officially how many submarines they have, but authoritative sources say there are four such submarines in the Israeli navy.

COAT OF ARMS

:03

INTERIORS OF SUBMARINE AND CREW HUSTLING
ABOUT ITS WORK
:20

This one is in for her periodic maintenance check and overhaul. A welcome interlude for her young crew, because they can spend a few days at home. But those on board doing the work are also running constant drills.

CAPT. ZOHA AT PERISCOPE
:06

Captain Zoha carries this responsibility at the age of only 25. He's running torpedo drill, to break in a few new members of the crew. Before joining the navy, he was an officer in the paratroops.

VIEW THROUGH PERISCOPE
:04

SAILOR AT WHEEL
:06
LONG CORRIDOR
:05

This ship is one of the old British T-Class subs from World War II — 287 feet long and 17-hundred tons. The Israeli Navy is small but well-trained and equipped. Its mission is primarily to protect the Israeli cities and industrial centers along the coast.

TORPEDO TUBE
:09

SUB EXTERIOR
SEAMANS (ON CAMERA):

:12

Her machinery overhauled, her young captain and crew trained to perfection, the *Leviathan* is now ready for another patrol somewhere in the Mediterranean. This is Bill Seamans, ABC News in Haifa.

SMITH (AND VIZMO):

Several Arab states complained bitterly today that Russia has begun helping Israel by easing the ban on Jewish emigration from Russia.

Lebanon's premier said that every Jew who moves to Israel is a more serious threat than a tank or a plane. And Jordan complained that Russia is allowing "experts in warfare" to move to Tel Aviv.

The Russians complained today that their diplomats in the United States are being constantly harassed by members of the Jewish Defense League who call them on the telephone all hours of the day and night. The Russians say the JDL wants to tie up their phone lines, and block all normal communication.

BILLBOARD

COMMERCIAL

REASONER (AND VIZMO):

There were these developments today in the still-confused story of northwest South Vietnam and Laos:

REVEAL: SPLAT

Enemy mortars and rockets hit Khe Sanh for the fifth straight day and are apparently getting more accurate: they seem to be aiming at helicopter landing and holding areas, and today when the fire was intensive, helicopters had to move out to bases to the east.

REVEAL: ARROW

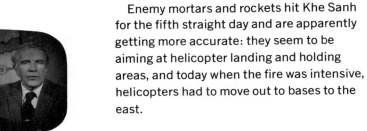

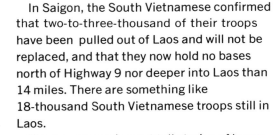

In Saigon, the South Vietnamese confirmed that two-to-three-thousand of their troops have been pulled out of Laos and will not be replaced, and that they now hold no bases north of Highway 9 nor deeper into Laos than 14 miles. There are something like 18-thousand South Vietnamese troops still in Laos.

The troops coming out tell stories of heavy fighting and of unremitting pressure from the enemy. ABC's Jim Giggans reports from the South Vietnamese command center just inside South Vietnam:

VTR OF SATELLITE FEED FROM GIGGANS.

GIGGANS (ON CAMERA AMID SOLDIERS):

:09

A short time ago, these South Vietnamese troops were fighting in the Tchepone area of Laos. But now they've been withdrawn back here to Vietnam.

'COPTERS LANDING, MEN ARRIVE

:12

NATURAL SOUND—'COPTERS

:03

This appears to be the most massive withdrawal yet of South Vietnamese forces from Laos. Hundreds of them were brought by helicopter here to Ham Nghi, the South Vietnamese command center for the Laotian operation. Most of these men had been in the Tchepone area since the Laotian operation began. They were obviously happy to be back home, but told tales of low morale, panic, and constant enemy fire during their stay in Laos.

CAMERA PAN FROM 'COPTERS TO FOLLOW SMILING

SOLDIERS DOWN ROAD

:07

MAN WEEPS, JOINS OTHER SOLDIERS

:15

This man is crying because his brother was killed during the withdrawal. He says that his unit suffered at least 30 percent casualties. He's disillusioned now, and bitter. But so are many of his fellow soldiers. Some told me they were withdrawn from Laos because they refused to fight any longer. They had had enough of being under constant enemy fire.

And they had threatened to surrender if they weren't withdrawn.

MEN GET OUT OF 'COPTERS

:12

'COPTERS IN AIR

:15

First, these helicopters went in to take out as many of the dead and wounded as they could. Those they couldn't take out were left in the Laotian jungles.

'COPTER UNLOADS WOUNDED

:09

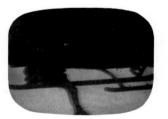

Next came the troop withdrawal. Many of these men say it was a hectic, harrowing experience, with soldiers clawing and fighting to get aboard. The South Vietnamese commanders here still will not refer to this as a withdrawal. They prefer terms such as "redeployment" and "rotation."

MEN WASH HANDS AND ARMS

:06

But they admit that these men will not be replaced in Laos. Despite their leaders' semantics, these men say they *were* withdrawn and that thousands more soon will be following them.

MEN WAIT AROUND AMBULANCES

:08

Jim Giggans, ABC News, Ham Nghi, South Vietnam.

REASONER (AND VIZMO):

The jury in the trial of Lieutenant William Calley had more testimony read to them today. The defense objected that the case is being re-tried, but the judge said the jury is just being properly careful in its deliberations. The jury will meet for a full day tomorrow and resume consideration of the case Sunday after church.

CHANGE VIZMO

Brigadier General George Young Junior accused the Army today of making him a "political scapegoat" by proposing to demote him for his role in the My Lai incident.

General Young said the Army's action was linked to a House speech by Congressman Samuel Stratton of New York, who complained that high-ranking officers were being let off in the My Lai case.

BILLBOARD

COMMERCIAL

SMITH (AND VIZMO):

The cost of living rose again last month, a familiar theme over the past three years. But this time there's cause for encouragement. The increase was only two-tenths of one percent. Added to the January figure of one-tenth of a percent, we have the smallest two-month rise in the last four years. Labor Secretary Hodgson said the figures prove the economy is now headed in the right direction, and the White House called it "encouraging news."

CHANGE VIZMO

There was also encouragement for the administration today on the touch-and-go issue of the S–S–T.

The House cut off funds for the plane yesterday, but the Senate Appropriations Committee voted today to restore them.

What's more, three members of the committee who opposed the project last year came out in favor of it. The question will be put to a vote before the entire Senate next Wednesday afternoon, and the outcome is still uncertain.

One of the big arguments for the S–S–T has been that the Russians and the French already have one. But ABC's Science Editor, Jules Bergman, reports those projects are still not a proven success:

VTR TRANSFER: BERGMAN V/O
CONCORDE TAKING OFF

:12

[BERGMAN]: If America's S–S–T is killed, it'll enhance the Concorde's chances of success — but economics are against the British-French S-S-T. It'll carry only 110 people — not enough to pay back its 30-million dollar cost. As TWA President F.C. Wiser told us, "It's a first-class plane in a tourist age." Somewhat slower than the American S–S–T's projected speed — flying at 14-hundred miles an hour — the Concorde has

DISSOLVE TO CONCORDE CRUISING

:18

succeeded technically. But that's not enough. The demise of the American S–S–T would clear the decks for the Super-Concorde—a bigger 250-passenger version that would make money but would cost almost as much to build—two billion—as the first Concorde itself. TWA and Pan Am say they'll buy a few Concordes—if they have to—to compete with Air France and BOAC.

CONCORD LANDING

:13

DISSOLVE TO TU-144 TAKE-OFF AND IN AIR

:09

The unknown is Russia's TU-144—which goes into operation this October—three years ahead of the Concorde. It's slightly faster, carries about the same number of passengers, and the Russians have launched an all-out sales drive. After chalking up sales in Japan—they're wooing India—and now a Louisiana aircraft broker claims to have been appointed U-S sales agent.

TU-144 CRUISING

:15

Pan Am has declared they might be interested. TWA thinks it unlikely they'd ever fly a Soviet-built plane. The big lure is price: the Russians—because they've buried the rubles—and are willing to take a loss to penetrate the Western market—can sell at discount prices. No firm figure has been announced—but reportedly the TU-144's price will be about half that of the Concorde.

DISSOLVE TO TU-144 LANDING VARIOUS SHOTS

:27

And for an airline that wants to be first with supersonics — that's a tremendous come-on. This is Jules Bergman, ABC News reporting.

SMITH (AND VIZMO):

Yesterday, the Penn Central revealed that it had lost 277 freight cars, and that some of them had been found on the tracks of an obscure line in Illinois. Today a lot of people, including the Justice Department, are asking,

CHANGE VIZMO

"How can you lose even one freight car so big?" Well, the answer is simple: You paint out the owner's name, you change the serial numbers, and you get the car rolling again. For more on this tale of intrigue on the Midwestern prairie, here is ABC's Kenneth Gale in LaSalle, Illinois:

SWITCH TO CHICAGO FOR FILM: GALE V/O

HIGH SHOT, BOX CARS

:06

[GALE]: The FBI says it has found and impounded 28 box cars on which Penn Central markings have been painted over with the initials of the LaSalle and Bureau County Railroad. They're suspected of being stolen through a scheme that involved the legitimate business to repair and rebuild old box cars.

MS, CARS WITH LS&BC MARKINGS

:10

Last July, a company called Magna Earth leased an office from the L-S-and-B-C Railroad and contracted to rebuild 466 old Penn Central box cars. The FBI says most of those cars were properly delivered. But Federal authorities also say that 277 freight cars, worth more than a million dollars, were apparently shuttled onto the L-S-and-B-C siding as contraband. The FBI says many of the cars could have been fed into other lines throughout the country.

LS&BC BLDG

:06

N.Y. CENTRAL CARS

:05

LS&BC LOCOMOTIVE PULLING FREIGHT TRAIN

:20

A secretary of the Magna Earth Company, the only person to be found in their office here, said L-S-and-B-C had agreed to let their initials be painted on the old box cars. But officials of the railroad say they're at a loss to explain the entire mystery. Railroad industry records show the L-S-and-B-C has 495 box cars. But a company official says he doesn't know just how much rolling stock his railroad has on inventory now.

VARIOUS SHOTS, N.Y.C. FREIGHT CARS PARKED

:25

Kenneth Gale, ABC News, LaSalle, Illinois.

SMITH:

We'll have more news in a moment.

BILLBOARD

GEER: ROGERS & EBAN
GIGGANS: ARVN PULLOUT
GALE: STOLEN BOXCARS
KOPPEL: PAKISTAN CRISIS ←
JARRIEL: DEWEY RITES
COMMENT: SPIN-OFFS

COMMERCIAL

REASONER (AND VIZMO):

Northern Ireland's Premier James Chichester-Clark has apparently postponed a decision to resign after today's emergency cabinet meeting in Belfast. The Prime Minister has been caught in the middle by extremists on both sides of the current crisis. A report now from ABC's John Rolfson in Belfast:

FILM: ROLFSON V/O
LS, PARLIAMENT
:05

[Rolfson]: Several thousand right-wing Protestants marched on Parliament, demanding the Prime Minister's resignation, just as he was reporting on the near-failure of his last-ditch appeal to the British government. Prime Minister Chichester-Clark was frustrated and bitter that the British government gave only a feeble reply to his demand for a vigorous British crackdown on rioting and terrorism here in Northern Ireland.

MS, MARCHERS
:07

DEMONSTRATORS AROUND PARLIAMENT
BUILDING, VARIOUS SHOTS
:16

PLACARDS

:14

The slogans of these demonstrators here in Belfast call for a far more extreme solution. They would have the Protestant majority take law and order into its own hands. Some Catholic leaders say it will mean civil war if these right-wing Protestants come to power or even if they are substantially represented in a new government. Moderate Protestant leaders insist that Northern Ireland is now alarmingly close to a complete breakdown of law and order, or a right-wing takeover. They insist that neither Mr. Chichester-Clark nor any other moderate Prime Minister can govern without a quick change of British policy.

DEMONSTRATORS SHAKE FISTS,

JUMP UP AND DOWN

:19

SOME MORE PLACID DEMONSTRATORS JUST STAND

AROUND

:12

John Rolfson, ABC News in Belfast.

REASONER (AND VIZMO):

Talks are going on in the capital of East Pakistan, trying to avoid complete chaos in an area that is very near to chaos.

The talkers are Sheikh Mujib Rahman, the major political leader of the eastern state, and President Yahya Khan, who is of West Pakistan as are most of the soldiers trying to keep order in the East.

ABC's Ted Koppel is in Dacca, the capital of East Pakistan, and sends this report from an area of disproportionate misery:

VTR OF SATELLITE FEED FROM KOPPEL,
SURROUNDED BY BENGALIS
KOPPEL (ON CAMERA):
  :17

Things in East Pakistan are so bad that its people — the Bengalis — are understandably tempted to believe that any change will be an improvement. And so, with a growing mood of national euphoria, they are being swept onto a collision course with West Pakistan — a course which may already be beyond change.

SIGNS ON STORES AND BUILDINGS
  :14

The only language that East and West Pakistanis have in common is English. English signs on shops have been painted or taped out of sight. Anything that smacks of communicating with West Pakistan is considered undesirable.

FLAGS FLUTTER FROM ROOFTOPS AND VEHICLES
:15

POSTERS WITH SHEIKH'S PICTURE
:08

SHEIKH SEATED IN YARD, FACING KOPPEL
:10

CU, SHEIKH—SOF:
:08

The black flag is now practically a national symbol. It's displayed on houses, shops, cars, trucks and bicycle rickshaws. It's in remembrance of the Bengalis who've been killed during the past three weeks by West Pakistani troops. The man who hoisted the black flag—the man who has brought East Pakistan to the very brink of declaring its independence from the west—is Sheikh Mujibur Rahman. In the east, Sheikh Mujib—as his followers call him—has a virtual monopoly on political power. But West Pakistan has the army.

The mechanized army cannot fight here. They might kill some people, of course. We know that. But ultimately, victory is the people's victory.

MS, KOPPEL—SOF:

:07

You realize, of course, Sheikh Mujib, that there is a spectre of violence now looming over East Pakistan. Does that frighten you?

CU, SHEIKH—SOF

:10

CU, SHEIKH

KOPPEL SOF

:07

CU, SHEIKH—SOF

:07

KOPPEL V/O DEMONSTRATORS CROWD SIDEWALKS AND FILL A TRUCK

:22

LOCKED GATE, ZOOM BACK TO SHOW LARGE BUILDING THAT SEEMS DESERTED

:06

[SHEIKH]: If they decide to use force, my people will resist it, with whatever resources they have.

[KOPPEL]: Other than 75 million people, do they have the resources in terms of arms to fight a very modern army?

[SHEIKH]: You have seen in many countries of the world—while there is tension, the people can wait.

[KOPPEL]: While Sheikh Mujib meets privately here in Dacca with Pakistan's President, Yahya Khan, his followers keep the machinery of protest limbered up. These demonstrations are relaxed, loosely organized—something to keep the people busy. Sheikh Mujib has closed down almost all government agencies. Most large businesses have been closed also. The demonstrations now have something of a carnival atmosphere to them, and the army remains out of sight.

TRUCKS LOADED WITH FLAG-WAVING PAKISTANIS,
SOME WITH GUNS

:19

But unless major concessions are made by both sides, and that does not seem likely at this time, East Pakistan will experience some of the worst violence in its brief and troubled history.

This is Ted Koppel, ABC News, Dacca.

REASONER (AND VIZMO):

An avalanche struck a mining camp set apart in the mountains 55 miles north of Lima, Peru, today, burying it in water and mud and rocks. Estimates are that as many as 600 of the one thousand persons in the camp may have been killed.

BILLBOARD

GEER: ROGERS & EBAN
GIGGANS: ARVN PULLOUT
GALE: STOLEN BOXCARS
KOPPEL: PAKISTAN CRISIS
JAPRIEL: DEWEY RITES
COMMENT: SPIN-OFFS

COMMERCIAL

REASONER (AND VIZMO—"PEOPLE PLACES AND
THINGS"):

In other news:

CHANGE VIZMO

REVEAL: BRAND NAMES

The Food and Drug Administration today
urged householders and restaurants to throw
away any package of meat tenderizer labeled
"Spice of Life" or "Country Tavern,"
purchased after March of 1969. The warning
had been issued five months ago, but the
death of a Maryland man last Sunday is
linked to the product. Its makers had
mistakenly filled some containers with the
poison, nitrite, instead of tenderizer. The
FDA thought all of the dangerous batch had
been accounted for, but some apparently got
sprinkled on garlic toast in a Maryland
restaurant on Sunday.

CHANGE VIZMO

With spring officially only two days away, a
heavy late winter storm has hit the Midwest,
leaving up to 16 inches of snow in some
areas. The storm is moving east, and gale
warnings are in force on the Great Lakes.

CHANGE VIZMO

In New York, there was rain this afternoon as many of the nation's leaders gathered for the funeral of Thomas E. Dewey. Among those present were President and Mrs. Nixon. ABC's White House Correspondent, Tom Jarriel, reports:

FILM JARRIEL V/O CHURCH EXTERIOR

:05

CROWD ON SIDEWALK

:04

LOWELL THOMAS ENTERS CHURCH

:05

[JARRIEL]: The funeral for Governor Dewey was held at St. James Church in midtown Manhattan. Several hundred spectators clustered beneath umbrellas along curbs to watch the arrival of dignitaries. Although Dewey has been largely retired from the political scene for the past decade, his influence of the '50s was evident by today's turnout.

OTHERS ENTER

:06

NIXONS OUT OF CAR AND INTO CHURCH

:07

President Nixon led an official entourage from Washington which included top cabinet officials plus Senators and Congressmen from New York.

ROCKY AND WIFE

:03

Governor Rockefeller came, along with Mayor Lindsay and former Vice President Hubert Humphrey. They heard the man who failed twice in his bid for the Presidency eulogized as a "good and faithful servant of the American people."

LINDSAY

:03

HUMPHREY AND WIFE

:04

CHURCH EXTERIOR

:03

DISSOLVING TO CASKET BEING CARRIED OUT

:18

Following simple rites from the Episcopal Book of Common Prayer, the body was taken to Dewey's home at Pawling, New York, for burial.

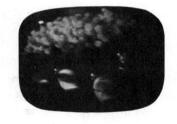

SIDEWALK CROWD

:04

NIXONS WALK OUT AND AWAY

:12

The late Thomas Dewey is best remembered for his narrow defeat by Harry Truman in 1948. However, Dewey's most significant contribution to national politics was his strength as an adviser and a behind-the-scenes man who is credited with having shaped the good political fortunes of such Republicans as Eisenhower and Nixon.

Tom Jarriel, ABC News, New York.

REASONER:

Howard will be back with tonight's
comment in a moment.

BILLBOARD

GEER: ROGERS & EBAN
GIGGANS: ARVN PULLOUT
GALE: STOLEN BOXCARS
KOPPEL: PAKISTAN CRISIS
JARRIEL: DEWEY RITES
COMMENT: SPIN-OFFS

COMMERCIAL

SMITH (AND VIZMO):

COMMERCIAL
COMMENTARY

There is now pretty much of a consensus
that, in a time of urgent human problems,
things like Defense and Space ought to be
cut to the bone, and most of those programs
have been. But nothing is simple any more.
Those cuts involve a tremendous danger.

Together, Defense and Space have caused
a huge basic research program in this
country. And due to it, we have learned
things, unrelated to Defense and Space, that
have become vital to our national life.

For example, finding out the miracle of
sending men to the moon and back forced us
to find ways of learning things we had no way
of knowing. It forced us—among other
things—to develop computers, now the basis
of our technical leadership in the world, to
unheard-of perfection. That is one of
thousands of spin-offs that have, to mix
metaphors, become the underpinning of our

output of wealth and our competitiveness in the world.

Well, with the cuts now, that research has almost stopped.

CHANGE VIZMO

Here is a measure to think about: Because of cuts, last year we graduated 140-thousand engineers and scientists to Russia's 250-thousand. At this rate, in five years we will graduate 180-thousand to Russia's 360-thousand. Ten or fifteen years of that and it will show and it will hurt.

CHANGE VIZMO

Once the U–S led the world in automotive technology. Now we buy more cars from other nations than we sell to them. Once we led in electronics. Now Japan does, and other nations are advancing.

CHANGE VIZMO

If desirable cuts persist, undesirable results will follow. We may cease to be competitive. We may not be able to create the wealth to meet those big human problems.

I don't know what to do about it. But we ought to think about it.

Harry.

REASONER (AND VIZMO):

Thank you, Howard.
That's tonight's news and comment. I'm
Harry Reasoner. Good night.

CBS EVENING NEWS
WITH WALTER CRONKITE
March 19, 1971

ANNOUNCER (IN BOOTH):

[KRAMER]: Direct from our newsroom in New York, this is the CBS Evening News with Walter Cronkite . . .

CLICKER*

and Bob Schieffer in Washington . . .
Nelson Benton in Washington . . .
Richard Threlkeld in Seattle . . .
Robert Pierpoint in New York . . .
Richard Wagner in LaSalle, Illinois . . .
David Schoumacher in Boston, and
Bill Stout in Los Angeles.

CRONKITE (ON CAMERA):

Good evening.
About one-thousand more battle-weary South Vietnamese were airlifted out of Laos today, to Khe Sanh in South Vietnam. And at Khe Sanh, the Communists kept up their shelling — forcing American helicopters to abandon the base from time to time because of the heavy fire.

*Names and datelines on the "clicker" are added one at a time, to coincide with copy being read.

CHANGE RP

This pullout leaves less than 15-thousand South Vietnamese still in Laos. At the operation's peak, some 24-thousand were there. At its deepest the South Vietnamese drive into Laos reached the key town of Sepone on the Ho Chi Minh trail—some 27 miles inside Laos. At one time they had six fire bases around Sepone. But since the start of the North Vietnamese counter-offensive, they have abandoned base after base, and now they have no bases left, north of Highway 9, and their defense outpost today—the farthest into Laos—is Fire Base Aluoi—just ten miles inside the border.

CHANGE RP

CHANGE RP

We've a report from Bob Schieffer on how some Pentagon people are evaluating the Laos campaign:

SCHIEFFER:

The senior Defense officials admitted for the first time today that the Laotian campaign is ending sooner than expected. These officials contended that the operation has been successful to a point, and that the enemy has paid heavily in men and material. And they contend the enemy timetable has been upset.

But they concede, in effect, that the South Vietnamese are being driven out of Laos by an overwhelming enemy force. Pentagon spokesman Jerry Friedheim declined comment except to say the South Vietnamese are still doing what they want to do — disrupt enemy supply lines. He said he would not be surprised if what he termed "a methodical redeployment" is now underway. He said he could not say when the operation will end. He said it may go on another month.

[SCHIEFFER]: These films, which arrived in New York today, show wounded South Vietnamese troopers being brought out of Laos by American helicopter earlier this week.

Meanwhile, field reports today told of South Vietnamese who said the fighting had been so fierce they were ready to surrender. Official spokesmen say between two- and three-thousand South Vietnamese troops have been brought out of Laos in the last 48 hours. Field reports told of other troops being removed, without announcement. About 15-thousand South Vietnamese troops are still believed inside Laos. Pentagon spokesmen from the beginning have stressed there was no plan to take and hold territory in Laos. But today, one source added: "We had hoped to hold some of the artillery positions a bit longer." He said the weather, which often kept American helicopters on the ground, was the main stumbling block. Another source said it has become obvious now that the South Vietnamese would have remained longer in Laos, if the enemy had not chosen to engage them in such force.

DISSOLVE TO FILM: 'COPTER LANDS. NATURAL SOUND UP BRIEFLY THEN UNDER

:06

SCHIEFFER V/O

WOUNDED MEN BEING CARRIED ON STRETCHERS AND HELPED TO WALK AWAY FROM HELICOPTERS

:40

FILM ENDS
SCHIEFFER (ON CAMERA):

Still, these sources insist that the enemy has been hurt badly. For the first time, they say, the enemy was forced to mass his troops. When that happened, the troops became easy targets for American bombers. They say thousands of enemy troops were killed in air strikes, and scores of enemy tanks and trucks were destroyed. These strikes, they say, were the main reason for most enemy deaths. They also say that, while enemy troops were tied down fighting the South Vietnamese, they were forced to virtually abandon their efforts to move supplies south.

This, officials here contend, will seriously hamper the enemy's ability to wage war in South Vietnam while the American troop withdrawals are underway. At least, that is the Administration hope.

Bob Schieffer, CBS News, Washington.

CRONKITE (AND RP):

In Cambodia today, the Vietcong captured an unguarded bridge on Highway 5, cutting off Pnom Penh from Badambang Province, where much of the city's rice comes from. Planes were called in to strafe the Communists while traffic piled up on the road. The local Cambodian commander said the bridge was seized during the night, after the guards went home.

CHANGE RP

Families of Americans held prisoner in North Vietnam have been complaining of not getting any mail from the men since Christmas. But today, a group with contacts in Hanoi said it has received a shipment of 193 letters. The group blamed the delay on the fighting in Laos which, it said, held up the messengers who take the P–O–W mail in and out of North Vietnam.

At a White House ceremony today, President Nixon proclaimed next week as a special period of observance for the 16-hundred Americans missing or held prisoner in Southeast Asia.

West Coast businessman, John Fairfax, has returned from almost a month in Vientiane, Laos. And there, representing a group of affluent Americans, including Bing Crosby, he approached Communist officials on a plan to free the U–S prisoners. In Los Angeles today, Fairfax said the offer to the North Vietnamese is to help finance the nation's postwar reconstruction, in trade for immediate release of the prisoners.

TITLE SLIDE

COMMERCIAL

CRONKITE (AND RP):

Moving quickly in the wake of House rejection, the Senate Appropriations Committee has set up still another Congressional battle over the supersonic transport.

By a vote of 7 to 5 today, the committee approved continued funding of the S–S–T and sent the issue to a floor battle scheduled for next Wednesday. Both supporters and opponents of the controversial plane say the Senate showdown will be close, and even if the supporters win, the issue would have to go back to the House — which, by a narrow margin, voted yesterday to cut off S–S–T funds.

CHANGE RP

The end of the S–S–T, being built by Boeing, would further aggravate one of the worst unemployment situations in the nation. From Seattle, Richard Threlkeld reports:

FILM: LS, PAN OF S–S–T MOCKUP

  :08

WORKERS ON ASSEMBLY LINE

  :10

[THRELKELD]: The only S–S–T that Boeing has put together at this point is an airplane that will never fly—an aluminum test mock-up. And now that there's a good chance the real S–S–T will never get off the ground, the skilled workers here on the assembly line are beginning to worry about their own future.

WORKER WITH NAME SUPERED

  :20

[HANSEN]: Well, you wonder whether the gates are going to be closed or not when you come in the morning.

[THRELKELD]: What's going to happen now if this plane is not funded? What'll happen to people like you?

[HANSEN]: Well, a lot of us will be downgraded somemore, and shifted around. Others will be going out the door.

2D WORKER WITH NAME SUPERED.

  :16

[BEARD]: Well, I imagine with the seniority I have here, I'll probably get laid off, because I don't have that much seniority with the company.

[THRELKELD]: What would you do then? About finding another job?

[BEARD]: Well, I don't know. I'd just have to scout around I guess. I don't know what I'd do. At my age, I don't know whether I can find a job or not.

ZOOM BACK FROM CU OF TAIL TO WIDE SHOT OF
MOCK-UP

:09

LS, BOEING PLANT

:05

747'S ON AIRPORT RUNWAY

:08

AERIAL SHOT, SEATTLE

:04

STREET SCENE

:05

EMPTY STORES, "FOR RENT" SIGNS

:09

MS, PLANT AND WORKERS

:10

SWEIHART:

:25

HIGH SHOT, S–S–T MOCK-UP

:06

WORKMEN ON ASSEMBLY LINE

:08

PAN OF MOCK-UP

:07

[THRELKELD]: There's good reason for concern now about the future of Boeing , too. The company has laid off more than half its work forces in the last three years, and there are more cutbacks to come. The 747 is not selling nearly as well as Boeing would like. It will take another year, and a lot of luck, before this plane will even begin to show a profit. And when Boeing gets the sniffles, Seattle catches cold. Unemployment here is approaching depression-era levels of 14 percent. Seattle is such a one-industry town that every time Boeing fires one worker, two others lose their jobs in related industries.

The demise of the S–S–T would force layoffs of 6-thousand more of Boeing's most skilled technicians, and Chief Engineer John Sweihart is angry about it:

Well, actually, the tragedy of this vote yesterday was that we have a team of men that we have assembled over a 12-year period that has advance the technology of the United States in airframe design. And this vote means that this team is going to be disbanded, so that the United States is going to lose 12 years of the best aeronautical development we've ever done.

[THRELKELD]: In pressing on with the S–S–T in the face of strong economic and environmental arguments, the U–S aircraft industry may have gambled away the future of supersonic transport altogether. Boeing admits it can't afford to build the S–S–T on its own, and right now, neither can the airlines.

THRELKELD (ON CAMERA):
:17

Such are the incredible cost factors in a project this size, that even if Congress does back out of the S–S–T program, it's still going to cost the government a lot of money — more than a hundred million dollars in penalty costs.

Richard Threlkeld, CBS News, Seattle.

CRONKITE (ON CAMERA):

A Federal audit of 61 defense contracts shows cost over-runs amounting to 33-and-a-third billion dollars — or about 40 percent more than anticipated. The study, by the General Accounting Office, involves weapons still in development or production — including the C–5–A super-transport and the Mark 48 torpedo. The auditors added, however, that under Deputy Defense Secretary Packard, the situation has improved in recent months. The G–A–O said the reasons for the excessive costs could range from unexpected development problems to deliberate under-estimating.

TITLE SLIDE

COMMERCIAL

CRONKITE (ON CAMERA):

Israeli Foreign Minister Abba Eban spent the day in Washington, talking over the Middle East deadlock with Secretary of State Rogers. Nelson Benton reports:

BENTON V/O EBAN WALKS WITH CROWD OF
NEWSMEN
  :05
DISSOLVE TO TWO-SHOT, EBAN AND ROGERS
  :15

[BENTON]: Eban met at the State
Department for nearly two hours of talks with
Rogers—talks that Eban said created a better
understanding between the two governments
on their differences on the approach to
peace in the Middle East. Secretary Rogers
had earlier cited an impasse in the Middle
East negotiations.

Leaving his meeting with Rogers, Eban held
a different view:

DISSOLVE EBAN SOF:
  :27

I think there is objectively no deadlock at
all. I think there are several ways in which the
Jarring mission could move forward. I
discussed some of them with Ambassador
Jarring yesterday.

CUTAWAY
  :03

There is, from our point of view, the
possibility of getting into a concrete and
detailed discussion of all questions of peace,
refugees, boundaries, withdrawal—all of
these things are now open, I think, for a
concrete and detailed discussion.

BENTON V/O EBAN DEPARTS
  :04
LS, NEWS CNF
  :03

[BENTON]: The State Department declined
comment on the apparent difference in views.
At a news conference later, the Israeli Foreign
Minister said there have been positive
developments in negotiations. He gave credit
to his own country, the United States, the
Arab states—but none to the Soviet Union.

MS, EBAN AND REPORTERS

:09

EBAN SOF:

:33

There is some progress toward realism, although that progress has not yet reached the point at which a final settlement is in view. Further movement, we think, is needed.

So we would say that these are the main factors. And I wouldn't give the Soviet Union credit for any of these positive developments, because its policy has been one of unilateral and massive rearmament of the Arab states — blind identification, unbalanced support for the Arab positions.

BENTON (ON CAMERA):

Eban also met with Presidential Adviser Henry Kissinger. He said he was not pressured to change his country's views on negotiations — that he came here to exchange views, not to change them.

Nelson Benton, CBS News, Washington.

CRONKITE (AND RP):

For the first time since the Middle East truce began last August, Egypt reported today its anti-aircraft guns fired at Israeli jets — two American-built Phantoms, the Egyptians say, were shot at when they flew over the north end of the Suez Canal.

Neither apparently was hit, and Israel has had no comment on the incident.

CRONKITE (RP OUT):

There's a story out of Beirut that the Lebanese premier has complained to the Russian ambassador about Moscow's letting Russian Jews go to Israel. The complaint was made at a banquet given by the Russians. The

Premier told the Russian that each Jew who enters Israel is a greater threat to the Arabs than a tank or a plane.

CRONKITE (AND RP):

Relations between Mexico and the Soviet Union are at their lowest point in years. Yesterday, Mexico recalled its ambassador to Moscow and ordered five Soviet diplomats out of its country. The Mexicans say they have uncovered a Soviet-financed plot to finance guerrillas intent on overthrowing the government. Some 50 Mexicans, it is said, went to North Korea for training in guerrilla warfare.

CHANGE RP

Turkey will soon have a new premier, ending a threat of a military takeover. Fifty-eight-year-old Nehat Erim, a political veteran with strong leanings toward the West, says he has the support of all political parties. Erim has the backing of the country's generals, as well. They were the ones who forced Premier Demirel to quit last week because of leftist disorders.

CHANGE RP

COMMERCIAL

CRONKITE (AND RP):

The cost of living went up two-tenths of one percent last month. That's double the figure for January. Food and clothing last month went up much more than other consumer items.

Nevertheless, the rise in February is much less than the recent inflationary rate. So, the White House calls today's report "encouraging news." And Labor Secretary Hodgson says the effort to stabilize prices is clearly headed in the right direction.

Two weeks ago, the Labor Department reported a slight drop in the unemployment rate. At the time, Hodgson called that drop "heartening." But simultaneously, at a press briefing, a professional underling, a statistician, called the figures "mixed." Today, the Department announced: No more briefings, for either cost of living or unemployment reports. The stated reason—to avoid embarrassing the professional staff with questions that make policy implications.

Funeral services were conducted in New York today for former Governor Thomas Dewey, twice the Republican presidential nominee. President Nixon was among the mourners. Robert Pierpoint reports:

CHANGE RP

CHANGE RP

PIERPOINT V/O CROWD AT CHURCH

:04

[PIERPONT]: St. James Episcopal Church, in midtown Manhattan, is in dramatic contrast to the other burial service President Nixon attended this week—the one Tuesday for Whitney Young at a small segregated cemetery outside Lexington, Kentucky.

LIMOUSINE ARRIVES, NIXONS GET OUT AND ENTER CHURCH

:16

LS, CHURCH AND CROWD
:09

SENS. BUCKLEY AND JAVITS, OTHER
WASHINGTONIANS
:12
HUMPHREY AND WIFE ARRIVE
:09

CHURCH EXTERIOR
:07
PEOPLE ON SIDEWALK WITH UMBRELLAS
:04
CASKET CARRIED OUT
:27

Thomas Edmund Dewey had been a vital factor in the President's early days in public life — had, in fact, urged General Eisenhower to put the young California senator on the ticket that resulted in Richard Nixon's becoming Vice President.

With him from Washington today, President Nixon brought two members of his cabinet, both New York senators, Supreme Court Justice Harlan, and several Presidential aides. Former Vice President Humphrey and his wife came separately.

Mr. Nixon did not speak at this ceremony. Instead, the eulogy was in the form of a prayer — delivered by the Reverend Ralph C. Lankler, pastor of the Church of Christ on Quaker Hill near Dewey's country retreat in Pawling, New York. The Reverend Lankler said of Dewey: "We are grateful for all good men who have sought public office — not for the power it represents or the prestige it gives, but for the opportunity it presents to serve the people and the public good. We consider Thomas Dewey," he added, "to be such a man."

Dewey will be buried near his country home in Pawling. President and Mrs. Nixon have returned to the White House.

Robert Pierpoint, CBS News, New York.

CRONKITE (AND RP):

Peruvian officials believe 400 to 600 lead and copper miners have been killed after an earthquake sent an avalanche and a flood roaring into a tiny mining town, high in the Andes mountains. A spokesman for the mining company says the town, northeast of the capital of Lima, has practically disappeared under the debris.

CHANGE RP

In the past three years, Congress has allocated almost 100-million dollars to help educate children of migrant farm workers. Well today, a private group interested in this cause asserted that about a fifth of the money has never been spent, and much of the rest has been ill-spent. A spokesman charged poor Federal administration, indifference by state agencies who would use the money, and tardiness by Congress in appropriating it. The predictable results, according to the report — poor food and medical services for the children, and few of them graduate from high school.

In Chicago, a member of the Federal task force on organized crime says theft, and not accidental loss, is involved in the diversion of Penn Central freight cars to a tiny spur line in Illinois.

CHANGE RP

That's where the investigation is now centered, and Richard Wagner reports:

FILM: WAGNER V/O
LS&BC BLDGS.
:08

[WAGNER]: The great LaSalle, Illinois, box car mystery now seems to be at least a little less mysterious. FBI officials in Chicago indicate they know the whereabouts of some of the 277 missing Penn Central freight cars. The Bureau says it has actually found 28 of them — along the short right-of-way of the LaSalle and Bureau County Railroad — 100 miles from Chicago. The L-S-and-B-C building also houses a mysterious firm called Magna Earth Enterprises, which has been bringing in old and damaged freight cars–repairing and refurbishing them. The LaSalle and Bureau County Railroad provided the shop facilities and the feeder track. What is still a mystery is exactly who was responsible for painting over

CU, RR TRACKS, TILT UP TO SHOW RR SHOPS
:06
PENN CENTRAL CARS,
:06

LS&BC BUILDING

:06

the emblems of the Penn Central and the old New York Central, thus making it appear that the cars really belonged to the little L-S-and-B-C Railroad. Officials of the LaSalle and Bureau County road deny any criminal intent on their part. They say they merely rented space to Magna Earth.

PEOPLE ENTER BLDG.

:03

FREIGHT CARS

:07

WIDE SHOT, LS&BC SHOPS

:05

CU, "PC" EMBLEM, MS OF SAME

:06

WIDE SHOT, LOCOMOTIVE WITH FULL NAME OF

LS&BC

:05

BOX CARS

:19

LS, RR BLDGS.

:04

The representative of Magna Earth in LaSalle has been unavailable for comment. So, as of the moment, the situation seems to be this: A small part of the loot has been found, but who did it and just how it was done, have yet to be determined.

Richard Wagner, CBS News, LaSalle, Illinois.

CRONKITE AND RP:

The averages were generally lower on the New York Stock Exchange today. Volume was 15-million 150-thousand shares.

CHANGE RP

The average price per share fell seven cents on the New York Exchange, and four cents on the American.

ZOOM IN, RP OUT

The Food and Drug Administration has repeated an urgent warning it issued last November: throw out any containers of meat tenderizer labeled "Country Tavern" or "Spice of Life." The brands were recalled when it was revealed that some containers were filled with a deadly poison. Officials believed that all the contaminated containers were recovered . . . and then, last Sunday, a Washington D.C. suburbanite died after consuming some of the mislabeled product in a restaurant.

CRONKITE (AND RP):

Trumpeter Louis Armstrong is reported to be improving and is now considered in satisfactory condition at the New York hospital where he is being treated for a heart ailment.

FILM: CRONKITE V/O COPS WITH GUNS AROUND
BANK
:09

GLASS DOORS, MAN ON OTHER SIDE WITH PISTOL
:11
MAN WITH PISTOL COMES OUT, SHIELDING
HIMSELF WITH A WOMAN, THEY GET INTO A CAR
:09

CRONKITE (ON CAMERA):

[CRONKITE]: Yesterday afternoon, in Orlando, Florida, police — alerted by a silent alarm — surrounded the local American Federal Savings and Loan branch. Inside, a man with a pistol — later identified as Joseph Malenowskous — was preparing to leave with 8-thousand dollars in loot and two hostages. Well, escape he did — in an unarmed sheriff's car, with two unwilling companions — a lady teller and a branch manager.

The rest of the story is somewhat anti-climactic. Soon, he let the lady go. Still holding the manager, he commandeered another car. Then he asked the manager, "Do you want to go to a movie?" According to the manager, Ralph Hassler, the movie at a drive-in they were passing was one he wanted to see anyhow. He said "Yes."

So while the manhunt for them continued, the two men watched the movie for a while, then shared pizzas and beer. Then Malenowskous let Hassler go. The robber drove off and was captured without a struggle a short time later.

COMMERCIAL

CRONKITE (ON CAMERA):

The news media, and particularly CBS News, have come under attack again by Administration spokesmen.

Vice President Agnew, on the East Coast, and the Republican party's national chairman, Senator Dole of Kansas, on the West Coast, focused particularly on the recent CBS News documentary, "The Selling of the Pentagon."

Agnew's remarks were delivered in a speech in Boston last night, and at a news conference there this morning. David Schoumacher reports:

[SCHOUMACHER]: For the second straight day, the Vice President set his sights on CBS News—this time at a briefing restricted to local Boston reporters. National correspondents could not participate.

Mr. Agnew carefully underlined that his quarrel is with one network—CBS—and its president, Dr. Frank Stanton.

FILM: SCHOUMACHER V/O
AGNEW ENTERS, CHATS WITH REPORTERS
:18

AGNEW SOF:
:27

I have no thoughts of intimidation. I have no thoughts of asking for stronger laws to see that any prosecutions would take place. My purpose was simply to tell the American people, and to show them through uncontroverted evidence, based on substantial and complete investigation, that they cannot rely on CBS documentaries for facts.

SCHOUMACHER V/O AGNEW AND REPORTERS
:07

[SCHOUMACHER]: The attack on CBS occupied well over half the briefing, and at only one point did Mr. Agnew seem to soften his criticism.

AGNEW SOF:

  :31

I don't say that CBS is untrustworthy, nor do I imply that Mr. Stanton is untrustworthy. I just say that the media are not infallible, and they have acted as though they were infallible. And it's time that they began to realize that their infallibility is something less than concrete and they began to admit to human failings that the rest of us have.

SCHOUMACHER V/O REPORTERS

  :03

AGNEW STANDS AND DEPARTS

  :08

[SCHOUMACHER]: Again today, Mr. Agnew's staff insisted President Nixon is playing no part in this—is not even being told beforehand what the Vice President plans to say.

David Schoumacher, CBS News, Boston.

CRONKITE (ON CAMERA):

Senator Dole's criticism came at a news conference in Los Angeles, in response to questions about Agnew's remarks. Bill Stout was among the questioners:

SOUND ON FILM: NEWS CNF. SCENE

  :03

CU, DOLE

  :97

(NO CUTAWAYS)

[STOUT]: Senator, you mentioned network coverage of the war. Now that the Vice President has reverted to his role as critic-at-large of television, what do you think of his comments last night?

DOLE:

I haven't read his complete comments, but what I heard I liked. We witnessed last week—some of us in the Senate—the coverage by CBS and NBC of Laos. And I just happened to, uh, in the nine days of CBS coverage of the Vietnam war from February 25 through March 5, there were 115 separate statements about the Laos incursion, reported in 25 separate news items, and only 16 did not state or strongly imply criticism—either that the North Vietnamese were strong and we were weak—we were widening the war—and comments of this kind by various CBS commentators. And I think the

American people have a right to make a judgment and it's difficult to make a judgment if they only hear biased coverage on the nightly news.

[UNIDENTIFIED REPORTER, NOT SEEN]: How does that constitute biased coverage?

DOLE:

Well, I think that bias — and I've got it fairly well documented here — I just happened to bring it along. I can almost recite it book, chapter and verse. And then if you're in the Senate and you witness daily coverage of Senators, and which Senators receive the coverage, it adds to your feeling that it just isn't completely objective coverage. And despite what Cronkite may say, or Mr. Stanton might say, I don't think CBS has been particularly objective.

CRONKITE (ON CAMERA):

The CBS News documentary on which Agnew's attack focused, "The Selling of the Pentagon," will be rebroadcast next Tuesday night.

And that's the way it is — Friday, March 19th, 1971.

This is Walter Cronkite, CBS News.

Good night.

NBC NIGHTLY NEWS
March 19, 1971

ANNOUNCER (IN BOOTH):

This is the NBC Nightly News — with David Brinkley in Washington and in New York, Frank McGee.

MCGEE (AND VIZMO):

Good evening.
    The South Vietnamese have evacuated about 3-thousand troops from Laos in the last two days. American helicopters brought out more today and landed them at the base at Khe Sanh.

CHANGE VIZMO

Even as this was going on, North Vietnamese gunners poured about 50 rounds of rocket, mortar and artillery fire on the base.

CHANGE VIZMO

The South Vietnamese now hold no areas north of Highway 9 in Laos. Severing that highway — an important part of the Ho Chi Minh trail — was the principal objective of the invasion. Dozens of trucks — some reports say more than a hundred — are moving equipmen out of the South Vietnamese command headquarters near Khe Sanh.

CHANGE VIZMO

CHANGE VIZMO

VARIOUS SCENES, CHILDREN AND ADULTS AMONG
RUBBLE AND IN RURAL SETTING

:30

[STREITHORST]: My Lai—a name seared in the American consciousness—is now classified as a "pacified" village.

My Lai-4 was part of the area known as "the street without joy"—an enemy stronghold since the days of the French. Now, cows graze on the ruins of Viet Cong bunkers.

My Lai-4 was completely demolished and the people who lived there were relocated. Now, some of them have returned to live in a nearby hamlet with a different name. Songmy, where My Lai-4 was located, is now officially listed as "pacified," but it is ranked in the lowest category of pacified villages.

You still hear firing. There are mines and booby traps reported. It's not advised for outsiders to remain here at night.

BOY AND COWS

:12

BOY POINTS, THEN WALKS TO BUNKER

:10

The little boy in the American baseball cap — Nguyen Van Da, 10 — herds cows for a living. He was doing the same thing here when the American helicopters arrived. He led us to the bunker where he and his sister, now 13, had hidden.

BOY POINTS, CAMERA PANS DOWN TO DITCH

:10

MCU BOY

:04

GRAVES

:04

He pointed out the ditch which figured so prominently in the testimony at the Calley trial. He said that his grandmother, mother and father were among those herded into the ditch. He pointed to three mounds, marked simply with three pieces of wood, and said, "There are their graves."

MS, GIRL

:10

This little girl, playing with the remnants of a mortar round, is another survivor. But she didn't want to talk about it, not even to give her name.

ANOTHER GIRL, MS AND MCU

:15

Doh Fi Foh said she ran when she heard the helicopters land, and that running saved her life. She lost her husband and six other members of her family in the My Lai-4 incident.

The government authorities weren't too happy about our coming here. The United States American Division refused to accompany us. As one South Vietnamese civilian said, "My Lai is like a piece of filth. Nobody wants to touch it."

STREITHORST (ON CAMERA IN FIELD):

:23

Tom Streithorst, NBC News, in the remains of My Lai-4.

MCGEE (AND VIZMO):

There is nothing to indicate the jury in the court martial of Lieutenant William Calley will soon reach a verdict. Calley's attorney complained today that the six jurors want too much of the testimony re-read. And, he said, they're not investigators, they're a jury.

If need be, a whole day of deliberations is scheduled for tomorrow and a half day on Sunday.

TITLE SLIDE ANNOUNCER (IN BOOTH):

This is NBC Nightly News — Friday, March 19th, 1971, brought to you by. . . .

COMMERCIAL

BRINKLEY (ON CAMERA):

Yesterday, the House voted "no" on the S–S–T airplane — to spend no more tax money on it. The Senate votes next Wednesday.

Today, the Senate Appropriations Committee met and voted "yes." But in the full Senate the vote certainly will be close, and it likely will vote "no," but no one is certain about that.

Last night, after the House vote, several newly elected members of the House who voted "no" on the S–S–T told why:

MAZZOLI:

I voted nay yesterday, nay to the S–S–T, on basis that from the economic standpoint, it wasn't the best use of the money.

SEIBERLING:

A very intensive lobbying effort was made. We had three briefings from the government on the S–S–T, just for freshman Congressmen, we heard a lot of ads on the radio. Some of the ads were absurd, such as that the S–S–T wouldn't make any more pollution than three Volkswagons. And there was another one I heard the day of the

S–S–T vote which said that the S–S–T
was the least polluting type of transportation
ever known — eliminating the horse, the
sailboat, the canoe, and everything else. This
turned people off. It was obviously overdone.

The same arguments were made in 1951
about what's going to happen to the jet
airliner industry — "If we don't help them,
we're going to fall behind." Well, we didn't
help them, and the airlines financed
themselves, and we went way ahead, we lead
the world. And it was all done by private
financing. This, too, should be done by private
financing.

ASPIN:

We've had a steady decline in surface
transportation for the people who live within
my district to the point where trains are being
discontinued, bus service being cut off, and
more than half the towns in my rural district
have no public transportation to the cities.
And I couldn't understand any reason why we
should vote for money for an airplane when
we can't even get to the city.

BERGLAND:

From the point of view of somebody living in
my state of South Dakota who is working on
the land for ten, fourteen, hours a day, who is
getting the same prices for his farm products
that he was getting in 1933, there was nobody
in my state of any significant number who
could support the S–S–T, and that includes
myself.

ABOUREZK:

Government auditors, employed by
Congress, have spent several months
studying the Pentagon's buying of new
weapons — how much they were supposed to
cost, and how much they actually did cost.
They told Congress that 61 new weapons

were estimated by the Pentagon to cost 83-billion dollars. But at last count, their actual cost had risen to 117-billion, and was still rising.

The report says these cost over-runs may result from unexpected trouble, bad planning, bad management, bad estimating, or deliberate under-estimating.

The biggest over-run of all was the Navy's Mark 48 torpedo. It cost three-billion more than predicted.

SLIDE: BRINKLEY V/O

BRINKLEY (AND VIZMOS):

Another example: The Air Force's Minuteman III missile. It cost 2-billion 900-million more than Congress was told it would cost.

ZOOM IN ON BRINKLEY, MCU

The report did not discuss the fact that many weapons bought at high prices were not used because they did not work. It also says the Pentagon's management of this has improved somewhat in recent months.

Frank . . . .

MCGEE (ON CAMERA):

A few years ago, there was a big fuss about the poor schooling being given the children of migrant workers. So Congress put up 97-million dollars to help the states do better by them. Today, a study was released showing things haven't changed much. Seventeen million dollars that could have been used were never spent, in part because the Office of Education didn't see to it that states wanting more money, got it. About a third of the money meant for food was not spent, nor was about another third meant for health services.

The cost of living rose two-tenths of one percent in February. That's double the rate of the previous month. But, even so, when the two months are taken together, it's the smallest two-month increase in four years. The White House calls this, ''encouraging news.''

TITLE SLIDE

COMMERCIAL

MCGEE (AND VIZMOS):

Egyptian anti-aircraft guns fired on Israeli planes they said were flying over the northern end of the Suez Canal today. They made no claims the planes were hit in the first such incident since the cease-fire began last August.

CHANGE VIZMO

VIZMOS OUT, ZOOM IN ON McGEE

MCGEE (AND VIZMO):

FILM: SUPER, "BELFAST" CROWD SHOT

P.M. EXITS BUILDING, ENTERS CAR

:14

BRITISH SOLDIERS PATROL BELFAST STREETS,
VARIOUS SHOTS OF MEN AND THEIR WEAPONS

:26

In Washington, Israel's Foreign Minister Abba Eban met with about 40 senators and made what one of them called "an impassioned presentation" of Israel's negotiating position.

Later, Eban spent nearly two hours with Secretary of State Rogers, in what both called "friendly talks" that, so far as we know, changed the opinion of neither.

Israel wants to keep certain Arab territories it took in the '67 war. Washington thinks it should give them up in exchange for international guarantees of security.

At the last minute, Northern Ireland's prime minister, James Chichester-Clark, postponed his expected resignation. Instead, he will meet with British defense officials about more British help in trying to put down terrorism in his country.

[Montgomery]: After almost two years in office, Major James Chichester-Clark is in big trouble as Northern Ireland's prime minister. Right-wingers in his Unionist Party are gunning for this amiable middle-of-the-road squire.

The Protestant right-wingers are enraged at the terrorist activities of the outlawed Irish Republican Army, and want British troops to get much tougher. Chichester-Clark has talked the British government into sending another 15-hundred soldiers to Northern Ireland, making a total of 97-hundred.

But the right-wing does not think the troops will get half tough enough.

DEMONSTRATORS OUTSIDE PARLIAMENT

:28

The right wing sent about two-thousand demonstrators to Storrmount, the Northern Ireland parliament, while Chicester-Clark was inside the building, outlining his new anti-terrorist plans.

He rejected right-wing demands for the immediate internment, or jailing without trial, of I–R–A leaders, and demands for an armed citizens' militia under local control.

CRAIG MOUNTS SPEAKER'S PLATFORM

:09

The demonstrators demanded Chichester-Clark's ouster. William Craig, a maverick right-wing Unionist member of Storrmount, got a big ovation from the crowd. Many hard-liners want him to become prime minister.

CROWD SHOTS BACKGROUND CHANT, "WE WANT

CRAIG," UP FULL

:08

CRAIG WITH BULLHORN, PAN TO CROWD

:14

MONTGOMERY (ON CAMERA):

:19

The crowd was peaceful enough on a wet day that reduced its size. But there were fears that hard line Protestant pressure for a crackdown on the I–R–A could lead to new fighting between Protestants and Catholics.

It looks as though Prime Minister Chichester-Clark's statement has pleased nobody — neither the Republican element nor the hard-line of his Unionist party. And it looks like his days as Prime Minister of Northern Ireland are numbered.

George Montgomery, NBC News, Belfast.

MCGEE (ON CAMERA):

There was a time when states wanted more people — cities wanted more industries — and almost any country all but worshiped tourists. But in London today, it was proposed that tourists be required to pay a one-dollar–and-20–cents bed tax—a tax of a dollar and 20 cents for each night they spent in a London hotel. An official of the Tourist Bureau called the proposal "monstrous."

David . . .

BRINKLEY (ON CAMERA):

A law professor has been named to head the new government of Turkey. And all political parties say they will support him. He is under orders from the Turkish army to pull the country back from the edge of chaos within one year, or the army says it will take over itself.

The U–S military bases in Turkey are still there, along the southern border of Russia. And for years the Americans and the Turks have got along very well. But now that is changing, and they seem to feel that too many Americans have been around for too long.

SUPERS OVER TROOPS MARCHING

:15

[KIKER]: Turkey is an old, reliable friend of the United States, and a valuable member of NATO. Turkish troops armed with American weapons guard the southern border of the Soviet Union. This nation is dotted with American military installations.

ANTI-AMERICAN SLOGANS ON WALLS AND
BUILDINGS

 :15

MARKET PLACE AND OTHER STREET SCENES

 :22

But the United States can no longer take the friendship of the Turkish people for granted. Anti-Americanism is on the rise in Turkey—on the rise with people of all political persuasions.

After left-wing extremists kidnapped four American airmen in Ankara, right-wing extremists beat up two American civilians and bombed American homes here in Istanbul.

SUPER

:05

OVER VARIOUS SHOTS OF SOLDIERS GETTING OUT
OF CAB, ON STREETS, USING BUSES

;29

The Turks are a proud, private people, and many of them simply believe too many Americans have been in their country, too long.

U–S officials here recognize the growing seriousness of this problem, and are trying to keep American visibility as low as possible these days. U–S military personnel wear uniforms only when they're on duty. The American flag is flown only on official holidays.

Fifteen-thousand American military men and their dependents now live in Turkey — half the number that was here only a few years ago. Within two years, another 50 percent reduction in American forces is expected.

But the Turks really are not going to be satisfied until the last American has departed from this country.

Douglas Kiker, NBC News, Turkey.

TITLE SLIDE

COMMERCIAL

BRINKLEY (ON CAMERA):

In the Great Box Car Heist, as reported, the Penn Central Railroad finally began to notice that when its box cars got onto the tracks of a tiny railroad in Illinois — called the LaSalle and Bureau County–the L-S-and-B-C—a lot of them never came back.

Well, today the FBI has found a number of them — repainted in the colors of the L-S-and-B-C—and their numbers changed.

SUPERS OVER LS&BC BLDGS. AND SIGNS

:12

RR TRACKS

:07

BOX CARS, RR PAINT SHOP, STENCILS FOR

PAINTING "LS&BC"

:20

FILM OF TOY TRAIN SET, WITH SIGNS ON BLDGS. AS

MODELS OF FREIGHT CARS MOVE FROM ONE BLDG.

TO ANOTHER

:80

[NOLAN]: The LaSalle and Bureau County Railroad is among the smallest in the country. Today, it is also probably the quietest. Not one train moved across its track this morning. Traffic was stopped by an FBI search for 277 stolen Penn Central Railroad freight cars, traced to the little L-S-and-B-C line. It was here in LaSalle, Illinois, that some of the stolen box cars were found. How they, and other Penn Central cars got here, is a confusing tangle of corporate business.

Late last year and early this year, Penn Central returned some of its leased freight cars to their owner — the Equitable Life Assurance Society.

Equitable is one of Penn Central's biggest creditors.

The insurance company, with little real need for trains, sold more than 400 of these cars to a New Jersey firm — Diversified Properties, Incorporated. Diversified Property officials prefer not to talk at the moment.

But the company apparently arranged to have the freight cars delivered to the LaSalle and Bureau County Railroad, a small line with inter-connecting track to bigger railroads. LaSalle then shipped the cars down its own 15 miles of track to the Magna Earth Company, which leases and operates the little line's repair shop.

Here, the old Penn Central cars were repaired and repainted.

Somehow, the legitmate transfer of 400 freight cars became mixed in with the theft of 277 other cars, which were still owned by the

Penn Central. They, too, were fixed, painted over — and those stolen cars were found operating in Illinois, under the wrong name, and on the wrong track.

Who sent them here, and why, are unanswered questions.

Peter Nolan, NBC News, Chicago.

BRINKLEY (ON CAMERA):

The Washington *Post* reports that the police in Montgomery county, Maryland, outside of Washington, set up a concealed television camera in the apartment of a 20-year-old woman, with her agreement and consent. Then the police, waiting in the apartment next door, watched on closed-circuit television when a physician, a general practitioner, came to see the woman, to pay a house call.

The testimony, at a preliminary hearing in court, is that when the doctor arrived, he gave his patient a shot which drugged her, and was about to commit a sexual assault when the police — from next door — burst in, arrested him, and charged him. How they knew in advance what was going to happen, they have not explained.

Frank . . . .

MCGEE (AND VIZMO):

HODGSON

Two weeks ago, Labor Secretary James Hodgson talked about some unemployment figures and said he found them "heartening." At the same time, a career employee of the Department — and an expert in statistics — was telling newsmen he found the same figures sort of "mixed."

Well today, the Department said its career employees would not longer provide briefings to newsmen.

ZOOM IN ON MCGEE

Why? Well, to get the news out faster — and to spare the professionals questions touching on policies.

For the second time, the Food and Drug Administration is urging people to destroy any packages of a meat tenderizer labeled "Spice of Life" or "Country Tavern." It is not a tenderizer, but a poison — nitrite. And a Maryland man died Sunday after eating some. Warnings against it were first issued five months ago.

SUPERS OVER CU, OLD RADIO, ZOOMING BACK FOR WIDE SHOT SHOWING COLLECTION

:18

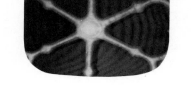

[TROTTA]: There seems to be a yearning in the country of late for old things — from earlier times — partly because it's thought that those times were simpler and easier. Well, that's hardly ever the case. But the mood has led to the collection of antique radios. But if you recognize the next voice you hear, you may not think they're all that old.

NATURAL SOUND UNDER TROTTA'S NARRATION OF 1930-TYPE RADIO PROGRAM, AUDIO QUALITY RESEMBLING THAT OF A MEGAPHONE. "AND NOW THE TIME HAS COME TO LEND THINE EAR TO AU REVOIR, PLEASANT DREAMS. . ." MUSIC FADES UNDER

Songs like this were popular almost half a century ago — in the years of what people now call, "The Golden Age of Radio."

They were also the good old days, when a corny joke got a belly laugh and radio was the nation's biggest entertainment.

PAN OVER TO MAN WORKING AT BENCH FULL OF
RADIOS
RICKEY-TICK MUSIC UP FULL
  :04

William Laverty collects old radios. As a child, he used to look at magazine pictures of radios but he could never afford them.

ANNOUNCER SAYS ". . .WITH THE OLD
MAESTRO. . ." MUSIC FADES UNDER AGAIN

SLOW PAN AROUND ASSORTMENT OF OLD RADIOS
AND PARTS
  :27

MUSIC UP FULL, VOICE SINGING ". . .YOU'LL MISS
ME, HONEY, SOME OF THESE DAYS. . ."
  :07
MUSIC FADES UNDER AGAIN

EXTREME CLOSE UP, HANDS WORKING ON INNARDS
OF AN OLD RADIO,
  :22

ANCIENT MUSIC SEGUES INTO 20 SECS. OF
1971-STYLE RADIO, ANNOUNCER PICKED UP BY OLD
RECEIVER SAYS: ". . .WILL ARRANGE BUDGET
TERMS. SO SAVE THE MONEY AND HAVE A GREAT
NEW HOME WITHOUT A CHANGE OF ADDRESS. CALL
M-A-7-6-700 FOR MORE INFORMATION ON THEIR BIG
PRE-SPRING. . ." ANNOUNCER FADES OUT AS
LAVERTY'S FINGERS ADJUST TUNER OF RADIO,
THEN BACK IN FOR ". . .AND DO MENTION MY NAME,
TOM BROWN. . ." RADIO SOUND FADES OUT.

Laverty knows he can't bring back the old sounds. But he can preserve and restore an Atwater-Kent or an old crystal set that was once the main attraction in the family parlor.

ZOOM BACK FOR TWO-SHOT OF TROTTA AND
LAVERTY
:20

CUTAWAY,
TROTTA,
:03
CU, LAVERTY, ZOOMING BACK FOR MS
:10

PAN, OLD RADIOS
:15

MUSIC COMES IN FULL, VOICE SINGING
". . .ANOTHER SEASON, ANOTHER REASON, FOR
MAKING WHOOPEE. . ."
:07
MUSIC FADES UNDER

ZOOM BACK TO SHOW LAVERTY WORKING ON
RADIOS
:10
MUSIC UP FULL
:04
MUSIC UNDER BRIEFLY
TROTTA:
MUSIC UP FULL TO CONCLUDE WITH SINGER
ENDING SONG, ". . .FOR MAKING WHOOPEE."
:03

[LAVERTY]: This is one of the earliest types of receivers, which was home-made. It was typical of the crystal sets which we used in the early '20s. Half the fun of this was to fiddle with this cat-whisker, to find a sensitive spot, so that you could get the music at the right volume.

[TROTTA]: How about music? Would you like to hear some of the old music if you could possibly do it?

[LAVERTY]: Yeah, I think so. Just for the heck of it. I think back and say, "Gee, I used to think that was good in the old days."

[TROTTA]: At 56, Laverty has a lot of memories and a lot of radios. And in his life, the two are often inseparable.

This is Liz Trotta, NBC News, reporting.

TITLE SLIDE

COMMERCIAL

MCGEE (ON CAMERA):

Funeral services for Thomas E. Dewey, twice a candidate for the Presidency, were held today in New York. President and Mrs. Nixon attended the services.

MCGEE (ON CAMERA):

The New York Stock Exchange closed out the week with a a loss.

VIZMO, FULL SCREEN*

The Dow Jones Industrials fell

CHANGE VIZMO

*This kind of visual is known as a "reveal." It begins with a graph that can be understood instantly. Additional details are revealed, to coincide with what the newsman is saying. Thus the viewer receives the identical information simultaneously through his eyes and ears.

CHANGE VIZMO

almost four points and
the value of an average share lost almost
seven cents.

DISSOLVE TO AMEX VIZMO

On the American Exchange, an average
share lost four cents.

MCGEE (ON CAMERA):

David . . . .

BRINKLEY (ON CAMERA):

One time an American diplomat was
negotiating something or other with Andrei
Gromyko, who is now Russia's foreign
minister, and on some sticky point the
American diplomat assured Gromyko he
really was sincere. Gromyko answered, "It is
possible for an individual diplomat to be
sincere, but countries never are."
   Well, right or wrong, that is the atmosphere
we have to work in. And so, in Washington, the
State Department's Foreign Service Institute
teaches a course for junior-and middle-grade
foreign service officers. And it doesn't
necessarily teach them how to lie or evade or
deceive, but how to negotiate with people
who often do.

FILM: SUPER

:05

OVER THOMAS

:15

[CHARLES THOMAS]: This will be Group A, this will be Group C. There are rooms outside for your groups. We will now give you 45 minutes to prepare yourself for the beginning of the game.

TEAM A AROUND TABLE

:15

[TEAM A, FIRST MAN]: I think we ought to start off cautiously, and re-evaluate it at every step.

[TEAM A, SECOND MAN]: I would argue that we're out to win the game. I would argue that we're all Foreign Service officers here and that they're going to be thinking, just the way you're thinking—that they're going to be cautious, and will proceed that way.

TEAM C AROUND TABLE

:12

[TEAM C, FIRST MAN]: We have to look at this in two ways, I suppose. I think we have to be careful not to tell them too much.

[TEAM C, SECOND MAN]: Yes, we can't assume that they're in the same good faith as we are in.

PAN DOWN CORRIDOR AND THRU DOOR OF
CONFERENCE ROOM, WHERE TEAMS FACE EACH
OTHER ACROSS TABLE

:36

[TEAM A MAN]: The reason why we asked for negotiating is that both of us have a common interest in avoiding an attack.

[TEAM C MAN]: Un-hunh.

[TEAM A MAN]: And in order to maintain trust, I think we should agree to make reciprocal moves.

[TEAM C MAN]: Well now, I don't quite understand how I can, uh, how I can count on your side to do that. [pause] What kind of guarantee can you give me that I would accept your offer in good faith, seek what you suggest, and then find that my side is suddenly attacked?

[CHAIRMAN OF TEAM A]: I suggest we attack immediately.

[MEMBER OF TEAM RESPONDS TO CHAIR]: No.

TEAM A AROUND ITS TABLE AGAIN, CAUCUSES AMID
A HUBBUB OF VOICES, THE CHAIRMAN'S EMERGING
ALONE FOR ONE SENTENCE

:09

TEAM C AROUND ITS TABLE

:18

[CHAIRMAN OF TEAM C]: I am convinced that our opposite numbers are bargaining in good faith. I cannot, I cannot, uh . . . It's difficult for me to believe that they are, as you accuse them of being.

TEAM C SEEMS TO BE TALKING ALL AT ONCE, WITH
MANY "OKAY'S" AND "ALL RIGHTS"
TWO TEAMS NEGOTIATING AGAIN.
CHAIRMEN FACE EACH OTHER

:17

[CHAIRMAN OF TEAM C]: Well now, to summarize, may I report back to my group that we agree to a gradual reduction of forces, so to speak.

[CHAIRMAN OF TEAM A]: That's my proposition. We'll have a referendum. We will of course get in touch with you if we have a change to suggest.

CHAIRMEN STAND UP, SMILING AT EACH OTHER   [CHAIRMAN OF TEAM A]: Shall we adjourn to the
    :05   cocktail party?

BRINKLEY: Good night, Frank.
MCGEE (ON CAMERA):   Good night, David.
                                                  Thank you, and good night for NBC News.

BIBLIOGRAPHY

INTERVIEWS

Barnes, Clive. Interviewed September 1970.

Broun, Heywood Hale. Interviewed March 1970 and again February 1971.

Brunton, Anthony (Executive Editor for CBS radio network news). Interviewed July 1970.

Crist, Judith. Interviewed February 1971.

Cronkite, Walter. Interviewed March 1970.

Curtis, Charlotte. Telephone interview, August 1970.

Friendly, Fred W. Formal interview in September 1970 in addition to numerous informal conversations about the writing of broadcast news.

George, Nicholas. Interviewed July 1970.

Hanser, Richard, Interviewed February 1971.

Hart, John. Interviewed August 1970.

Jackson, Allan. Interviewed March 1970.

Joyce, Ed. (News Director of WCBS-TV, New York.) Interviewed July 1970.

Kuralt, Charles. Interviewed September 1970.

Newman, Edwin. Interviewed September 1970.

Stone, Emerson. Interviewed March 1970 and again October 1970.

Tornabene, Russell C. (of NBC News). Interviewed July 1970.

Westfeldt, Wallace. Interviewed August 1970.

BOOKS AND RECORDS

Agee, Warren K., ed. *Mass Media in a Free Society* (essays by six media specialists). Lawrence, University Press of Kansas, 1969.

Arlen, Michael J. *The Living-Room War*. New York, Viking Press, 1969.

Barnouw, Erik. *The Television Writer*. New York, Hill and Wang, 1962.

—— *A Tower in Babel*. New York, Oxford University Press, 1966.

—— *The Golden Web*. New York, Oxford University Press, 1968.

—— *The Image Empire*. New York, Oxford University Press, 1970.

Barrett, Edward W., ed. *Journalists in Action*. Manhasset, N.Y., Channel Press, 1963.

Barrett, Marvin, ed. *Survey of Broadcast Journalism 1968–1969*. New York, Grosset and Dunlap, 1969.

——*Survey of Broadcast Journalism 1969–1970*. New York, Grosset and Dunlap, 1970.

Bernstein, Theodore M. *Watch Your Language*. New York, Atheneum, 1965.

—— *The Careful Writer*. New York, Atheneum, 1967.

Bliss, Edward, Jr., ed. *In Search of Light: The Broadcasts of Edward R. Murrow, 1938–1960*. New York, Knopf, 1967.

Bluem, A. William. *Documentary in American Television*. New York, Hastings House, 1965.

Bryson, Lyman. *Time For Reason—About Radio*. New York, George W. Stewart, 1948.

—— *The Communication of Ideas*. New York, Harper, 1948.

Burlingame, Roger. *Don't Let Them Scare You: The life and Times of Elmer Davis*. Philadelphia, J.B. Lippincott, 1961.

Callihan, E.L. *Grammar for Journalists*. Revised ed. Philadelphia, Chilton, 1969.

CBS News. *Television News Reporting*. New York, McGraw-Hill, 1958.

Chase, Stuart. *Power of Words*. New York, Harcourt, Brace & World, 1954.

Crist, Judith. *The Private Eye, the Cowboy and the Very Naked Girl*. New York, Holt, Rinehart and Winston, 1968.

Coons, John E., ed. *Freedom and Responsibility in Broadcasting*. Evanston, Ill., Northwestern University Press, 1961.

Crosby, John. *With Love and Loathing*. New York, McGraw-Hill, 1963.

Edwards, Verne E., Jr. *Journalism in a Free Society*. Dubuque, William C. Brown, 1970.

Emery, Edwin, Phillip H. Ault, and Warren K. Agee. *Introduction to Mass Communications*. 3d ed. New York, Dodd, Mead, 1970

Faulk, John Henry. *Fear on Trial*. New York, Simon & Schuster, 1964.

Flesch, Rudolf. *How to Write, Speak, and Think More Effectively*. New York, Harper & Bros., 1960.

Fowler, H.W. *A Dictionary of Modern English Usage*. London, Oxford University Press, 1964.

Friendly, Fred W. *Due to Circumstances Beyond Our Control*. New York, Random House, 1967.

Garst, Robert and Theodore M. Bernstein. *Headlines and Deadlines*. New York, Columbia University Press, 1961.

Geddes, Donald Porter, ed. *Franklin Delano Roosevelt, a Memorial* (broadcasts upon the death of the 32d President). New York, Pocket Books, 1945.

Gordon, Matthew. *News Is a Weapon* (with an introduction by Elmer Davis). New York, Knopf, 1942.

Greene, Maury. *Television News: Anatomy and Process.* Belmont, Calif., Wadsworth, 1969.

Greene, Robert S. *Television Writing.* New York, Harper & Bros., 1956.

Hilliard, Robert L. *Understanding Television: An Introduction to Broadcasting.* New York, Hastings House, 1964.

—— *Writing for Television and Radio.* New York, Hastings House, 1967.

Hohenberg, John. *The Professional Journalist.* New York, Holt, Rinehart and Winston, 1969.

—— *Free Press, Free People—The Best Cause.* New York, Columbia University Press, 1971.

I Can Hear It Now (1933–1945). Produced by Edward R. Murrow and Fred W. Friendly, narrated by Murrow. Columbia Records, about 1948.

I Can Hear It Now: The Sixties. Produced by Fred W. Friendly and Walter Cronkite, narrated by Cronkite. Columbia Records, 1970.

Ives, Sumner. *A New Handbook for Writers.* New York, Knopf, 1960.

Jackson, Allan. "You Have to Write, Too! (unpublished lecture), 1969.

Kaltenborn, H.V. *Fifty Fabulous Years.* New York, Putnam, 1950.

Kendrick, Alexander. *Prime Time.* Boston, Little, Brown, 1969.

Kittross, John M. and Kenneth Harwood. *Free and Fair: Courtroom Access and the Fairness Doctrine.* Philadelphia, Association for Professional Broadcasting Education, 1970.

Klapper, Joseph T. *The Effects of Mass Communication.* New York, The Free Press, 1960.

Lippmann, Walter. *Public Opinion.* New York, The Free Press, 1965.

MacDougall, Curtis D. *Interpretative Reporting.* 5th ed. New York, Macmillan, 1968.

MacNeil, Robert. *The People Machine.* New York, Harper & Row, 1968.

Morgan, Edward P. *Clearing the Air.* Washington, Luce, 1963.

Murrow, Edward R. *This Is London.* New York, Simon & Schuster, 1941.

Perrin, Porter G. *Writer's Guide and Index to English.* 4th ed. Glenview, Ill., Scott, Foresman, 1965.

Priestley, J.B. *All England Listened.* New York, Chilmark Press, 1967.

Report of the National Advisory Commission on Civil Disorders. New York, E.P. Dutton & Co., 1968.

Rivers, William L. *The Adversaries.* Boston, Beacon Press, 1970.

Rivers, William L. and Wilbur Schramm. *Responsibility in Mass Communication.* Rev. ed. New York, Harper & Row, 1969.

Schramm, Wilbur, ed. *Mass Communications.* Urbana, Ill., University of Illinois Press, 1949.

Sevareid, Eric. *In One Ear.* New York, Knopf, 1952.

—— *Small Sounds in the Night.* New York, Knopf, 1956.

—— *This Is Eric Sevareid.* New York, McGraw-Hill, 1964.

Skornia, Harry J. *Television and the News.* Palo Alto, Calif., Pacific Books, 1968.

Small, William. *To Kill a Messenger.* New York, Hastings House, 1970.

Stahr, John. *Write to the Point.* New York, Macmillan, 1969.

Stein, M.L. *Write Clearly, Speak Effectively.* New York, Cornerstone Library, 1967.

Steinberg, Charles S., ed. *Mass Media and Communication* (selections from 26 authors on the subject). New York, Hastings House, 1966.

Strunk, William, Jr. and E.B. White. *The Elements of Style.* New York, Macmillan Paperbacks, 1962.

Swing, Raymond. *"Good Evening!"* New York, Harcourt, Brace and World, 1964.

Thomas, Lowell. *History As You Heard It*. New York, Doubleday, 1957.

Wagner, Geoffrey. *On the Wisdom of Words*. New York, Van Nostrand, 1968.

White, Paul. *News on the Air*. New York, Harcourt, Brace, 1947.

Willis, Edgar E. *Writing Television and Radio Programs*. New York, Holt, Rinehart and Winston, 1967.

INDEX